JEWISH LEGENDS

by

STEFAN ZWEIG

Translated by
Eden and Cedar Paul

with a new introduction by
Leon Botstein
Bard College

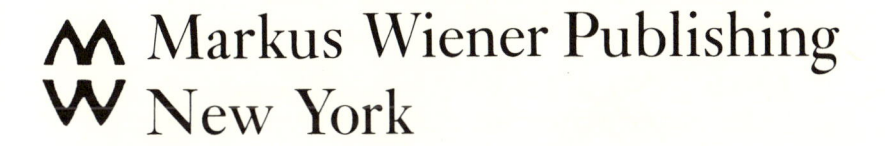

Markus Wiener Publishing
New York

First Markus Wiener Publishing Edition 1987
The first publication of the German original in book form, under the title LEGENDEN, was issued by Bermann-Fischer Verlag in 1945 in Stockholm. This is the first American edition of LEGENDEN. The stories included have been previously published in various English-language volumes; here they appear together in English for the first time.

© Copyright 1987 by Leon Botstein for the introduction.

© Copyright 1937 by Viking Press for The Buried Candelabrum. Renewed in 1965 by Viking Press. Reprinted with permission of the copyright owner.

© Copyright 1934 by Viking Press for Kaleidoscope. Renewed in 1961 by Viking Press. Kaleidoscope includes the following stories: Rachel Arraigns with God, Virata, Buchmendel.

Reprinted with permission of the copyright owner, Atrium Press, Ltd. London. All rights reserved.

Cover Design: Cheryl Mirkin

Library of Congress Cataloging-in-Publication Data
Zweig, Stefan, 1881–1942.
   Jewish legends.

(Masterworks of modern Jewish writing series)
Translation of: Legenden.
Contents: The buried candelabrum—Rachel arraigns with God—The legend of the third dove—[etc.].
   1. Jews—History—Fiction. I. Title. II. Series.
PT2653.W42L4413   1987   833′.912   86-40569
ISBN 0-910129-59-2

Printed in The United States of America

Table of Contents

Introduction by Leon Botstein   vii

The Buried Candelabrum   3

Rachel Arraigns with God   147

The Legend of the Third Dove   167

Virata or The Eyes of the Dying Brother   175

Buchmendel   227

First publications

The Buried Candelabrum, *Der begrabene Leuchter*, 1936

Rachel Arraigns with God, *Rachel rechtet mit Gott* (in the anthology *Neue Deutsche Erzähler*), 1930

The Legend of the Third Dove, *Die Legende der dritten Taube* (in Stefan Zweig, *Legenden*), 1945

Virata or The Eyes of the Undying Brother, *Die Augen des ewigen Bruders*, 1922

Buchmendel, *Buchmendel* (in Stefan Zweig, *Kleine Chronik*), 1929

Introduction
by Leon Botstein

Stefan Zweig and his work constitute a powerful symbol of a vanished but often disparaged community of assimilated and proudly secular Central European Jewish intellectuals who, before 1939, resisted Zionism and clung to a dream of the eventual social and moral triumph in history of a cosmopolitan European culture based on learning and enlightenment. This community of Jews embraced and engaged the traditions of European art and civilization and sought that culture's victory over ordinary modern politics, with its divisive ideological commitments, not to speak of its virulent nationalisms. Rereading Stefan Zweig is an almost harrowing journey back—not to the lost world of the mass of Yiddish-speaking, poverty-stricken, and deeply religious Jews of Eastern Europe, whose Shtetl world has, until now, provided the lion's share of symbols and cliches for the extermination of the Jews during World War II—but to a different Jewish world that Hitler also destroyed, an affluent, middle class and assimilated community, Eastern as well as Western European. Its traditions and conceits trigger less sympathy; its faith in the power of

Jewish Legends

language, reason, and culture and its status as the nearest equivalents of Nietzsche's "good Europeans" render its members not facile objects of compassion, but a forgotten milieu inspiring ambivalence and discomfort.

Stefan Zweig's career was hardly dependent on Jewish matters or on Jewish readers. But ironically, the Jewish community from which he came and whose characteristics and sympathies he so unabashedly displayed was a collective ideal type, in Max Weber's methodological sense, of the European bourgeois reading public—Gentile and Jewish—that Zweig sought to reach; of an educated, urbane European public's notions of language and history before 1939 and its expectations of culture and learning. A few remnants of this Jewish community remained or returned to Germany and Austria after the war. They have engaged, often reluctantly, the continuing experience of anti-semitism in a Central European world essentially without Jews.

Some of those who emigrated to America and Israel in the 1930s and 1940s have sustained, with pride, the centuries-old culture of German-speaking Jewry. The Leo Baeck Institute in New York and Israel, with its crucial scholarly focus on German Jewry, is one of their achievements. In New York, this segment of survivors, many of whom in the 1930s and 1940s ended up living in Washington Heights, read the newspaper *Der Aufbau* ("Reconstruction"), not the Yiddish dailies. The Jewish author they admired most was not Sholom Aleichem; nor would it have been the Singer brothers and the world of *The Brothers Ashkenazi*. Other emigre survivors from this community of European Jewry dealt with the trauma of

Introduction by Leon Botstein

Nazism by turning on the past, exchanging a heritage of assimilation into German culture with a parallel but fierce effort to become undeniably and undistinguishably American. Differences in the experiences of this community after the war notwithstanding, the Jewish writer closest to the hearts of cultivated, assimilated European Jews before 1939—even affluent Polish Jews who read German and were proud possessors of their *Bildung*—was Stefan Zweig. Ironically, even a portion of the Yiddish-speaking intellectual elite admired Zweig. One of I. B. Singer's first professional assignments as a writer was a translation into Yiddish of Zweig's biography of Romain Rolland, a book whose contemptuous dismissal of ordinary political movements such as nationalism, and therefore, by implication, Zionism, did not at all sit well with Singer.

The career of Stefan Zweig presents a difficult challenge. It has remained an enigma for critic and historian alike. Born in 1881 in Vienna, Zweig earned recognition early in his life as a new, young literary talent in the competitive and brilliant world of *fin de siècle* Vienna. In his late fifties, as a celebrated man of letters, Zweig was forced to flee Austria and the Nazis. He eventually emigrated to Brazil where he and his second wife, Lotte, committed suicide in 1942, before Stalingrad and the first believable glimmers of hope that Hitler might be defeated. Zweig's suicide came as a shock, even to those who knew him well, for unlike most emigres, Zweig had no material concerns and was recognized and honored all over the world, even in Brazil. But as his later writings reveal, particularly his analysis of Michel de Montaigne,

Zweig understood that Hitler and the war amounted to more than a loss of a homeland in Europe and the irreversible transvaluation of the language he loved, German. Zweig accepted the events around him as a devastating defeat for his fundamental political and social assumptions and the vocation of the writer as he defined it. After all, he had sought to do more than exercise his imagination in service of literary originality and beauty. As teacher and exemplar—as the voice of the meaning of history and the crucial importance of the idea of the individual, both of which he sought to vindicate—Zweig responded to the terror of the recognition of his failure to wield influence despite success and to the seeming bankruptcy of his beliefs by the act of ultimate resignation, which at the same time still appeared to affirm the possibility of personal freedom: suicide.

Many of Zweig's contemporaries, including Karl Kraus and Thomas Mann, realized that Zweig's writing never broke free from a stylistic self-consciousness—the explicit cultivation of a "literary" language of expression able to carry learning and intellectual ambitions overtly and undisguised—or a superficiality in thought—a repetitive reliance on facile reductions of near psychoanalytic insights and primitive notions of the logic of history. Nevertheless, Zweig was never entirely dismissed as a serious literary figure. He was clearly more subtle than his closest rival in the popular biography arena, Emil Ludwig. His short stories, while not of the calibre of those of Thomas Mann or Joseph Roth, Zweig's compatriot and friend, were finely crafted. His poetic and dramatic work, including his controversial collaboration

Introduction by Leon Botstein

with Richard Strauss on *Die schweigsame Frau*, was, likewise, respectable. Zweig was skillful and prolific.

More important, however, not even Zweig's well-known contemporary, Franz Werfel, came as close as Zweig to linking the popular and commercial worlds of readers and books with the more complex and rarified milieu of twentieth-century modernism in literature. The extent to which Zweig did so enabled him to act, throughout his entire life, as a broker between the world of journalism and politics and that of the intellectuals, as a spokesman to a wider audience for the concerns of writers and thinkers. Zweig was active in PEN, participated in pacifist crusades, traveled all over the world giving speeches covering a daunting range of subjects, and wrote gladly for popular consumption. Early in his career he developed the pattern of associating himself with individuals whom he admired not only as intellects but also as historically significant individuals. Emile Verhaeren, Belgium's leading poet, and Romain Rolland were two examples. Zweig maintained contact with an astonishing variety of figures within the arts and public life. He recognized his own pivotal role as popularizer of those ideas, individuals, and movements he regarded as somehow more crucial than his own work as a writer.

During his last years, Zweig even accepted a commission to write a pot-boiler paean about Brazil as the "eldorado" (which unfortunately and unwittingly ended up falling prey to the satirical sense of Eldorado best known through Voltaire's *Candide*) of mankind. Zweig's decision took Brazil's intellectual community by surprise, considering the repression of writers by the Brazilian regime of

Jewish Legends

Getulio Vargas, not to speak of its generally illiberal and unsavory character.

Despite his fame and wide-ranging output, Zweig is almost forgotten nearly half a century after his death. The literary figures to whom we turn from the culture of early twentieth-century Vienna include Robert Musil and Hermann Broch, neither of whom ever experienced the recognition and fortune of Stefan Zweig. Schnitzler and Hofmannsthal have retained their standing; men such as Hermann Bahr, despite their importance in their own time, never approached the international stature of Zweig, and they remain significant historical figures but not writers whose work demands re-reading as literature. The appreciation of and fascination with Karl Kraus and Joseph Roth have only increased since their deaths in the 1930s. Roth in particular provides a striking contrast. He died in 1939, perhaps by suicide, despondent and forgotten. Yet his work is experiencing critical revival here and in Europe as a result of the renewed and broadly-based fascination with the world of *fin de siècle* Vienna. Even though Stefan Zweig's works remain in print in German, today's romance with *fin de siècle* Viennese culture (despite a series of centennial Zweig celebrations in 1981) has not led to serious attention (except by a cadre of devoted scholars) being paid to either Zweig's fiction or his historical writings.

This lack of interest stems, in part, from the discomfort contemporary intellectuals sense when they confront that in-between world—one neither of subtle art and complex ideas nor of vulgar popular culture—that Zweig dominated. The career of Stefan Zweig reminds us of a

Introduction by Leon Botstein

world of serious readers, middle-class consumers of culture, which existed in Europe from the late nineteenth century to World War II. Zweig's readers were the first generations of Europeans with widespread literacy and a yearning for knowledge. In the German-speaking world they were avid readers of cultural criticism in daily newspapers and subscription periodicals. They were the patrons of concerts, theatre, and museums, in whose homes sets (specially designed for this market) of the great works of the essential classical authors—Goethe, Schiller, Heine, and Shakespeare (translated by Schlegel)—were conspicuously on display.

The reappearance, in English, of stories and legends by Stefan Zweig—particularly those based on Jewish subject matters—forces us, therefore, to reflect on the character of the reading public, the largely middle-class audience for culture in the early twentieth century. Stefan Zweig was, in his lifetime, among the most popular and widely read European authors. This fact bears emphasis, given the relative disregard and even obscurity Zweig's work has experienced since his death. The case of Stefan Zweig, his success and subsequent eclipse provides a window on how extensively the world of books and reading has changed since 1945. Between the two World Wars Zweig's reputation and financial success as an author (and that of Insel Verlag, his publisher) were at their height and extraordinary. Zweig wrote more than fiction and poetry. His reputation rested on the fact that he produced an extensive series of books in a dated and historically significant but now discredited genre, the popular historical biography. No other individual writing in German was so well known or so widely respected as popularizer of narratives of the past and of their seemingly timeless psychological and moral insights.

Zweig's historical subjects rarely had to do with Jews or Judaism. The subjects of his most well known works ranged from Marie Antoinette, Magellan, and Mesmer to Erasmus, Balzac, and Joseph Fouché. Few, if any, of these books are read today. Zweig's carefully constructed dramatic and narrative renditions of individuals, their inner character and personal crises were more than facile and entertaining. They always contained a message, a view of past and present that made the reader sense that history was comprehensible. History was both a matter of accident and the moment and yet still a process in which individuals, even insignificant individuals, could make a mark. In part, Zweig's popularity rested on his capacity to make passive understanding by individual readers of a rational presentation of the patterns of the past appear as a social accomplishment of some ethical and political value all its own. The implicit and easily grasped preaching about the ultimate meaning and consequence (or lack thereof) of intentions and historical actions seemed only to enhance the popularity of Zweig's books.

No matter what his subject, Zweig persistently sought to lure his readers into an all-encompassing allegiance to humanity. Taste, discernment, and knowledge, through an encounter with history and culture, could help fashion, within the disparate nations of Europe, tolerant citizens of the world, not of discrete and competing

Introduction by Leon Botstein

nations. Cosmopolitan humanism, led and fostered by a literary and intellectual elite, could displace the common motives behind primitive collective social conflict and shape the political, economic, and social arrangements of the future. Making the past, its patterns, and its actors comprehensive and familiar through the writing and reading of popular but clearly didactic biographical narratives constituted an ethical initiative on behalf of a better world.

Within this grandiose *Weltanschauung*, Zweig's biographies and renditions of historical vignettes always celebrated the idea of the individual and, indirectly, the significance of the act of reading. Central to Zweig's credo was the primacy of the spirit over the body, mind over matter. No matter how grim historical reality at any single moment of time might be, the ultimate meaning of life resided in the mind, the imagination—in culture, art, and science. Man's gift of reason, whether employed passively by the average consumer of learning and culture or by the man of genius was, finally for Zweig, the only reason for hope, the true basis for a creditable notion of human progress. Creative genius and the actual moments of creative inspiration were twin obsessions for Zweig. He became a persistent but shrewd collector of original manuscripts by great minds because he thought that the manuscripts would reveal the magical process of inspired individual artistic and intellectual creation—the aspect of life that justified being-in-the-world. Zweig's priceless collection was given to the British Museum. Cultivated individuality, particularly in mass society, was offered by

Jewish Legends

Zweig to his readers as a reminder of the humanly possible, as the redeeming feature in an often cruel and violent modern world.

A reassessment of Stefan Zweig as writer and historical personality, however, offers more than a unique opportunity to encounter the sensibilities and habits of the reading public of twentieth-century Europe before World War II. We are reminded how profoundly the following that Zweig cultivated has been eclipsed since 1945 by the enormous growth of professional intellectuals employed by a network of academic institutions far more extensive than in Zweig's day, and also by a powerful popular culture that makes no pretense of a connection to the traditions of art and culture so dear to Zweig. Both modern popular culture and the professionalization and institutionalization of high culture (with its conceit of theoretical subtlety) have rendered Zweig's popularizing and didactic writing inappropriate objects for serious consideration. The professionals have little use and the public no patience for Zweig's work. The space once occupied by Stefan Zweig, André Maurois, Emil Ludwig, and Will Durant—is now occupied by public television and fictional and scholarly writing for the few—.

Zweig's commitment to the burgeoning segment of middle class readers—professionals, businessmen, educated housewives, and civil servants—was not cynical. He believed that education, *Bildung*, was the only plausible key to ethical and political progress. Furthermore, Zweig, like many in his generation, had been deeply influenced by the pessimistic assessment of modernity and ordinary politics that emanated from Nietzsche. The

Introduction by Leon Botstein

first World War and the collapse of the Habsburg Monarchy, not to speak of the chaos and incompetence that hounded the Austrian Republic, only underscored Zweig's pre-1914 apprehensions about the course of the future. Although Zweig became increasingly pessimistic after 1918, he persisted in the hope that the pen might in fact be mightier than the sword. He became devoted to pacifism and to schemes of international cooperation. He held on to the dream of a humanism; of a cosmopolitan society that might take the place of a militarism and nationalism. Culture, art, and a sense of history remained, for Zweig, instruments of political transformation.

Zweig rejected reductionist definitions of effective political action both in the sense of Machiavellianism, and of an acceptance of economic and historical determinism. By spreading appreciation for great literature, broadening an understanding of man's common psyche, and preaching the lessons of history—all of which demonstrated, for Zweig, the curse and futility of violence, the harm wreaked by patriotism and national separatism, the irrationality of the ambition for power and the potential for seemingly insignificant individuals to play a decisive role (an adroit extension and democratization of Hegel's notion of the centrality of the world-historical individual)—modernity might succeed in reconciling itself with true culture and civility.

By the 1930s the tension between Zweig's inner and implicit pessimism and his tireless overt optimistic activity as writer and public figure became intense. In his essays from the late 1920s and 1930s, Zweig warned increasingly of the destruction of individuality, the demise of art and culture under the weight of an American-style commercial uniformity. Monotony, uniformity, and boredom were part of a poisoning of modern Europe's moral character. By the time Zweig landed in Brazil, the only shred of hope was the new world, not the United States but a yet uncorrupted paradise south of the equator. But that too, on the eve of his suicide, seemed threatened by the world-wide military triumph of fascism.

From a post World War II perspective, Zweig's elevation of culture, his contempt for ordinary politics, and his conceit that a mass middle class could only be rendered civilized, if at all, in the ethical sense only through learning and a carefully nurtured sense of beauty seem at best naive. Zweig's investment in culture centered on the notion of style as a virtue. The self-conscious assertion of high minded reflections, well within extant intellectual traditions, were emblems of the finest human activity.

But it is not only from the convenient perspective of over half a century that Zweig's agenda and voice as a writer appear both strangely simplistic and unsettling. Most of the stories and legends contained in this new edition were published in German in a slender volume in Stockholm at the end of the war in 1945. Jody Suter, reviewing the collection in December 1945 in the Zuerich newspaper, the *Tages-Anzeiger*, sensed, with impressive immediacy, the rapid and radical break that had occurred between the world before 1939 from which Stefan Zweig wrote and the contemporary world that would encounter his work. "But the times have changed

Introduction by Leon Botstein

and transformed us since then, and we read today with different eyes," she wrote. Reading Zweig as early as 1945, just three years after his death, was "something akin to passing by the home of our childhood after many years, which remained big but in the new reality appeared small and strange. So it is with Stefan Zweig's legends. Their wisdom has changed for us, and much that seemed to offer solutions has become irrelevant or invalid. We sense strongly his virtuosic use of language, all too noticeably and all too forcefully for an age in which virtuosity and routine—how closely related these two qualities are!—bear a great deal of the guilt for the great horrible cultural collapse."

In Zweig's case virtuosity meant the sense one derived from his style that an overtly elegant literary language, one readily grasped as cultivated, lent weight to ideas. For Zweig style, as a visible technical vehicle, could serve to vindicate thought. If the reader sensed the author's skill, grace, and subtlety, so much the better, for that sensibility gave the reader confidence that he could demarcate the vulgar from the refined. Yet the effort to rise above the commonplace, the ordinary, which, in terms of art, seemed synonymous with the vulgar, doomed Zweig to deracinate his overt claim to humanism. He misconstrued the notion of the vulgar. By excluding the mundane, Zweig embraced the universal without ever adequately grasping the simple facts of the everyday; without candidly and sympathetically embracing humanity, as it might be as a consequence of what it was.

The glorification of style and refinement in the name, so to speak, of a notion of a common culture of humanity

Jewish Legends

itself became a routine for Zweig and his readers. This routine justified a variety of self-delusions of the part of Zweig and his middle-class readers. Apparent knowledge of the past, the psychological processes of genius, as well as a taste for beauty encouraged a smug sense of superiority about the concerns of day-to-day existence, particularly the nature of everyday politics. It became easy and even elegant to traffic with utopian notions of pacifism and a world without nationalisms and hate without addressing the practical challenges posed by economic and social realities.

The routine, in Suter's sense, became the habitual assertion that the spirit, independent of the material in life—the actual context of existence, its economic and social pressures and opportunities—could remain unsullied and free through the act of one's own love of art and truth. The world of readers, writers, artists, and scientists constituted an ideal commonwealth within a corrupt world. The conceit of membership in this imaginary international commonwealth became a routine, a complacent reflection that before 1933 and 1939 lured many, particularly Jews, to accept their exclusion from European politics, reject Zionism, and at the same time dismiss the threat of fascism as transitory and possibly not so terrifying. Arrogant virtuosity in the command of language as a tool of style created a routine habit of complacent reading and passive assent to perceptions and credos bearing the exterior appearance of humanism but the inner character of a pathetic yet elaborate self-deception regarding the power of culture—the presumed link between learning, ethics and human progress. The sur-

Introduction by Leon Botstein

render to these illusions transformed an educated middle class, to its own members, into an historically significant force in history, merely through its pursuit of self-cultivation and its role as carrier of the traditions of so-called high culture.

From the narrower Jewish perspective, Zweig embodied a specific dimension of this illusion: the notion that through affluence, learning, and certainly fame one could render being Jewish an irrelevant fact in the world of modern Europe. The Jew could take his place in the commonwealth of the cultured and gain equal standing with other European nationals even in an environment in which widespread political anti-semitism flourished, as it did in turn-of-the-century France, Germany and, significantly, the city of Vienna. Zweig, like Franz Werfel and Joseph Roth, never shed his nostalgic attachment to the historical premise of Habsburg unity, the equality of all subjects despite membership in different nationalist groups under a system based on dynastic loyalty.

The multi-national and nearly federal character of the Monarchy during Zweig's youth and early adulthood led him naturally to despise modern nationalism and retain a hope that it could be transcended or competed with as a basis for the modern political state. The Austrian ideal was the supranational state. The Jews could be equals, as Jews, even though they lacked a territorial focus within the state. This vision conformed to the idea embodied, in Zweig's view, in Romain Rolland's *Jean Christophe*. Jean Christophe, for Zweig, was a model "European," who followed "the path by which the nationalist becomes a citizen of the world and acquires a 'European soul.'"

Jewish Legends

That path had already been traveled successfully by the cultured European Jew.

Zweig never converted. He never denied his Jewishness. He was sensitive enough to the mystical and the ambiguities and false choices implicit in commonplace distinctions between the rational and irrational to sustain a respect for and fascination with religion and faith. His confidence that national identity was ultimately a secondary characteristic entirely compatible with international humanism made denial of Jewishness unnecessary. "To the citizen of the world . . . all nations are alike," Zweig wrote. "In each his soul can make itself at home."

As this collection reveals, Zweig regarded his Jewish identity as a spiritual asset. As he defined it, being Jewish did not involve a commitment to an exclusionary nationalism. Therefore, a radical acceptance of claims of political Zionism revealed, in the case of Max Brod, his "human limitation." In contrast, Zweig took the idea of the diaspora and extended it into an ideal. Until very late in his career, in the mid 1930s, the Jewish experience with and prospect for eternal homelessness (in the narrow sense of a people lacking a fixed and local attachment to specific geographic place on the globe) became, as Zweig scholar Klara Carmely has noted, "an ideal of supranational freedom." It seemed to be the proper precondition of the highest evolution of culture and morality.

The Jew was, consequently, the pioneer in showing modernity the way to the triumph of mind over body, spirit over the physical, culture over crass materialism, humanism and tolerance over sectarianism and rabid

Introduction by Leon Botstein

prejudice. For Zweig it was possible to think that the historical purpose of Judaism was "to prove through the centuries that community can exist without native soil, only through blood and spirit, only through world and belief, and for us to relinquish this uniqueness means for me to resign willingly from the high office which we have accepted from history which, written on a thousand pages, still has room for thousands and thousands of years of wandering." The Jew was the present and future embodiment of the premise and promise of Zweig's formulation of cosmopolitan humanism.

Yet Stefan Zweig, despite evident shortcomings in his creative work and his philosophical assumptions, still manages, almost a half century after his death, to command our attention. An alluring mastery of the art of storytelling and a poignant sensitivity for the individual permeate his work, particularly his short stories. Zweig, not only his autobiography, *The World of Yesterday* (now perhaps his most cited work), manages to cast light onto the human condition. This is particularly so when he unself-consciously concentrates on rendering concrete circumstances and details. The legends in this collection constitute a crystalline distillation of Zweig's character, talent, and limitations. As examples of his command of the craft of short fiction, they place him in the best possible light for the modern reader.

"Buchmendel" is the finest story in the collection. Its place and subject are drawn from Vienna and Zweig's youth. A compelling authenticity of voice and material can be sensed in the story. Zweig's psychological portraits of Mendel and of himself as narrator are subtle and

Jewish Legends

ring true. "Buchmendel" is primarily about a matter of lifelong concern to Zweig: the nature of true genius. In this story Zweig displayed a rare example of self-understanding. He recognized early in his career that within the tradition and the contemporary world of literature he was little more than a brilliant epigone. He knew that he was not the equal of Hofmannstal in the command of language, the peer of Schnitzler as storyteller or dramatist, or a rival to Rilke as poet. As a prose writer he could not match the great Russian novelists or Thomas Mann. Neither was he an original in the sense of Freud or Mozart. He had no aspirations to scholarship.

Precisely because of his own self-recognition, his reluctant but accurate estimate of himself, "Buchmendel" possesses an authentic match between subject and narrative style rare in Zweig. Mendel, in a much more limited arena, is the self that Zweig might like to have been but was not—an unrivaled genius. Yet Zweig is careful to distance himself socially from Mendel in the story to cast some ambiguity on the narrator's awe of Mendel. Mendel was a foreigner from the provinces, like most of Vienna's *fin de siècle* poor and *petit bourgeois* Jews, who were born either outside the city or as first-generation Viennese and retained evident marks of provincialism in accent and dress. By contrast, Zweig was born to an affluent and assimilated family who had come to Vienna directly to an elegant apartment on the Schottenring. His parents came to Vienna not in search of a livelihood but as a consequence of their material success.

One can detect Zweig's visceral distaste for and distance from the *Ostjude* in his characterization of Mendel.

xxiv

Introduction by Leon Botstein

Mendel was but a few steps removed from the masses of Jews who flooded Vienna to attend Theodor Herzl's funeral and who seemed to Jews of Zweig's class embarrassingly strange. Inside the city there were at least three distinct groupings of Jews, the old pre-1867 German-speaking Jewish community (which included the fabled elite banking and merchant families), the newer assimilated affluent community, of which Schnitzler and Zweig were members, and the evidently foreign and immigrant Jews. Mendel was an anomaly from that third grouping whose origins could somehow never be masked.

If Zweig displayed ambivalence toward Mendel physically and as a Jewish type, he revealed a more telling but authentic mixture of attraction and repulsion for his talent. On the one hand Mendel was a genius. He had the single-minded love and fanaticism for his work that genius demanded. He was oblivious to everything around him except books. His virtuosity and creativity in his world were unmatched. But this had its costs, not only in human terms. Was the sacrifice worth it? How dangerously close was Mendel to being an *idiot savant?* Might not the same have been said of Mozart? Zweig never committed himself to any one genre or any one field, in the sense of Mendel, sufficiently to test his own talent. He was constantly aware of the outside world. He engaged it. For Zweig, the urbane manner, breadth of interest, and signs of cultivation he possessed were as much marks of his talent as symptoms of his lack of genius.

Zweig's intense scrutiny of Buchmendel's mind is matched in the story by his will to portray, through

Mendel, the dehumanizing brutality of World War I and the decay of the post-war years. Zweig gives narrative meaning to Joseph Roth's lament contained in *Radetzkymarsch* that "Then, before the Great War . . . it was not yet a matter of indifference whether a man lived or died . . . All that grew, needed much time to grow; and all that disappeared, required much time to be forgotten. But everything that once existed left traces behind, and one lived during those times from the memories, just as one lives today from the capacity, quickly and pointedly, to forget." The narrator in the story remembers Buchmendel only with difficulty. He must press through the cheap veil of post war change that has come over the coffeehouse. Only one poor survivor, the cleaning lady, also remembers Mendel. Buchmendel becomes Zweig's metaphor for the transformation of life and the abrupt change brought about by the collapse of the Habsburg Monarchy. To the extent that Buchmendel embodied a specific enterprise of the mind devoted to learning, it had been supported by a spontaneous, non-bureaucratic network, requiring no home, office, station, advertisement or certification but merely a regular table in a cafe—a way of life to which the homeless but spiritually superior Jew could aspire. Such miracles were only possible in the days before the war. Zweig, through this authentic tale, implicitly challenges his romantic notion of the possibilities of a humanistic world for modernity in which the exotic genius might still find a home. "Buchmendel" is an example of how Zweig's artistry and insight as storyteller triumph over his direct rhetorical celebrations of global humanism. The brutal realities of

Introduction by Leon Botstein

power, politics, and money succeeded in extinguishing the fragile and carefully nurtured gleam of spiritual genius that Mendel represented.

"Rachel Arraigns with God" is, in contrast, an explicit extension of a biblical story. Here one encounters Zweig at his weakest. The tone is artificial, the consequence of Zweig's self-conscious effort to approximate the character of the Old Testament. The psychological struggle Zweig depicts is as crass and artificially antique in its sexual predicament as it is incongruous with the Biblical narrative. Here Zweig overplays his sense of stylistic virtuosity. He feigns the tone of the Bible, in search for a modern equivalent, without simulating the power of the Bible. The moral of the tale is the mercy of God in response to the mundane conflicts of love, desire, and envy. Zweig sets Rachel up in the tradition of the literary elevation of the feminine as eternally ethically superior. The pain inflicted by life—by parents, by courtship, marriage, and sexual attachments among individuals—is appropriated awkwardly into the larger calculus of the covenant, the theology of human history, and the obligations of faith and virtue. Banality and myth clash, as do the mundane and the sacred. Zweig's stylistic imitation is undifferentiated and unrelenting; his evident delight in the pseudo-prophetic voice grates on the reader. The cadences and rhetoric of the Bible and its sweeping and moralizing tone—the work of Zweig the stylist—somehow undercut Zweig the storyteller in the effort to render Rachel a powerful individual, a "personality" in the twentieth-century sense.

"The Legend of the Third Dove" is a somewhat more

Jewish Legends

successful effort on the part of Zweig to command the form of the brief fable and parable. It is more effective because it is more modest and contains no human characters. Here too we sense Zweig's assertive presence as stylist. The language seeks the attention of the reader as artfully produced. One is not permitted to forget the sequence of well-turned phrases. Once again, the moral of the tale is nearly undercut by the sanctimonious tone and the self-congratulatory high-mindedness of a tale whose message is the continuing struggle of man to find peace and harmony, to overcome destruction and conflict, and to find a stable resting place.

In this tale, man is like the third dove sent by Noah, who forgets his master and is faithless. The dove is overcome by a "violent" sense of power and joy at the prospect of life and freedom from confinement. As a secondary myth of the linkage between the exercise of free will and the fall from grace, it is weak, for the meaning of the dove's ultimate achievement of a resting place remains unclear. Zweig's prophetic lamentation that humankind, like the dove, is mired in struggle, darkness, and self-delusion with respect to its own power leads to his conclusion that, in the sense of Biblical history and sacred teleology, "a hand" will be "put forth to take her [the dove] waiting for the knowledge that the trial has been at last enough."

This legend, more than the others, helps to illuminate Zweig's alluring relationship to his readers. Here was a fable that aestheticized the sufferings and wanderings of human history. The educated reader could delight in his profound recognition of man's condition as rebellious

Introduction by Leon Botstein

wanderer without either sensing the pain or assuming responsibility for resolution. A passive hope for a magical rescue, stripped from any coherent theological content, is put forth. All the pathos, weighty symbolism, and meaning do little more than inspire a sense of facile recognition of the terrifying. A cosmic and profound essential truth is compressed into a palatable and cultured morsel, easily digested and appropriated. Pretty phrases about the troubled career of human history since the Flood emerge. Zweig replaces the opportunity for discomfort, recognition, and a sense of actual ethical responsibility for the human plight with a decorative, literary and secular version of the hope for messianic redemption.

The two remaining tales are the most substantial and challenging. The earlier of the two, "Virata or the Eyes of the Undying Brother," is the finest precis of Zweig's grasp of the predicament of the individual's being-in-the-world. Written before World War I, it reflects the widespread fascination with India and the East among Zweig's *fin de siècle* contemporaries. By 1910 Zweig had been to India. He saw himself in a tradition of discourse about Eastern Philosophy that extended back to Schopenhauer. The reconciliation of Western notions of freedom and judgment with Eastern traditions was attempted by the retelling of the career of a great Eastern holy man in a manner that dovetailed readily with comparable Western moral and philosophical ruminations of the early twentieth century. In particular, "Virata" takes on the challenge of Leo Tolstoy with respect to ethical purity and the demands of the everyday; the conflict between the absolute dictates of conscience and the real, compromis-

Jewish Legends

ing contexts of life in which practical responsibility must normally be exercised. This legend can be compared to Max Weber's characterizations of the tension between politics and pure ethical behavior and thought in his 1919 lectures, *Science as a Vocation* and *Politics as a Vocation*. Weber, like Zweig, sought to understand the problem of competing values, particularly between those of engagement in the world (with its pragmatic standards and persistent call to sacrifice ultimate values) and those associated with the search for a higher standard of personal ethical purity, self-recognition, and integrity.

In this legend, Zweig strikes a compelling balance between his didactic and narrative impulses. He tells the story economically, with an unobtrusive elegance. Zweig rivets the reader with Virata's experience and personal struggle. At the same time Zweig manages to frame the philosophical paradoxes. Like Weber, Zweig concludes that an assumption of ethical purity within the world is self-deceptive. He challenges one of the basic assumptions behind his own work, the capacity of language to communicate among people with clarity and agreement. Even the specific terms of judgment, let alone their consequences, never carry equivalent moral meaning for all people; nor do they always take the same shape or maintain the same truth values. Zweig contemplates the denial and negation of the power of his only tool, language.

Unlike Weber, Zweig even doubts the ethical validity of silence and the ascetic withdrawal from the world, for they too, as in the Virata legend, can lead inadvertently to evil and suffering. However, the moral of the tale, as is

Introduction by Leon Botstein

often the case with Zweig, remains troublesome. Self-denial, blind obedience to a menial task, and the rejection of fame and recognition—the search for inconsequential obscurity—seemed the only answer for Virata. But that choice came after a life history of action, both good and evil. It was a choice at life's closure, after marriage and children. Was Virata's conclusion, his flight into obscurity, an option for one's beginning encounter in the world?

The legend, therefore, works best as a parable of the stages of life. Virata moves from courageous violent action based on loyalty, confidence, and skill to withdrawal within society before death. But throughout, the eyes of the dying brother—the metaphor for the inescapable recognition of the fact that unexpected tragic consequences derive from one's life and that one always affects one's fellow human—follow Virata.

This legend, finally, frames the issue of the meaning of history and man's role in it. If action in one's own time has unpredictable consequences and easily changes its ethical significance, then over the larger sweep of time ethical judgment regarding the good and bad action, past or present, is nearly impossible. It is no longer a matter of decoding the "cunning of reason" in history. Rather, the legend demands that we relinquish what Zweig doubtless regarded as the prevalence, in the West, of excessive confidence by individuals in the historical value of their actions. This implication was as encouraging of Zweig's pacifism as it was of his disregard for organized efforts to intervene, through politics, in the social and

Jewish Legends

economic order. Here once more was an elegant and authentic justification of a refined and wise passivity and political detachment.

What makes this legend beautiful is the fact that, as in the case of "Buchmendel," Zweig used it to engage in some evident autobiographical self-criticism. He confronts his own conceits and ambitions. As with Mendel, he uses Virata as a mirror for his own personality and prejudices. Zweig's Virata legend draws on more than Zweig's flirtation with the Indian and the Oriental. It stems from his own spiritual odyssey as a man in his twenties in search of a justification for his literary work in relation to the pressing political and moral dilemmas of his time.

Although it does not possess any overt connection to Judaism or the Jewish tradition, it is sufficiently similar in subject to the Rachel and Third Dove legends to warrant inclusion in this collection. Furthermore, the Virata legend, in the cast given it by Zweig, approaches the dilemmas of mankind in a manner comparable to Zweig's version of the Biblical voice. The Virata legend exhibits the same narrative pattern as "The Buried Candelabrum." But the Virata legend, despite its attempt to transmit an authentic sensibility of India (much in the manner of Hesse's *Siddhartha*), also exhibits an unwitting distance from the real community from which the original legends are taken. The same distance is visible in the cases of the Jewish legends. Curiously, in none of these three legends is Zweig's self-image or awareness as a Jew crucial or even perceptible.

The opposite is the case in "The Buried Can-

Introduction by Leon Botstein

delabrum." This, the longest of the selections in this volume, is Zweig's most overtly personal statement with respect to Judaism and Jewish history. Written after the seizure of power by Hitler in 1933, it is Zweig's fullest and final expression of his sense of Jewish identity and the historical role and predicament of the Jewish people. "The Buried Candelabrum" also documents Zweig's slight shift toward Zionism. Before the 1930s, he held on to the notion of the Jew as bearer of an identity which transcended nationalism and which could provide a model for a new basis of world citizenship. Zweig's admiration for Theodor Herzl was based not on Herzl's ideas but his personality. Before Hitler, political Zionism seemed yet another species of divisive nationalism. Given Zweig's distance from a traditional religious identity as Jew, the vision of a secular and peculiarly spiritual people, bonded together by a common history of dispersion, study and suffering, who as sojourners in the lands of others emerged as the party of humanity and peace and not of hate and violence, was the only plausible alternative. Until the mid-1930s, it fit well with Zweig's vocation and his personal success.

It is ironic that it took Hitler to force Zweig to reconsider his distance from Zionism. After all, he had grown up in the city of Karl Lueger, a Vienna marked by extensive public and private anti-semitism. Since Zweig was both assimilated and affluent, the anti-semitism touched him only slightly. It seemed irrelevant, particularly within the literary and intellectual circles of Viennese society. Unlike Schnitzler and Felix Salten, Zweig chose not to engage the pressing Jewish question

Jewish Legends

or the significance of anti-semitism in Viennese political life after the *fin de siècle*. Zweig, well into the 1930s, held onto a near-fictional and nostalgic image of Vienna as a cosmopolitan and almost idyllic center of culture and toleration.

The extent to which Hitler's success came as a shock, and not a confirmation of a long historical process, can be seen in "The Buried Candelabrum." Zweig sets aside his allegiance to the image of the Jew as world citizen. He strikes a nearly nationalist sentiment and projects the end of the wanderings of the Jewish people through the image of the future discovery of the light-bearing Menorah which, having been buried in the sands of Palestine, would be dug up "when the Jews come once more into their own, and that then the Seven-Branched Lampstand will diffuse its gentle light in the temple of peace."

Despite this shift, Zweig tries to remain true to his past beliefs. The Jews continue to play a unique historical role for humanity. They are still the bearers of light. Their nationalist triumph will come only after centuries of struggle, at the moment of the triumph of peace. Zweig's accommodation with Zionism was only partial. The legend makes clear that his vision was not of the Jews returning home as a normal modern nation, or of their taking a place in an ordinary world with commonplace political means, including power, persuasion and war.

"The Buried Candelabrum" in fact expresses explicitly Zweig's sense of the special place in history occupied by Jews. Their survival during their dispersion, as depicted in the legend, depends on the triumph of spirit over

Introduction by Leon Botstein

force. Young Benjamin is in fact permanently physically maimed in the effort to rescue the symbol of the Jewish people. Yet he outlives all his brethren. Benjamin embodies the superiority of the spirit over the body. An aged cripple manages to lay the basis for a new age, the age in which the "gentle" (as opposed to fierce) light of the Menorah will herald an age of peace. Furthermore, the crucial dramatic twist of the story revolves around the triumph of imagination and skill over brute force. A false copy of the Menorah is substituted, cheating Justinian's commands of their power, outsmarting the most powerful man in the world. The Jews become the preservers of secret authenticity in a world duped by seductive falsehoods. The experience of powerlessness and homelessness only enhances the humanity of the Jews.

Perhaps the most poignant aspect of the legend is Zweig's assertion that the prospect of the rediscovery of the genuine treasured symbol of Jewish nationhood was a reason for collective hope. Zweig renders concrete the teleological promise inherent in Zionism. He concedes for the first time that Europe may not be home; that a home is necessary, even in a utopian world at peace; and that the Jewish homeland will be in Palestine. Most crucially, Zweig argues that the return *will* occur, for otherwise Benjamin's heroic rescue of the Menorah would make no sense. God and human history finally must reveal an ultimate and ethical logic. Tragically, Zweig's sense of this hope was fragile. His eloquence on its behalf was impersonal and detached. Zweig's "Buried Candelabrum" stands in stark contrast to Zweig's suicide.

Zweig's utopian and abstract version of Zionism in

Jewish Legends

"The Buried Candelabrum" frames the essential twentieth-century tension between the traditions of modern European secular Jewish culture from the diaspora and the actual evolution of modern Israel. Israel has become a political entity, a nation, in the normal sense. Political Zionism experienced success in transforming the Jew from the abnormal—the people apart from the everyday, bereft of a political arena capable of normalizing the abnormal Jew and shaped by a history of dispersion and persecution—into the Jew as entirely human, undifferentiated in either the sense of good or evil. This has been part of Israel's triumph. From the perspective of Stefan Zweig, however, the historic abnormality of the Jew had been a virtue. He cherished the idea of the Jew as spiritual pioneer of a better world containing nations free of hate and discrimination. Zweig, like so many others, sought in Jewish nationalism a different, new, and ethically higher definition of community. The task of Zionism, as portrayed in Zweig's image of the Menorah, was to lead the world of the future to the point at which the historically abnormal qualities of the Jews (by comparison with the nationalities of Europe tied to soil and race)—the Jews' traditional cultivation of spirit, ethics, culture and finally humanism—would become the normal.

The role in history given to the Jews by Zweig through this legend of the successful preservation of the national symbol is ultimately as bearers of the "gentle" light, the enlightenment of mankind. The Jew should *not* become like the others. The others should become like the Jews of the diaspora. Like the long-suffering, physically-im-

Introduction by Leon Botstein

paired Benjamin, the flower of European Jewry possessed in its heart the symbolic image, not only of yet another nation, but of its own unique capacity to shed light. The task of history was to make its secret public, to rekindle the light for mankind.

With the staggeringly extensive extermination of European Jewry during World War II, the diaspora, with its traditions of secular Jewish culture has shrunken. Given the religious revival of the late twentieth century in America, the continuing process of radical assimilation among diaspora Jews, and the evolution of Israel as a distinct and powerful political entity, shaped by Western and Oriental Jewish traditions alike, the spiritual and nearly cosmopolitan Zionism which represented the most profound expression of Jewish identity by Stefan Zweig appears to be an anachronism.

But "The Buried Candelabrum" does more than evoke the world of Stefan Zweig and his allegiance to the nineteenth and early twentieth century triumph of European Jews in European culture and civilization. Zweig's embrace of enlightenment, learning, and pacifist utopianism—his celebration of the life of the mind and spirit, of art, science, and culture as the highest expressions of human life—reminds us of an instinctive idealism that demands admiration. It may have been part of the dangerous delusions shared by hundreds of thousands of European Jews. But that idealism is a key to a glorious era of Jewish history in Europe. Zweig lived in that era. The other legends and stories in this collection bring that era with all its shortcomings into sharp focus.

Despite the destruction of his world, Stefan Zweig's

Jewish Legends

innocent and naive hopes for humanity ought not be dismissed too readily. Beneath Zweig's facile sentimentality and often maudlin prose lies one of the simplest but noblest of aspirations for humankind. For this reason alone, "The Buried Candelabrum" and its companion stories merit a fresh reading. When these stories and legends were first published in a collection in 1945, one unenthusiastic critic noted, "Now is not the time to determine the ultimate place of Stefan Zweig in literary history. We know that much of his work will remain alive and therefore it is good to preserve it for the future. For along with our own metamorphoses, his work will change its appearance to us again—and to our benefit."

March 8, 1987

The Buried Candelabrum

Illustrated by Berthold Wolpe

IN THE Circus Maximus, on a fine June day in the year 455, a combat between two tall Heruli and a sounder of Hyrcanian boar had reached its sanguinary close when, in the third hour of the afternoon, disquiet spread among the thousands of onlookers. At first it was only those seated near the imperial box who noticed that something was amiss. A horseman, dusty and travel-stained by a long ride, descended the stairway with its statues on either side, and approached the bedizened dais where Maximus lolled, surrounded by courtiers. The Emperor listened to the tidings, sprang to his feet, and—disregarding the convention which forbade him to leave while the games were in progress—hastened out, followed by his train. The senatorial benches likewise and those of the other dignitaries quickly emptied. The cause must be

Jewish Legends

grave indeed for such a breach of etiquette. Naturally the common folk grew uneasy.

Attempts were made to distract the attention of the crowd. Trumpet blasts announced a new "turn." The grid rose. A roar issued from the dark interior as a black-maned lion was goaded into the arena to encounter the short swords of a troop of gladiators. In vain, for the show had lost interest. Waves of alarm, crowned by a spume of anxious and excited faces, spread irresistibly from tier to tier. Quitting their places, the plebs gathered in knots and pointed to the empty seats of the mighty; they questioned one another eagerly; catcalls were heard; the amusement had ceased to amuse; and at length (how or where started no one knew) a rumour ran through the vast amphitheatre, a name of ill-omen, "The Vandals!"—"The Vandals!"

Genseric and his men, the dreaded pirates of the Mediterranean, had landed at Portus, to attack the heart of the Empire. Vast numbers of them were already marching along the Via Portuensis. "Vandals, Vandals." The whisper became a shout, and changed itself into the still more terrible word, "Barbarians, barbarians." Hundreds screamed it; thousands screamed it, in the huge circus. Panic-stricken, disorderly, the crowds raced along the stone courses toward the exits, driven by fear like leaves before the wind. Janitors, marshals, and soldiers of the watch forsook their posts, fighting through the press with fists, staves, and swords; women and children were trampled underfoot; the outlets were funnels, each containing a mass of shrieking humanity. Within a few minutes the enormous edifice of stone and marble was empty, save for the corpses of those who had been struck down, or trampled to death. The gigantic oval, still glowing beneath the summer sun, was vacated, save for the lion, whose antagonists (death-defying gladiators though they were) had also fled. Puzzled and forsaken, the black-maned king of beasts once more roared his challenge into the void.

The Vandals were approaching. Messenger after messenger spurred into the imperial city, each bringing worse news than the last. The barbarians had landed from a fleet of a hundred sailing ships and galleys, a lightly equipped and swiftly moving multitude. Cavalry as well as infantry, for white-robed Berbers and Numidians, riders from the nomadic tribes of Northern Africa, were speeding along the road to the capital in advance of their Teutonic allies. On the morrow, or the next day, the whole invading force, fired by the lust for plunder, would assail the doomed town. The Roman army (captives and mercenaries) was far away, fighting near Ravenna; and the walls of Rome had never been repaired since Alaric breached them. No one even dreamed of defence. The minority, who had property to lose as well as life, made ready to escape, loading their valuables into mule-carts, for they hoped to get away with at least some of their possessions. Their hopes were vain. The long-suffering populace rose in wrath against those who had lorded it over them in time of peace, and now tried to flee in time of war.

When Maximus, the Emperor, set forth from the palace with such baggage as he had time to get together, curses were volleyed at him and were soon reinforced by deadlier missiles—stones. Growing fiercer, the mob assailed the cowardly deserter, and made an end of him with bludgeons and hatchets. The warders followed the customary routine, and closed the gates at nightfall. Alas, the shutting of the gates served only to prison fear within the city. Like a pestilential vapour, forebodings of a terrible fate hovered over the silent and shadowed houses, while darkness fell like a pall upon the once glorious but now decadent and trembling Rome. Yet the stars shone as usual, serenely indifferent to human woes, and the crescent moon sank as tranquilly as if no barbarian invasion threatened. Sleepless and desperate, the Romans awaited the coming of the Vandals, as a man about to be executed lays his head on the block awaiting the fall of an axe already poised for the stroke.

Slowly, surely, purposefully, victoriously, the main force of the Vandals advanced along the deserted road leading from Portus to Rome. The blond, long-haired Teutons marched in good order, century by century, while in front of them, wheeling and curvetting, rode their dark-skinned auxiliaries from the desert, mounted on thoroughbreds, bare-footed and stirrupless. In the midst of his army was Genseric, King of the Vandals. From the saddle he smiled good-humouredly at his warriors. Now middle-aged, inured to battle from earliest youth, he had learned from his spies that there was no likelihood of serious resistance; that his forces were on their way, not to a strenuous fight, but to a week or two of easy and pleasurable looting.

In truth, no Roman stood to arms. Not until the King reached the gate of the city, did anyone attempt to stay his progress. Here there appeared Pope Leo, first of the Leos, Leo the Great, in full pontificals, attended by the senior clergy. Leo hoped to repeat the success of three years earlier, when he had persuaded Attila, King of the Huns, to depart from Italy without sacking Rome. At sight of the imposing greybeard, the club-footed Genseric politely dismounted and limped to meet the Holy Father. But he did not kiss the hand of the priest who wore the Fisherman's ring, nor make obeisance, for, being an Arian, he looked upon the Pope as a heretic and a usurper. Coldly and unresponsively he listened to the Latin oration, in which Leo begged the Vandal monarch to spare the Holy City. Through an interpreter he replied that, being himself a Christian as well as a soldier, he did not propose to burn and destroy Rome—though Rome herself, ambitious and greedy for power, had razed thousands of cities to the ground. In his magnanimity he would spare the possessions of the Church and the bodies of the women, and would merely have the place looted "sine ferro et igne," in accordance with the right of the stronger to work his will upon the vanquished. "But," he said menacingly, as his equerry held the stirrup for him to remount, "you will do well to hearken to my counsel, and open the gates to me without more ado."

His orders were obeyed. Not a spear was pointed, not a sword brandished. Within the hour, Rome was at the mercy of the Vandals. But the victorious raiders did not fling themselves lawlessly upon the defenceless town. They marched in quietly, restrained by Genseric's iron hand, these tall, upstanding, flaxen-haired warriors, striding along the Via Triumphalis, staring curiously at the marble statues, whose mute lips seemed to promise such an abundance of loot. His goal was the Palatinum, the imperial residence. He ignored the rows of waiting senators, who had timidly assembled to do him reverence, and he did not even accept a banquet, or so much as glance at the splendid gifts which some of the wealthier citizens had brought to appease him. No, what the stern soldier had in mind was how best, most swiftly, and most methodically to get possession of the riches of the capital. Poring over a map, he allotted a century to each district, making the centurions responsible for the good conduct of their men. There was to be no indiscriminate and lawless looting. Genseric had in view a systematic spoliation of Rome. The gates were closed and guarded, the breaches in the walls were manned, that not an ingot or a coin should be removed. Then his men commandeered boats, carts, and beasts of burden, pressing thousands of slaves into the service, to make sure that as speedily as possible the treasures of imperial Rome should be removed to the pirates' lair on the southern coast of the Mediterranean. The work of plunder was carried out methodically, coldly, and noiselessly. For thirteen days the quivering city was disarticulated and stripped bare.

Parties of Vandal warriors went from house to house, from temple to temple, each detachment led by a nobleman and accompanied by a clerk. They seized whatever was valuable and transportable; gold and silver chalices, ingots, coins, jewels, necklaces from the Amber Coast, furs from Transylvania, malachite from Pontus, swords from Persia. Deft workmen were constrained to remove mosaics from the walls of the temples and porphyry slabs from the peristyles of the mansions. All was done according to plan, with the utmost care. With the aid of windlasses, the bronze chariot-teams were taken down from the triumphal arches; the interior of the temple of Jupiter Capitolinus was cleared of its valuables; and slaves were sent onto the roof to remove the gilt tiles one by one.

As for the bronze pillars, which were too large to take away intact without the sacrifice of much time and trouble, Genseric had them knocked to pieces or sawn in sunder, that he might ship the metal in fragments. Street after street, house after house, was cleared by these locusts; and when the plunderers had done with the habitations of the living, they turned to break open the tumuli, the abiding-places of the dead. Out of the stone sarcophagi they took the jewelled combs which had been thrust into the now mouldering hair of dead noblewomen; they tore golden anklets and bracelets from skeletons; silver mirrors too, they found, and signet-rings which had been interred with the corpses; they impounded even the obols which, in accordance with ancient custom, had been placed in the mouths of the deceased to pay Charon the ferryman for the voyage across the Styx.

As had been arranged by the King, the booty was piled in orderly heaps. The golden-winged Nike was prostrate between a gem-studded casket containing the bones of a saint and an ivory dice-box that had belonged to a lady of rank. Silver ingots lay upon purple garments, and precious glassware adjoined fragments of base metal.

Each article thought worth taking to Carthage was recorded by the clerk on one of his parchments, not only to keep tally, but to give this wholesale theft a veneer of legality. Followed by his notables, Genseric hobbled through the medley, poking at various objects with his stick, scrutinizing the jewels, well pleased, and distributing praise. He was delighted as he watched the heavily freighted carts and the boats deep in the water leave the capital. But no house in the city was fired and there was no bloodshed. Quietly and in regular succession, as in a mine, the loaded wagons and boats went from the town to the harbour and came back empty from Portus to Rome. Never within the memory of man had there been so great a plundering effected in thirteen days as in this bloodless Vandal sack of Rome.

For thirteen days no voice was raised above a whisper in the myriad-housed city, nor did anyone laugh. The lutes were silent in the dwelling-rooms, and the chanting was stilled in the churches. The only noises were made by the hammers and crowbars of the devastators, the wains that creaked under their load, the oxen that grunted as they tugged, the mules that tightened the traces, the drivers as they cracked their whips. Sometimes, indeed, a neglected cur would whine for food, which his master was too busy or too anxious to provide; or the sound of a trumpet would come from the wall, where the guard was being relieved. But in the houses men, women, and children held their breath. Rome, which had conquered the world, lay prostrate at a conqueror's feet; and when, at night, the breeze blew through the deserted streets, the sound was like the groans of a wounded man who feels his lifeblood flowing from his veins.

On the thirteenth evening of the Vandals' plunder-raid, the Jews of the Roman community were assembled in the house of Moses Abtalion, on the left bank of the Tiber, where the yellow river curves slothfully like an overfed serpent. Abtalion was a "small man" among his co-religionists, nor was he learned in the Law, being only a middle-aged craftsman whose hands were stained by his occupation as dyer; but they had chosen his house for a meeting-place because his workshop on the ground floor was more roomy than the attic chambers in which most of them dwelt. Since the coming of Genseric and his hordes, they had assembled day after day, wearing their white shrouds, to pray in the gloomy shuttered shops, stubborn and almost stupefied, amid rolls of carpet, bales of brightly coloured cloth, and well-filled barrels of oil and wine. So far, the Vandals had not troubled them. Twice or thrice, a century, accompanied by noblemen and clerks, marched through the Jewish quarter, which was low-lying, so that its narrow streets showed abundant traces of repeated inundations, and walls and flagstones sweated damp. One disdainful glance sufficed to convince the treasure-hunters that they would waste their pains here. No peristyles paved with marble, no triclinia glittering with gold, no bronze statues or costly vases. The Vandals did not tarry, but went elsewhere in search of spoil.

Nevertheless the hearts of the Roman Jews were heavy. Generation after generation, ever since the Diaspora, these exiles from the Holy Land had found that disaster to the country of their adoption betokened disaster to them also. When fortune smiled, the Gentiles forgot them or paid them little heed. The princes wore sumptuous clothing and gave themselves up to their craze for architecture and display; while the coarser lusts of the mob were satisfied with the chase and gambling and the unceasing round of gladiatorial shows. But always, when trouble came, the cry was "Blame the Jews." It was unlucky for the Jews when the Gentiles among whom they lived sustained a defeat; bad for them when a town was sacked; bad for them when a pestilence broke out. No matter what evil should befall, it would be laid to their charge. To rebel against this injustice was futile, for they were few and weak, no longer men of war as their valiant forefathers had been. Their only resource was prayer.

Throughout this fortnight when Rome was being despoiled by the Vandals, the Jews, therefore, prayed evening after evening, and on into the small hours. What else could a righteous man do, in an unrighteous and violent world where might was held to be right, than turn away from earth and look to Jehovah for aid? These barbarian invasions had been going on for decades. From the north and the south, from the east and the west they came, fair-haired and dark, speaking divers tongues, but robbers without exception. Hardly was one conquest finished when the next began, for the invaders trod on one another's heels. The ungodly were at war throughout the world, and continued to harry the pious. Jerusalem had fallen, Babylon and Alexandria; now it was Rome's turn. Where the Chosen People sought rest, unrest came; where they desired peace, they were afflicted by war. Who could escape his destiny? In this tormented world, refuge, tranquillity, and consolation could be found only in prayer. Yes, prayer dispelled alarm with words of promise, appeased terror through the chanting of litanies, enabled the heavy-hearted to wing their way Godward. Hence it was meet to pray in time of trouble, and better still to pray when gathered together, for God's good gifts came most abundantly to those who sought them in common.

So the Jews of the Roman confraternity had assembled to pray. The pious murmur flowed from their bearded mouths gently and unceasingly, just as outside the windows the current of the Tiber rippled gently and unceasingly past the planking of the levee—eating away the bank wherever it was undefended. The men did not look at one another, and yet their rounded shoulders moved in unison, since the time was set by the familiar words of the psalms they were intoning, the psalms which their fathers and forefathers had intoned hundreds and thousands of times before them. So automatic was it that they scarcely realized their lips were moving, hardly understood the significance of the words they uttered. The despairful and prayerful monotone issued, as it were, from a trance, from an obscure land of dreams.

Then they came to themselves with a jerk, straightening their bent backs, for the door-knocker had been violently sounded. Even in good times the Jews of the Diaspora were wont to be alarmed by any sudden or unexpected happening. How could good come of it when a stranger demanded admittance in the middle of the night? The murmur ceased, as if cut with shears, so that the plashing of the river sounded louder than before. They listened, their throats tense with alarm. Again the knocker thundered, and an impatient fist banged on the door.

"Coming," answered Abtalion, rising and scuttling forth into the entry. The flame of the wax candle, which was stuck to the table by some of its own meltings, flickered as the craftsman threw open the workshop door while the hearts of all those present throbbed under stress of fear.

They recovered, however, on recognizing the new arrival. It was Hyrcanus ben Hillel, master of the imperial mint, a man of whom the community was proud, since he was the only Jew who had the right to cross the threshold of the palace. By special favour of the court he was allowed to live beyond Trastevere, and might even wear the coloured robes reserved for Romans of distinction;' but now his raiment was torn, and his face besoiled.

They crowded round him, eager to hear his tidings, all the more because his expression showed that they were evil.

Hyrcanus ben Hillel drew a deep breath and struggled vainly to speak. At length he managed to pant:

"Ruin has befallen us, the greatest of disasters. They have found it; they have seized it."

"Found what, Hyrcanus?"—"Seized what?"—A similar cry came from every mouth.

"The Candelabrum, the Menorah. When the barbarians entered the city, I hid it beneath the garbage in the kitchen. Purposely I left the other holy things in the treasury: the Table of Shewbread, the Silver Trumpets, Aaron's Rod, and the Altar of Incense. Too many of the servants in the palace knew about our treasures, and it would have courted a search had I hidden them all. One thing only did I hope to save from among the temple furniture—Moses' Seven-Branched Candlestick, the Lampstand from Solomon's House, the Menorah. The rogues had taken what I had left for them to see, the room was stripped bare, they had ceased hunting and were about to leave, and I was glad at heart in the conviction that we had saved the Candelabrum, at least. But one of the slaves (a murrain seize him) had watched me hiding it, and betrayed the hiding-place—in the hope of a reward which would enable him to buy his freedom. He showed them, and they discovered it. Now everything is gone which once stood in the Holy of Holies, in the House of Solomon: the Altar and the Vessels and the Mitre of the

Jewish Legends

Priest and the Menorah. This very evening the Vandals are carrying off the Candelabrum to their ships."

For a moment, silence followed. Then came a wailing chorus:

"The Lampstand ... Woe, and yet again woe.... The Menorah ... God's Seven-Branched Candlestick.... Woe, woe.... The Lampstand from God's Altar ... the Menorah."

The Jews staggered like drunken men; they beat their breasts; they held their hips and screamed as though in pain; as if struck blind, the reverend elders lamented.

"Silence!" commanded a powerful voice, and the distraught men did as they were bid. He who spoke was the senior member of the community, the oldest and the wisest, the most learned in the Law, Rabbi Eliezer, whom they called Kab ve Nake, which being interpreted means "the pure and clear." Nigh upon eighty years of age was he, with a huge snow-white beard. Seamed was his visage by the painful ploughshare of unrelenting thought; but the eyes beneath the bushy brows were bright as ever, and full of kindness. He raised his hand, the skin being yellowed like parchment with the tale of his years, and waved it as if to dispel the clamour and make room for the thoughtful words he was about to utter.

"Silence!" he repeated. "Children scream in alarm. Grown men consider what is to be done. Let us resume our seats and hold counsel together. The mind is more active when the body is at rest."

Shamefacedly the men sat down on stools and benches. Rabbi Eliezer talked to them, in low tones, almost as if communing with himself.

"Indeed we have suffered a terrible misfortune. Long since, the holy furnishings of the Tabernacle were taken away from us, to be kept in the Emperor's treasury, and none of us save Hyrcanus ben Hillel was permitted to set eyes on them. Still, we knew they had been in safe-keeping since the days of Titus. In the imperial treasury, they were at least close at hand. These Roman aliens seemed more congenial to us when we remembered that the sacred emblems which had wandered for a thousand years—had been in Jerusalem, then in Babylon, had come back thence to Zion—were at rest in the capital of the Empire where we abode, we who had been despoiled of them. No longer were we allowed to lay bread on the Table of the Lord, but of this Table we thought as often as we broke bread. We could not kindle the lamps on the Lampstand; but whenever we lighted a lamp we remembered the Menorah, which stood untended and dark in the house of the stranger. The holy furniture of the Tabernacle was ours no longer, but we were more or less at ease since it was well guarded. Now the wanderings of the Candelabrum are to begin again. It is not, as we had hoped would happen some day, returning to the home of our fathers, but going elsewhere, and who can say whither? Still, let us not complain. Lament is unavailing. Let us bethink ourselves."

The men listened, wordless, with bowed heads. Eliezer, stroking his beard from time to time, went on, again as if talking to himself:

"The Candelabrum is of pure gold, and often have I wondered why God commanded it should be made of such costly metal. Why did he enjoin upon Moses to make it so heavy, of a talent of pure gold, seven-branched, with its knops and its flowers, all of beaten gold? Often I have pondered whether being so valuable did not endanger the Menorah, for wealth attracts evil, and precious things are a lure to robbers. But now I am aware that I was thinking vain thoughts, and that what God commands has a sense and a purpose which pass our shallow understanding. It has been revealed to me that because they were so precious have these holy things been preserved through the ages. Had they been of base metal, and unadorned, the robbers would have destroyed them unheeding, to make of them chains or swords. Instead they preserved the precious things as precious, though unaware of their holiness. Thus one robber steals them from another, but none venture to destroy them; each remove is but a stage in the journey back to God.

"Let us reflect a while. What can barbarians know of the Menorah? Only what they see for themselves, that it is made of gold. If we could appeal to their cupidity, could offer twice or thrice the value of the gold, perhaps we could buy it back. We Jews are no fighters. Sacrifice alone is our strength. We must send messengers to the dispersed communities of our people, asking them to join forces and purses with us for the redemption of the sacred Candelabrum. This year we must double or triple what we usually contribute for the Temple, stripping the clothes from our backs and the rings from our fingers. We must buy the Menorah, even if we have to pay seven times its weight in pure gold."

He was interrupted by a sigh; from Hyrcanus ben Hillel, who looked up, sad-eyed, and said softly:

"No use, Rabbi; I've tried that in vain. It was my first thought. I betook myself to their valuers and clerks, but they were rude and harsh. Then I forced my way into Genseric's presence and offered to redeem the Lampstand with a great sum. He was wroth, would scarcely listen to my words, and shuffled impatiently with his feet. Thereupon, beside myself, I wrestled with him in speech, assuring him (fool that I was) that the Menorah had once stood in Solomon's Temple, and had been brought back by Titus as the most splendid object with which to grace a triumph. The barbarian monarch laughed scornfully, saying:

" 'I do not need your money. So much gold have I seized here in Rome that I can pave my stables with it, and have my horses' hoofs set with jewels. If the Seven-Branched Candlestick once stood in King Solomon's Temple, it is not for sale to you or to any other. Titus, you say, had it carried before him here in Rome when celebrating his triumph after the conquest of Jerusalem? Well, it shall be carried before me when I celebrate my triumph in Carthage after the conquest of Rome. If the Menorah served your God, it shall now serve the true God. I have spoken. Go!' "

"You should not have gone, Hyrcanus ben Hillel," protested the assembled Jews. "You should have been firmer."

"Do you think I gave way so readily? I flung myself on the floor in front of him and embraced his knees. But his heart was as hard as were his iron-shod shoes. He kicked me away as contemptuously, as mercilessly, as he would have kicked a stone. At a sign from him, his menials beat me with staves and thrust me forth. Barely did I escape with life, and not with a whole skin."

Only now did they understand why Hyrcanus ben Hillel's raiment was torn and bedraggled, why his face was bruised and besoiled, and why there was clotted blood on his brow. Voices were stilled. In the silence they could hear from afar the rattle of the carts in which the plunder was being driven away through the night. Then, reverberating from one end of the city to the other, came trumpet blasts from the departing Vandals. Profound silence followed, while the same thought struck one and all:

"The sack of Rome is finished. The Menorah is lost to us for ever."

Rabbi Eliezer raised his head wearily, and asked:

"Tonight the barbarians remove it?"

"Yes, tonight. They are taking the Menorah in a wagon, which is being driven along the Via Portuensis while we sit here. Those trumpets must have been the signal for the rearguard to assemble. Tomorrow morning the Lampstand will be shipped."

Eliezer bowed his head once more and seemed to fall into a doze. For a few minutes he was absent-minded, paying no heed to his companions' perturbed glances. At length he looked up and said tranquilly:

"Tonight? Well and good. Then we must go with it."

They gazed at him in astonishment. But the old man repeated, firmly:

"Yes, we must go with it. Our duty is clear. Recall what is prescribed for us in Holy Writ. When the Ark of the Covenant was borne before us, we had to follow;

only when the Ark rested, could we rest. If the insignia of God wander, we must wander likewise."

"But, Rabbi, how can we cross the sea? We have no ships."

"Let us make for the coast. It is but one night's march."

Hyrcanus rose to his feet, saying:

"As always, Rabbi Eliezer's words are wise. We must go with the Menorah. 'Tis but another stage of our unending journey. When the Ark of the Covenant moves onward, and the Candelabrum, we must follow, the whole congregation of the Chosen."

Came a plaintive voice from a corner of the room. It was Simeon the carpenter, a hunchback, who trembled with fear.

"But what if the Vandals should seize us? Hundreds, already, have they carried into bondage. They will beat us, will slay us, will sell our children as slaves—and nothing will be gained."

"Silence, poltroon!" rejoined another. "Control your fears. If any one of us is seized, he is seized. If any one of us should be killed, he will die for the holy emblem. We must all go, and we will."

"Yes, all, all," they cried in chorus.

Rabbi Eliezer waved his hand to arrest the clamour. Again he closed his eyes, as usual when he wanted to reflect. After a while he resumed:

"Simeon is right. You do ill to revile him as a coward and a weakling. He is right. We should be foolish to venture the lives of the whole confraternity among these nocturnal marauders. Is not life the greatest gift of God,

Jewish Legends

who does not wish the least of his creatures to throw it away? Simeon is right, the barbarians would lay hands on our children, to make bondmen and bondwomen of them across the sea. Neither our young men nor our boys shall go forth with us into the night. But we who are old are useless to ourselves and to others. They will not make slaves of us, who cannot pull lustily in their galleys, who have hardly strength to dig our own graves, and whom even death can rob of little. It is for us to go with the furniture of the Tabernacle. Let those only make ready whose age is above threescore years and ten."

At the word, the old, those whose beards were white, severed themselves from the rest of the company. There were ten, and when Eliezer, "the pure and clear," joined them, the number was made up to eleven. "The Fathers of our People," thought the younger men, looking at them reverently, the veterans of a generation most of whom had passed away. Rabbi Eliezer detached himself from them once more, to mingle with the young and the middle-aged. He spake:

"We, the elders, are going, and you need not be troubled about our fate. But stay, while I consider. One who is yet a boy must go with us, to bear witness to those of the next generation and that which will follow. We shall not long survive, our light burns low, our course is nearly run, our voices will soon be hushed. Needful is it that one should live on for many years, one who will have set eyes upon the Lampstand from the Altar of the Lord, that in tribe after tribe and in generation after generation knowledge shall endure concerning the most sacred of our treasures, which shall not be lost for ever, but shall move onward upon its eternal pilgrimage. A child, a little boy, too young to understand what he is doing, must accompany us that he may testify in days to come."

There was silence for a space, while each of his auditors thought of a son whom he dreaded to send forth into the dangers of that night. But Abtalion the dyer did not hesitate long.

"I will fetch Benjamin, my grandson. He is seven, having lived as many years as there are branches on the Menorah. Is not that a sign? Meanwhile prepare for the journey, making free of such victuals as my poor house can offer."

He departed. The elders seated themselves at the table, and the younger men served them with wine and food. Before breaking bread, the Rabbi uttered the prayer which their forefathers had repeated thrice every day. Thrice, now, in the thin voices of old age, the others said after Eliezer the heartfelt petition:

"Be merciful, O Lord, unto thy people Israel; in thy loving-kindness restore thy sacred emblem to Zion and bring back to Jerusalem the service of the sacrifice."

Having said this prayer three times, the elders made ready to depart. Calmly and deliberately, as though performing a sacred task, they took off their shrouds and made them into a bundle with their praying-shawls and their phylacteries. The younger men, meanwhile, brought bread and fruit for the journey, and strong staves for support. Each of the intending travellers then wrote upon parchment directions as to the disposal of his property should he fail to return, and these documents were duly witnessed.

Abtalion the dyer, after removing his shoes, mounted the wooden staircase as silently as possible, but he was stout and solidly built, so the treads groaned beneath his weight. Cautiously he lifted the latch and opened the door that led into the living-room. Since they were poor folk, this was for the joint use of the head of the family and his wife, their son and daughter-in-law, their daughters, and their grandchildren. The shutters were closed, but between the chinks the silver moonbeams made their way mistily into the crowded apartment. While walking on tiptoe Abtalion could see that, for all his precautions, his wife and his son's wife had awakened, and were staring at him in alarm.

"What's the matter?" asked one of them.

Abtalion made no reply. Gropingly he went to the left corner at the back, where Benjamin slept. The grandfather leaned solicitously over the pallet. The little boy was sound asleep, but his fists were clenched and his features twitched. He must be having a nightmare. Abtalion stroked his disordered hair, to wake him up; but he slept on, quieted by the caress. The little fists relaxed, so did the lips; the sleeper smiled and stretched his arms contentedly. Abtalion was remorseful at the thought of having to waken the youngster from what were now pleasant dreams. But, having no choice, he shook the child. Benjamin awoke, terror-stricken. A Jewish child in exile soon learned to dread the unexpected. His father was startled when an unheralded visitor knocked loudly at the door; the elders were startled when a new edict was read in the streets of Rome; they were alarmed when an emperor died and a new one took his place. Every child of the Jewish quarter had come to anticipate evil as the outcome of change. Before he knew his letters and could spell out the shorter words of Scripture, the Hebrew youngster had learned this much—to dread everyone and everything on earth.

Confusedly little Benjamin stared at the nocturnal visitor, and was about to scream when Abtalion clapped a hand upon the opened mouth. Then, recognizing his grandfather, the child was appeased. Abtalion bent low, and whispered:

"Gather up your clothing and your shoes, and come with me. Quietly. No one must hear."

The boy sprang out of bed, reassured and proud. Secrets between him and Grandfather. That was fine. He asked no questions, but fumbled for the necessary garments and footgear.

They were creeping to the door, when the boy's mother raised her head from the pillow. She sobbed as she asked:

"Where are you taking Benjamin?"

"Peace," answered Abtalion menacingly. "It is not fitting for a woman to question me."

He closed the door behind him. All the women in the upstairs room were awake now. Through the thin door came a buzz of chattering mingled with sobs. As the eleven old men and the youngster emerged into the street, it was obvious that tidings of their strange and perilous mission had soaked through the walls. The alley was on the alert. Fears and plaints came from every house. But the elders did not look up at the windows nor yet at the house-doors on either side. Silently and resolutely they set forth. It was close on midnight.

Great was their surprise to find the city gate unguarded. The tucket they had heard had assembled the last of the Vandals. These were now marching westward along the Via Portuensis; but the Romans, behind barred doors, did not yet venture to believe that their troubles were over. Thus the road leading to the harbour was deserted; no wains or packhorses, not a man or a shadow; nothing to be seen but the white milestones shimmering in the moonlight. The pilgrims, therefore, strode unchallenged through the open gate.

"Let us hasten," said Hyrcanus ben Hillel. "The carts freighted with plunder must be far on the road to Portus. Perhaps they had already started before the trumpets were sounded. We will speed in pursuit."

They put their best foot foremost, marching three abreast. In the front rank were Abtalion on the left, Eliezer on the right, and between the septuagenarian and the octogenarian tripped along the seven-year-old boy, a little frightened by this adventure, sleepy too, but kept awake by excitement. In three more ranks followed the rest of the elders, each gripping his bundle in the left hand, holding his staff in the right; heads all bowed, as if they were bearing an invisible coffin on their shoulders. The haze of the Campagna enveloped them. No refreshing breeze dispelled the marshy vapour, which hung heavily athwart the plain with its reek of decaying vegetation, and gave a greenish tinge to the waning moon. It was uncanny, on so suffocating a night, to be striding towards insecurity, past the scattered burial mounds looking in the half-light like dead animals on either side of the way, and past the pillaged houses, emptied of their inhabitants, with unshuttered windows as if staring at the strange spectacle of the hoary pilgrims. For a long while, however, there was no hint of danger. The road slumbered like the countryside through which it led, its white surface beneath the moonlit mist recalling that of a frozen river. Except for the open windows of deserted houses there was nothing to show that the barbarians had gone by, until, down a side-track to the left, the wanderers sighted a Roman villa in flames. No farm this; but a patrician's country mansion. The roof-tree had already fallen in; the coils of smoke that rose above where it had been were tinged red by the fires that still raged amid the walls; and to each of the eleven old men came the unspoken thought:

"It is as if I were looking upon the pillar of cloud and the pillar of fire which went before the Tabernacle of the Lord when our forefathers followed the Ark of the

Covenant, even as I and my companions now follow the Menorah."

Between Grandfather Abtalion and Rabbi Eliezer, trotted the boy, panting, in his eagerness not to be a drag on his elders. He was silent because the others said not a word, but his little heart fluttered against his ribs. He was afraid, now that the excitement of novelty was passing; mortally afraid because he could not guess why they had dragged him out of bed at such an hour, afraid because he did not know where the old men were taking him; most afraid of all because never before had he been in the open country after dark, and beneath the open sky. He was familiar with night in the alleys of the Jewish quarter; but there the blackness of the sky was but a narrow strip in which two or three stars twinkled. No reason to dread that ribbon of sky, which familiarity had robbed of its terrors. He knew it best as he glimpsed it between the slats, which broke it up into tiny fragments, too small to be alarming; while he listened, before he fell asleep, to the prayers of the men, the coughing of the sick, the shuffling feet of those who went by in the alley, the caterwauling on the roof, the crackling of the logs as they burned on the hearth. On the right was Mother, on the left Rachel; he was safe, warm, cosy; never alone.

But here the night was threatening, huge, and void. How tiny felt the little boy beneath the vast expanse of heaven. Had not the old men been with him to protect him, he would have burst into tears, would have tried to crawl into some hiding-place where he could escape from the huge dome which marched with him as he marched, always the same, always oppressive.

Happily there was room in his breast for pride as well as fear; pride because the elders in whose presence Mother dared not raise her voice, and before whom the children quaked—because these great and wise men had chosen him, little Benjamin, to accompany them upon their quest. What did it mean? What could it mean? Child though he was, he felt sure that something tremendous must account for this procession through the night. Most eager, therefore, was he to show himself worthy of their choice, trying to take manly strides with his little legs, and refusing to admit even to himself that he was afraid. But the test of his courage and endurance lasted too long. He grew more and more tired, frightened of the very shadows of himself and his companions; alarmed by the sound of their footsteps upon the paved road. Now, when a bat, blundering through the night, almost touched his forehead, he shuddered and screamed at the black, unknown horror. Gripping Abtalion's hand, he cried:

"Grandfather, Grandfather, where are we going?"

Without even turning to look at the lad, his grandfather growled:

"Hold your tongue, and don't drag back. Little boys must be seen and not heard."

The youngster shrank, as if from a blow, ashamed at having given vent to his terror. In thought he scolded himself: "Of course, I ought not to have asked." Still, he could not restrain his sobs.

But Rabbi Eliezer, the pure and clear, looked reproachfully at Abtalion over the little one's head, saying:

"Nay, friend, it is you who are to blame. How natural that the child should ask that question! What could he do but wonder at our taking him from his bed and bringing him forth with us into the night? Moreover, why should he not learn the object of our pilgrimage? We bring him with us because he is of our blood, and therefore partaker in our destinies. Surely he will continue to sustain our sorrows long after we have been laid to rest? He is to live on, bearing witness to those of a coming time as the last member of our Roman community to see the Lampstand from the Table of the Lord. Why should you wish him to remain in ignorance? We have brought him with us to watch and to know, and to give tidings of this night in days to come."

Abtalion made no answer, feeling justly reproved. Rabbi Eliezer tenderly stroked Benjamin's hair, and said encouragingly:

"Ask, child, ask freely, and I shall answer with the same freedom. Better to ask than to be ignorant. Only through asking can we gain knowledge, and only through knowlege can we win our way to righteousness."

The boy was elated that the sage whom all the community revered should talk to him as an equal. He would gladly have kissed the Rabbi's hand, yet was too timid. His lips trembled, but he uttered no sound. Rabbi Eliezer —whose wisdom was not only the wisdom of books, since he had also the wisdom of those who know the human heart—understood, despite the darkness, all that Benjamin thought and felt. He sympathized with their little companion's impatience to know the whither and the why of this strange expedition, so he fondled the hand which lay as light and tremulous as a butterfly in his own withered palm.

"I will tell you where we are going, and will hide nothing. There is naught wrongful in our purpose, though it must be hidden from those whom ere long we shall join. God, who looks down on us from heaven, knows and approves. He knows the beginning as clearly as we know it ourselves; and he knows what we cannot know, the end."

While speaking thus to the child, Rabbi Eliezer did not slacken his pace. The others quickened their steps for a moment, to draw nearer, and hearken to his words of wisdom.

"We walk along an ancient road, my child, on which our fathers and forefathers walked in days of yore. In ages past we were a nation of wanderers, as we have become once more, and as we are perhaps destined to remain until the end of time. Not like the other peoples have we lands of our own, where we can grow and harvest our crops. We move continually from place to place; and when we die, our graves are dug in foreign soil. Yet scattered though we are, flung like weeds into the furrows from north to south and from east to west, we have remained one people, united as is no other, held together by our God and our faith in him. Invisible is the tie which binds us, the invisible God. I know, child, that this passeth your understanding, for at your tender age you can grasp only the life of the senses, which perceive nothing but the corporeal, that which can be seen, touched, or tasted, like earth and wood and stone and brass. For that very reason the Gentiles, being children in mind, have made unto themselves gods of wood and stone and metal. We alone, we of the Chosen People, have no such tangible and visible gods (which we call idols), but an invisible God whom we know with an understanding that is above the senses. All our afflictions have come from this urge which drives us into the suprasensual, which makes us perpetual seekers for the invisible. But stronger is he who relies upon the invisible rather than on the visible and the palpable, since the latter perisheth, whereas the former endureth for ever. Spirit is in the end stronger than force. Therefore, and therefore alone, little Benjamin, have we lived on through the ages, outlasting time because we are pledged to the timeless, and only because we have been loyal to the invisible God has the invisible God kept faith with us.

"Child, these words of mine will be too deep for you. Often and often we elders are troubled because the God and the Justice in whom we believe are not visible in this our world. Still, even though you cannot now understand me, be not therefore troubled, but go on listening."

"I listen, Rabbi," murmured the boy, bashful but ecstatic.

"Filled with this faith in the invisible, our fathers and forefathers moved on through the world. To convince themselves of their own belief in this invisible God who never disclosed himself to their eyes and of whom no image may be graven, our ancestors made them a sign. For narrow is our understanding; the infinite is beyond our comprehension. Only from time to time does a shadow of the divine cast itself into our life here below. Fitfully and feebly a light from God's invisible countenance illumines our darkness. Hence, that we may be ever reminded of our duty to serve the invisible, which is justice and eternity and grace, we made the furniture of the Tabernacle, where God was unceasingly worshipped—made a Lampstand, called the Menorah, whose seven lamps burned unceasingly; and an altar whereon the shewbread was perpetually renewed. Misunderstand me not. These were not representations of the divine essence, such as the heathen impiously fashion. The holy emblems testified to our eternally watchful faith; and whithersoever we wandered through the world, the furnishings of the Holy Place wandered with us. Enclosed in the Ark of the Covenant, they were safeguarded in a Tabernacle, which our forefathers, homeless as are we this night, bore with them on their shoulders. When the Tabernacle with its sacred furniture rested, we likewise rested; when it was moved onward, we followed. Resting or journeying, by day or by night, for thousands of years we Jews thronged round this Holy of Holies; and as long as we preserve our sense of its sanctity, so long, even though dispersed among the heathen, shall we remain a united people.

"Now listen. Among the furnishings of the Holy Place were the Altar of the Shewbread, which also bore the fruits of the earth in due season; the Vessels from which clouds of incense rose to heaven; and the Tables of Stone whereon God had written his Commandments. But the most conspicuous of all the furniture was a Lampstand whose lamps burned unceasingly to throw light on the Altar in the Holy of Holies. For God loves the light which he kindled; and we made this Lampstand in gratitude for the light which he bestowed on us to gladden our eyes. Of pure gold, of beaten work, was the

Lampstand cunningly fashioned. Seven-branched was it, having a central stem and three branches on each side, every one with a bowl made like unto an almond with a knop and a flower, all beaten work of pure gold. When the seven lamps were lighted, each light rose above its golden flower, and our hearts rejoiced to see. When it burned before us on the Sabbath, our souls became temples of devotion. No other symbol on earth, therefore, is so dear to us as this Seven-Branched Lampstand, and wherever you find a Jew who continues to cherish his faith in the Holy One of Israel, no matter under which of the winds of heaven his house stands, you will find in that house a model of the Menorah lifting its seven branches in prayer."

"Why seven?" the boy ventured to ask.

"Ask, and you shall be answered, child. To ask reverently is the beginning of wisdom. Seven is the most holy of numbers, for there were Seven Days of Creation, the crowning wonder being the creation of man in God's own image. What miracle can be greater than that we should find ourselves in this world, be aware of it and love it, and know something of its Creator? By making light in the firmament of heaven, God enabled our eyes to see and our spirit to know. That is why, with its seven branches, the Lampstand praises both lights, the outer and the inner. For God has given us also an inner light in Holy Writ; and just as we see outwardly with our eyes, so does Scripture enable us to see inwardly by the light of the understanding. What flame is to the senses, that is Scripture to the soul; for in Scripture all is recounted, explained, and enjoined: God's doings, and the

The Buried Candelabrum

deeds of our fathers; what is allowed to us and what forbidden; the creative spirit and the regulative law. In a twofold way God, through his light, enables us to contemplate the world: from without by the senses, and from within by the spirit; and thanks to the divine illumination we can even achieve self-knowledge. Do you understand me, child?"

"No," gasped the little boy, too proud to feign.

"Of course not," said Rabbi Eliezer gently. "These things are too deep for a mind so young. Understanding will come with the years. For this present, bear in mind what you can understand of all I have told you. The most sacred things of those we had as emblems on our wanderings, the only things remaining to us from our early days, were the Five Books of Moses and the Seven-Branched Lampstand, the Torah and the Menorah. Bear those words in mind."

"The Torah and the Menorah," repeated Benjamin solemnly, clenching his fists as if to aid his memory.

"Now listen further. There came a time, long, long ago, when we grew weary of wandering. Man craves for the earth, even as the earth craves for man. After forty years in the wilderness, we entered the Promised Land, as Moses had foretold, and we took possession of it. We ploughed and sowed and harvested, planted vineyards and tamed beasts, tilled fruitful fields which we surrounded with hedges and hurdles, being glad at heart that we no longer sojourned among strangers to be unto them a scorn and a hissing. We believed that our wanderings were finished for ever and a day, being foolhardy enough to declare that the land was our very own—

Jewish Legends

whereas to no man is land given, but only lent for a season. Always are mortals prone to forget that having is not holding, and finding is not keeping. He who feels the ground firm beneath his feet builds him a house, fancying that thus he roots himself as firmly as do the trees. Therefore we built houses and cities; and since each of us had a home of his own, it was meet that we should wish our Lord and Protector likewise to have an abiding-place among us, a House of God which should be greater and more splendid than any human habitation. Thus it came to pass during the years when we were settled at peace in the Land of Promise that there ruled over us a king who was wealthy and wise, known as Solomon—"

"Praised be his name," interposed Abtalion gently.

"Praised be his name," echoed the others, without slackening in their stride.

"—who builded a house upon Mount Moriah, where aforetime Jacob, dreaming, saw a ladder set up on the earth, and the top of it reached to heaven; and behold the angels of God ascending and descending on it. Wherefore on awaking Jacob said: 'Holy is this place, and holy shall it be to all the peoples of the earth.' And here Solomon built the Temple of the Lord, of stone and cedar wood and finely wrought brass. When our forefathers looked upon its walls they felt assured that God would dwell perpetually in our midst, and give us peace to the end of time. Even as we rested in our homes, so did the Tabernacle rest in the House of God, and within the Tabernacle the Ark of the Covenant, which we had borne with us for so long. By day and by night burned unceasingly before the Altar the seven flames of the Menorah, for this and all that was sacred to us were enshrined in the Holy of Holies; and God himself, though invisible as he shall be while time endures, rested peaceably in the land of our forefathers, in the Temple of Jerusalem."

"May my eyes behold it once again," came the voices in a litany.

"But listen further, my child. Whatever man possesses is entrusted to him only as a loan, and his happiness is unstable as a shadow. Not for ever, as we fancied, was our peace established, for a fierce people came from the east and forced a way into our town, even as the robbers whom you have seen forced a way into the city of the Gentiles among whom we have sojourned. What they could seize, they seized; what was portable, they carried away; what they could destroy, they destroyed. But our invisible goods they could not take from us—God's word and God's eternal presence. The Menorah, however, the holy Lampstand, they took from the Table of the Lord and carried it away; not because it was holy (since these sons of Belial knew naught of holiness), but because it was made of gold, and robbers love gold. Likewise they took the Altar and the Vessels, and drove our whole people into captivity in Babylon——"

"Babylon? What is Babylon? Where is Babylon?"

"Ask freely, child, and with God's will you shall be answered. Babylon was a great city, big as Rome, lying nearly as far to the east of Jerusalem as Rome lies to the west. Look you, we have walked for three hours since leaving the gate of Rome, and already we ache with weariness, but that march was a hundred times as long.

Think, then, how far to the east the Menorah was taken by the robbers, and we driven with it into captivity. Mark this, also, that to God distance is nothing. To man it is otherwise; but perhaps the meaning of our unending pilgrimage is that what is sacred to us grows more sacred with distance, and our hearts are humbled by affliction. However that may be, when God saw that his Word was still holy to us in exile, that we stood the test, he softened the heart of one of the kings of that alien people. Aware that we had been wronged, he let our forefathers return to the Promised Land, giving back to them the Lampstand and the furniture of the Tabernacle. Then did our forefathers leave Chaldea and make their way home to Jerusalem across deserts, mountains, and thickets. From the ends of the earth they returned to the place which they had never ceased to cherish in their memories. We rebuilt the Temple on Mount Moriah; again the seven lamps of the Seven-Branched Lampstand flamed before God's Altar, and our hearts flamed with exultation. Now mark this, Benjamin, that you may grasp the meaning of our pilgrimage which begins tonight. No other thing made by the hands of men is so holy, so ancient, and so travelled hither and thither, as this Seven-Branched Menorah, which is the most precious pledge of the unity and purity of the Chosen People. Always when our lot is saddened the lamps of the Menorah are extinguished."

Rabbi Eliezer paused. At this the boy looked up, his eyes flaming like the lamps of the sacred emblem, eager with expectation that the story should be continued. The Rabbi smiled as he noticed this impatience, and stroked the lad's hair, saying:

The Buried Candelabrum

"Have no fear, little one. The tale is not ended. Our destiny marches on. I could talk to you for years and fail to recount a thousandth part of all that has happened to us and all that awaits us. Listen then, since you are a good listener, to what befell after our return to Jerusalem from Babylon. Once more we thought that the Temple had been established for ever. But once more enemies came, across the sea this time, from the land where we now sojourn as strangers. A famous general led them, son of an Emperor, and himself in due time to be Emperor; Titus was he called—"

"Accursed be his name," intoned the elders.

"—who breached our walls and destroyed the Temple. Impiously he entered the Holy of Holies and snatched the Lampstand from the Altar. He plundered the Lord's House, and had the sacred furnishings carried before him when he celebrated his triumph upon his return to Rome. The foolish populace rejoiced, thinking that Titus had conquered our God, and that this was one of the captives who marched before him in fetters. So proud of his victory was the miscreant, that he had an arch built to commemorate it, with graven images that showed forth how he had ravaged the House of God."

"Rabbi," asked the boy, "tell me, is that the arch decorated with so many stone images? The arch in the great square, the arch which Father said I must never, never go through?"

"That's the one, child. Never go through it, but pass by without looking, for this memorial of Titus's triumph is likewise the memorial of one of the most sorrowful days in our history. No Jew may walk beneath the Arch of Titus, on which are graven images to show how the Romans mocked what was and always will be holy to us. Remember unfailingly——"

The old man broke off, for Hyrcanus ben Hillel had sprung forward from the rear to lay a hand upon his lips. The others were terrified by this irreverent freedom, but Hyrcanus silently pointed forward. Yes, there was something partially disclosed by the fog-bedimmed moon—a dark shape that seemed to wriggle along the white road like a huge caterpillar. Now, when the elders halted and listened, they could hear the creaking of heavily laden carts. Above these or beside them there flashed spears which looked like blades of grass that shine in the dew of morning—the lances of the Numidian rearguard escorting the spoil.

They kept good watch, the lancers, for a number of them wheeled their horses, to gallop back with levelled weapons and uttering shrill cries. Their burnouses streamed in the breeze, so that it seemed as if their chargers were winged. Involuntarily the eleven old men drew together in a bunch, the child in their midst. The lancers did not tarry until the steel points were close to the suspect pursuers; then they drew rein so suddenly that their mounts reared. Even in the faint light, the cavalrymen could see that these were no warriors, designing to recapture the booty, but peaceful whitebeards, infirm and old, each with staff and scrip. Thus in Numidia, too, did pious elders make pilgrimage from shrine to shrine. The fierce lancers, suspicions allayed, laughed encouragingly, showing white teeth. The leader whistled, once more the troop wheeled, and thundered down the road after the carts they were convoying, while the old men stood and trembled, hardly able to believe they were to be left unharmed.

Rabbi Eliezer, the pure and clear, was the first to regain composure. Gently he tapped the little boy's cheek.

"You're a brave lad, Benjamin," he said, leaning forward over the youngster. "I was holding your hand, and it did not shake. Shall I go on with my story? You have not yet heard whither we are going, or why we did not seek our beds as usual."

"Please go on, Rabbi," answered the boy, eagerly.

"I told you, you will remember, how Titus (accursed be his name), having laid impious hands on our holy treasures, carried them off to Rome and, in the vanity of his triumph, made a display of them all over the city. Thereafter, however, the Emperors of Rome put the

Menorah and the other sacred objects from Solomon's Temple for safe-keeping in what they called the Temple of Peace—a foolish name, for when has peace ever lasted in our contentious world? Nor would Jehovah permit the furniture of the Tabernacle which had adorned his own Holy House in Zion to remain in a heathen temple, so one night he sent a fire to consume that building with all its contents, save only our Lampstand and other treasures which were rescued from the devouring flames, to show once again that neither fire nor distance nor the hand of a robber has power over the Menorah. This was a sign, a warning from God, that the Romans should restore the sacred emblems to their own sacred place, where they would be honoured, not because they were made of gold, but because they were holy. But when did such fools understand a sign, or when did men's stubborn hearts bow before the light of reason?"

Having paused to sigh, Rabbi Eliezer resumed:

"Thus the Gentiles took the Lampstand and put it away in one of the Emperor's other houses; and because it remained there in safe-keeping for years and for decades, they believed it to be theirs for all eternity. Nevertheless it is untrue to say that there is honour among thieves. What one robber has stolen will be taken from him forcibly by another. Just as Rome sacked Jerusalem, so has Carthage sacked Rome. Even as the Romans plundered us, they themselves have been plundered, and as they defiled our sacred places, so have their sacred places been defiled. But the robbers have also taken away what was ours, the Menorah, the emblem which used to stand on God's Altar in King Solomon's House. Those wains

The Buried Candelabrum

which drive westward through the darkness are carrying to the coast that which is dearest to us in the world. Tomorrow the barbarians will put the Lampstand on one of their ships, to sail away with it into foreign parts, where it will be beyond the reach of our longing eyes. Never again will the Lampstand shed its beams upon us who are old and near to death. Nevertheless as those who have loved anyone when alive escort the body upon its last journey to the tomb, thus testifying their affection, so today do we escort the Menorah upon the first stage of its journey into foreign parts. What we are losing is the holiest of our treasures. Do you understand, now, little one, the meaning of our mournful pilgrimage?"

The child walked on with hanging head, and made no answer. He seemed to be thinking things over.

"Never forget this, Benjamin. We have brought you with us as witness, that in days to come, when we are beneath the sod, you may bear testimony to the way in which we were loyal to the sacred emblem, and may teach others to remain faithful. You will fortify them in the faith which sustains us, the faith that the Menorah will one day return from its wanderings in the darkness, and, as of old, will with its seven flames shed a glorious light upon the Table of the Lord. We awoke you from your slumbers that your heart might also awaken, and that you will be able to tell those of a later generation what befell this night. Store up everything in your mind that you may console others by telling them how your own eyes have seen the Menorah which has moved onward for thousands of years among strangers, even as our people have wandered. Firmly do I believe that it will never perish so long as we remain alive as God's Chosen People faithful to the Law."

Still Benjamin answered not a word. Rabbi Eliezer, the pure and clear, sensed the resistance which must underlie this stubborn silence. He leaned forward, therefore, over the little boy, and asked, gently as was his manner: "Have you understood me?"

The child was froward. "No," he said curtly. "I don't understand, Rabbi. For if . . . if the Menorah is so dear to us and so holy . . . why do we let them take it away from us?"

Heaving a sigh, the old man said: "There is reason in your question, my boy. Why do we let them take it away from us? Why don't we resist? When you are older, you will learn that in this world, alas, might is right, and that the righteous man can seldom prevail. Men of violence establish their will upon earth, which is a place where piety and righteousness have little power. God has taught us to suffer injustice, not trying to establish the right with the strong hand."

Rabbi Eliezer said these words as he marched forward with bowed head. Thereupon Benjamin snatched away his hand and stopped short. Bluntly, almost masterfully, did the boy, in his excitement, apostrophize Eliezer:

"But God? Why does he permit this robbery? Why does not he help us? You told me that he is a just God and almighty. Why does he favour the robbers instead of the righteous?"

Except for Eliezer, the old men were outraged by these words. They all stopped in their stride, feeling as if their hearts had ceased to beat. Like the blast of a trumpet

The Buried Candelabrum

the little boy's defiance had been hurled into the night, as if he were declaring war against God. Ashamed of his grandson, Abtalion shouted:

"Silence! Blaspheme not!"

But the Rabbi cut him short:

"Be you silent, rather. Why should you find fault with the innocent child? His unsophisticated heart has but blurted out a question which, in truth, we ask ourselves daily and hourly, you and I and the rest of us; a question which the wisest of our people have asked since the beginning of time. From of old the Jewish sages and prophets have inquired why Jehovah should deal so harshly with us among the nations, seeing that we serve him more fervently than any others. Why should he thrust us beneath the feet of our enemies that they may trample us into the dust, we who were the first to know God and to praise him in his unfathomable ways? Why does he destroy what we build; why does he frustrate our dearest hopes? Why does he drive us forth into exile whenever we think we have found rest; why does he incite the heathen to rage against us ever more furiously? Why does he visit us with supreme affliction, we whom he made his Chosen People, we whom he first initiated into his mysteries? Far be it from me to deceive this simple child. If his question be blasphemous, then I myself am a blasphemer every day of my life. Look you, I acknowledge it to you all. I also am froward. I also continually arraign God. Day after day do I, now eighty years of age, ask the question which has just been asked by a seven-year-old boy. Why should God visit upon us more than upon all others such unceasing tribulations? Why does he allow us to be despoiled, helping those who plunder us to gain their ends? Often and often do I beat my breast in shame, but never can I stifle these urgent questionings. I should not be a Jew, I should not be a human being, if these meditations did not torment me day after day, these blasphemies as you call them which will continue to trouble me for as long as I draw breath."

The rest of the elders were astounded, nay, horrified. Never had any of them seen Kab ve Nake, the pure and clear, so greatly moved. This arraignment must have surged up from depths which were ordinarily concealed. They could scarcely recognize him as he stood there quaking with emotion and distress, and shamefacedly turning his head away from the child who looked up at him with wonder. Speedily, however, Rabbi Eliezer mastered his emotion, and, bending once more over the little boy, he said appeasingly:

"Forgive me for speaking to these others, and to one who stands over us all, instead of answering your question. In the simplicity of your heart, little one, you ask me why God should permit this crime against us and against himself. In my own simplicity I answered you, as frankly as I could: 'I do not know.' We do not know God's plans; we cannot read his thoughts; and his ways are past finding out. But ever and again, when I arraign him in the madness of my suffering and in the extremity of our general distress, I try to console myself with the assurance that perhaps, after all, there is some meaning in the afflictions with which he visits us, and that maybe each of us is atoning for a wrong. No man can say who hath committed it. Perhaps Solomon the Wise was unwise when he builded the Temple at Jerusalem, as if God were a man coveting a habitation here on earth and among one of its peoples. It may have been sinful of Solomon to adorn the Holy House as he did, as though gold were more than piety and marble more than inward stability. May not we Jews have departed from God's will by desiring, like the other nations, to have house and home of our own, saying 'This land is ours' and speaking of 'our Temple' and 'our God' even as a man saith 'my hand' and 'my hair'? Perhaps that was why he had the Temple destroyed, and tore us away from our homes, that we might cease to turn our affections towards things visible and tangible, and remain faithful in the spiritual field alone to him the unattainable and the invisible. Maybe this is our true path, that we shall be ever afoot, looking sorrowfully back and yearningly forward, perpetually craving for repose, and never able to find rest. For the only road of holiness is that pursued by those who do not know their destination, but continue to march on steadfastly, as we march onward this night through darkness and danger, not knowing our goal."

The boy listened attentively, but Rabbi Eliezer was drawing to a close:

"Ask no more questions, Benjamin, for your questions exceed my capacity to answer. Wait patiently. Some day, perhaps, God will answer you out of your own heart."

The old man was silent, and silent likewise were the other elders. They stood motionless in the middle of the road; the silence of the night enwrapped them, while they felt as if they were standing in that outer darkness which lies beyond the realm of time.

Jewish Legends

Then one of them trembled and raised his hand. Seized with anxiety, he signed to the others to listen. Yes, through the stillness came a murmur. It was as if someone had gently plucked the strings of a harp; an obscure tone, but gradually swelling like the wind blowing out of the obscurity that hid the sea. Quickly, quickly, it rose to a roar, for now the wind raged, tossing the branches of the trees, making the bushes rustle loudly, while the dust whirled up from the road. The very stars in the sky seemed to tremble. The old men, knowing that God often spoke out of the storm, wondered if they were about to hear his voice in answer. Each looked timidly on the ground. Unthinkingly they joined hands, clasping one another for joint support in face of the threatening terror, and each could feel the alarmed throbbing of another's pulses.

But nothing happened. The flurry-scurry of the brief whirlwind subsided as rapidly as it had arisen; the rustle in the bushes and the grass ceased. Nothing happened. No voice spake; no sound broke the renewed and intimidating stillness. When they ventured to raise their eyes from the ground, they perceived that, in the east, an opaline light was showing on the horizon. The flurry of wind had been nothing more than that which usually precedes the dawn. Nothing more? We take it lightly, but is it not a daily miracle that day should tread upon the heels of night? As they stood there, still disquieted, the crimson in the eastern sky strengthened and spread, while the outlines of surrounding objects began to detach themselves from the gloom. Yes, the night was finished, the night of their pilgrimage.

"Dawn cometh," murmured Abtalion. "Let us pray."

The eleven old men drew together. Benjamin stood apart, being too young to share in this ritual, though he looked on with interest and excitement. The elders withdrew the praying-shawls from their scrips to wrap them round head and shoulders. Their phylacteries, too, they strapped on, round the forehead and the left hand and wrist which lie nearest the heart. Then they turned eastward, towards Jerusalem, and prayed, expressing thanks to God who created the world and enumerating the eighteen attributes of his perfection. Intoning and murmuring, they swayed their bodies forward and backward in time with the words. The boy found many of these words too difficult to understand, but he saw the ardour with which the worshippers waved their bodies in the exaltation of the prayer as, shortly before, the grass had waved in God's wind. After the solemn "Amen," they made obeisance one and all. Then, having taken off the praying-shawls and the phylacteries, they put them back in their scrips and made ready to resume their march. They looked older, now, these old men, in the pitiless light of dawn; the furrows on their faces seemed deeper, the shadows beneath their eyes and at the corners of their mouths were darker. As if newly arisen from their own deathbeds, accompanied by the child who, though tired, was fresh and vigorous in comparison, they wearily proceeded upon the last stage of their journey.

Bright and limpid was the Italian morning when the eleven old men and the little boy reached the harbour of Portus where the yellow waters of the Tiber mingled sluggishly with the sea. Only a few of the Vandals' ships were still in the roads, and one after another was on its way to the offing, pennants flying gaily at the mastheads and holds full of loot. At length only one remained at anchor close to the shore, greedily swallowing the contents of the overloaded wagons, the remnants of the plunder from Rome. One cart after another drove onto the jetty, and slaves took load after load across the gangplank, carrying the burden on head or shoulders. Swiftly they bore chests packed with gold and amphoræ filled to the neck with wine or oil. But hasten as they might, they were not quick enough for the impatient captain, who signed to the overseer to speed the embarkation with the lash. Now the last of the wains was being unloaded, the one which the pilgrims had been following throughout the night because it contained the Menorah. To begin with, its contents had been hidden by straw and sacking, but the old men shook with excitement as these wrappings were removed. Now had come the decisive moment, now or never must God work a miracle.

Benjamin's eyes were elsewhere. This was the first time he had seen the sea, which filled him with amazement. Like an enormous blue mirror it looked, arching to the sharp line of the horizon where sea passed into sky. Even larger it appeared to him than the dome of night with which he had so recently made acquaintance, the starry expanse of heaven. Spellbound he watched the play of the waves on the shore, chasing one another up the beach, breaking into foam, receding and continually reforming. How lovely was this sportive movement, such as he had never dreamed of in the dull, dark alley where he had been brought up. He threw out his chest, tiny though this chest was, vigorously breathing in the air which had a tang he had never before experienced, determined to make the fresh sea-breeze invigorate his timid Jewish blood and fill it with a new joy. He longed to go close to the edge of the troubled waters, to stretch out his slender arms and embrace the wide and wonderful prospect. As he looked at the beautiful blue waters sparkling in the early sunshine, he was thrilled by a new sense of happiness. How splendid and free and untroubled was everything here. The wheeling gulls reminded him of the white-winged angels of whom he had been told; gloriously white, too, were the sails of the ships, sails bellied by the wind. Then, when he closed his eyes for a moment and threw his head back, opening his mouth wide to inhale more of the salt-tasting air, there suddenly occurred to him the first words of Scripture he had been taught: "In the beginning God created the heaven and the earth." Never before had the name of God, mentioned so often by Rabbi Eliezer during the night walk, been full, as now, of meaning and form.

Then a loud cry startled him. The eleven elders screamed as with one voice, and instantly he ran to join them. The sackcloth had just been removed to uncover the contents of the last wagon, and as the Berber slaves bent to lift a silver image of Juno, a statue weighing several hundredweight, one of them who was standing in the cart kicked the Menorah out of his way. The Seven-Branched Lampstand fell from the wagon onto the ground. That was why the old men had uttered their cry of terror and wrath, to see the sacred emblem—on which Moses' eyes had rested, which had been blessed by Aaron, which had stood upon the Altar of the Lord in the House of Solomon—desecrated by falling into the dung from the team of oxen, defiled by dirt and dust. The slaves looked round inquisitively, wondering why the onlookers had screamed so dolorously. They could not understand why the foolish greybeards had yelled with horror, seizing one another by the arms to make a living chain of distress. No one had done them any harm. But the overseer, who would not suffer any pause in the work, lashed the toilers' naked backs with his whip, so once more subserviently they buried their arms in the straw of the load, this time to disengage a sculptured slab of porphyry, followed by another huge statue which, sustaining it by a pole and a rope round the head and the feet, they bore across the gangplank as they might have carried a slaughtered enemy. Speedily they emptied the wagon. Only the Lampstand, eternal symbol, still lay disregarded where it had fallen, half hidden by one of the wheels. The old men, still clasping one another's hands, were united also in the hope that the robbers, whom the overseer continued to speed at their task, would in their haste overlook the Menorah. Might it not be God's will, at the last moment, to save this precious object for his devoted worshippers?

But now one of the slaves caught sight of it, stooped, and lifted it onto his shoulders. Brightly it gleamed in the sunshine, so that the brightness of the morning grew yet more bright. This was the first time in their long lives that any of the elders save Hyrcanus ben Hillel had set eyes upon the lost treasure; and how lamentable that it should be only at a moment when the beloved object was again passing into the hands of the Gentiles, about to voyage into a foreign, a far-away land. The Berber slave was a big, strong, broad-shouldered man, but the golden Menorah was heavy, and he needed both hands to steady his burden as he walked across the swaying plank. Five steps, four steps, and it would have vanished for ever from their eyes. As if drawn by a mysterious force, the eleven elders, still clasped together, moved forward to the gangplank, their eyes blinded with tears, mumbling incoherently as spittle dribbled from their mouths. Drunken with sorrow they stumbled forward, hoping to be allowed to implant at least a pious kiss upon the holy emblem. One only among them, Rabbi Eliezer, though suffering no less than his brethren, remained clear-headed. He gripped Benjamin's hand, so firmly that the little boy found it hard to repress a cry of pain.

"Look, look well. You will be the last Jew alive to set eyes upon what was our most precious possession. You will bear witness how they took it away from us, how they stole it."

The child could hardly understand what the Rabbi meant; but sympathy with the old men's manifest agony surged up within him, and he felt that an unrighteous deed was being done. Anger, the uncontrollable fury of a child, boiled over. Without realizing what he was about, this seven-year-old boy snatched his hand away from Eliezer's and rushed after the Berber, who was at this moment crossing the gangplank, and who, strong though he was, tottered beneath the weight. This alien, this Gentile, should not take away the Lampstand. Benjamin flung himself upon the mighty porter, trying to snatch away his burden.

The slave, heavily laden, was staggered by the unexpected shock. It was only a little child who hung upon his arm; but, losing his balance upon the narrow plank, he fell beneath his burden, both of them on the quayside. The child fell with him. Furiously the Berber struck with all his strength at Benjamin's right arm. Feeling the pain, which was intense, Benjamin yelled at the top of his little voice, but his cry was drowned in the general hubbub. All who saw what had happened were shouting and yelling: the Jewish elders horror-stricken at the sight of the Menorah being once more rolled in the mud, and the Vandals on the ship shouting with wrath. The enraged overseer rushed up to flog the Jewish elders away with his whip. Meanwhile the slave, greatly incensed, had risen to his feet. Delivering a hearty kick (fortunately he was unshod) at the groaning child, he shouldered his burden once more and hastily but triumphantly bore it along the gangplank into the ship.

The elders paid no heed to the youngster. Not one of them noticed the writhing little body on the ground, since they had eyes only for the Menorah as it was carried on board, its seven lamps pointing upward as if in appeal to heaven. Shudderingly they watched how, as soon as the Berber had crossed the plank, other hands carelessly relieved him of his burden and threw it upon a pile of the general spoils. The boatswain sounded his whistle, the moorings were cast off, and from between decks, where the galley-slaves were chained to their benches, at the word of command forty oars took the water, one-two, one-two. Instantly the galley responded, and moved away from the quay. Foam curled on either side of the prow; noiselessly it departed, except for the plashing of the oars; as it crossed the bar it began to pitch and toss upon the waves as if it were breathing and alive; pursuing the fleet, the other galleys and the sailing ships, it steered southward towards Carthage.

The eleven old men stared after the vanishing galley. Again they had clasped hands, again they were trembling, a live chain of horror and distress. Without holding counsel together, without mutually confiding their secret thoughts, they had all hoped for a miracle. But the galley had hoisted sail, was running before a favourable wind, and as she grew smaller and smaller, so did their hopes even of a miracle decline, to be submerged at last in the huge ocean of despair. Now the vessel on which their gaze was fixed seemed no larger than a seagull, until at length, their eyes wet with tears, they could discern no further trace of her on the forsaken surface of the waters. They must abandon hope. Once again the Menorah had wandered off into the void, unresting as ever, utterly lost to the Chosen People.

At length, ceasing to look southward in the direction of Carthage, they bethought them of Benjamin, who lay where he had been struck down, groaning with the pain of his broken arm. Having gently raised the bruised and bleeding form, they laid him on a litter. They were all ashamed at having left it to this little boy to make a bold attempt at recovering the Lampstand; and Abtalion had good reason to dread what the women of his household would say when he brought back his grandson thus crippled. But Rabbi Eliezer, the pure and clear, consoled them, saying:

"Do not bewail what has happened, nor pity the lad. He has come well out of it. Recall the words of Holy Writ, how, upon the threshing-floor, Uzzah put forth his hand to the Ark of God, and took hold of it; for the oxen shook it. And the anger of the Lord was kindled against Uzzah; and God smote him there for his error; and there he died by the Ark of God—for God does not wish that things which are most holy shall be lightly touched by human hands. But he spared this child, who has suffered no more than a broken arm instead of being smitten to death. Perhaps there is a blessing in this hurt, and a calling."

The Rabbi bent low over the weeping boy.

"Be not wroth because of your pain, but accept it thankfully. Indeed it is a boon and our common heritage. Only through suffering doth our people thrive, and naught but distress can give us creative energy. A great thing hath happened to you, for you have touched a most holy emblem, without worse hurt than a broken arm when you might well have lost your life. Maybe you are set apart by this pain, and a sublime meaning is hidden in your destiny."

The boy looked up at Rabbi Eliezer, strengthened and full of faith. In his pride at having such words addressed to him by the sage, he almost forgot the pain. Not another groan passed his lips through the long hours during which they carried him home.

For decades after the sack of Rome by the Vandals there was continual unrest in the Western Empire—more than usually happens in seven generations. For twenty years there was a rapid succession of emperors: from Avitus, Majorian, Libius Severus, and Anthemius, each of them slaying or driving out his predecessor; through another Teuton invasion of Italy from the north and a plundering of Rome; to the brief day of the last emperors of the West, Glycerius, Julius Nepos, and Romulus Augustulus. Another Teuton, Odoacer, King of the Heruli, took Rome, overthrew the Western Empire in 476, took the title of King of Italy, and reigned until he in turn was overthrown by Theodoric, King of the Goths. These Gothic invaders fancied that their kingdom, established by mighty warriors, would endure for ever; but it too passed in a generation while other barbarians continued to come down from the north, and in Byzantium the Eastern Empire, the only successor of Rome, stood firm. It seemed as if there were to be no peace in the thousand-year-old city beside the Tiber since the Menorah had been carried away through the Porta Portuensis.

The eleven old men who had followed the Menorah upon its journey from Rome to Portus had long since passed away in due course of nature; so, likewise, had their children, and their children's children had grown old: but still there lived on Benjamin, Abtalion's grandson, who had witnessed the Vandal raid. The boy had become a stripling, the stripling had grown to manhood, and was now exceedingly old. Seven of his sons had died before him, and of his grandchildren one had been smitten to death when, during the reign of Theodoric, the mob burned the synagogue. Benjamin lived on, with a withered arm, the outcome of a badly set fracture. He lived on as a forest giant may survive the storms that lay low the trees on either side. He saw emperors reign and perish, kingdoms rise and fall; but death spared him, and his name was honoured, almost holy, among all the Jewish exiles. Benjamin Marnefesh did they call him, because of his withered arm, the name meaning "one whom God has sorely tried." He was venerated as the last survivor of those who had set eyes upon Moses' Lampstand, the Menorah from Solomon's Temple which, its lamps unlighted, was buried in the Vandals' treasure house.

When Jewish merchants came to Rome from Leghorn and Genoa and Salerno, from Mainz and Treves, or from the Levant, they made it their first business to call on Benjamin Marnefesh, that they might see with their own eyes the man who had himself seen the holy emblem on which the eyes of Moses and of Solomon had rested. They made obeisance before him as one of the chosen of the Lord; with a thrill of terror they contemplated his withered arm; and with their own fingers they ventured to touch the fingers which had actually touched the Menorah. Though everyone knew the story (since in those days news spread by word of mouth as readily as it now spreads in print), they all begged him to tell them his memories of that wonderful night. With unfailing patience, old Benjamin would recount the expedition the twelve of them had made on the fateful occasion; and his huge white beard seemed to glisten as he repeated the words that had been spoken by the long-dead Rabbi Eliezer, the pure and clear.

"Nor need we of the Chosen People despair," he would conclude. "The wanderings of the sacred emblem are not yet finished. The Lampstand shall return to Jerusalem, shall not for ever be separated from those who reverence it. Once again shall our nation come together around it."

When his visitors left him, it was with gladdened hearts; and one and all they prayed that he might live many years yet, he, the consoler, the witness, the last of those who had seen the Menorah.

Thus Benjamin, the sorely tried, the child of that night hallowed by ancient memories, lived to be seventy, to be eighty, to be eighty-five, to be eighty-seven. His shoulders were bowed beneath the weight of his years, his vi-

Jewish Legends

sion was dimmed, and often he was tired out long before the day was done. Yet none of the Jews of the Roman community would believe that death could strike him down, seeing that his life bore witness to so great a happening. It was unthinkable that the eyes of him who had

seen the Lampstand of the Lord could be closed in death before they had seen the return of the Seven-Branched Menorah, and they cherished his survival as a token of God's favour. His presence must grace every festival, and he must join in every religious service. When he walked the streets of the Jewish quarter, the oldest bowed before old Benjamin, everyone whom he passed blessed his footsteps, and wherever the faithful assembled in sorrow or rejoicing he must be seated in the first place.

Thus did the Jews of the Roman congregation do honour as usual to Benjamin Marnefesh when, as custom prescribed, they assembled at the cemetery on the saddest day of the year, the Black Fast, the ninth of Ab, the day of the destruction of the Temple, the gloomy day on which their forefathers had been made homeless and had been dispersed among all the lands of the earth. They could not meet in the synagogue, which had recently been destroyed by the populace, and it therefore seemed meet to them that they should draw near to their dead on this day of supreme affliction—outside the city, at the place where their fathers were interred in alien soil, they would come together to bemoan their own severance from the Promised Land. They sat among the tombs, some of them on gravestones already broken. They knew themselves to be inheritors of their forefathers' grief, as they read the names and the praises of the deceased. Upon many of the tombstones, emblems had been chiselled: crossed hands for one who had been a member of the priesthood; or the vessels of the Levites, or the lion of the tribe of Judah, or the star of David. One of the upright gravestones had a sculptured image of the Seven-Branched Lampstand, the Menorah, to show that the man buried beneath it had been a sage and a light among the people of Israel. Before this tombstone, with his eyes fixed on it, sat Benjamin Marnefesh amid his companions —all of them with torn raiment and ashes scattered upon their heads, all bent like weeping willows over the black waters of their sorrow.

It was late in the afternoon, and the sun was sinking behind the pines and the cypresses. Brightly coloured butterflies fluttered round the crouching Jews as they might have fluttered round decaying tree-stumps; dragon-

Jewish Legends

flies with iridescent wings settled unheeded upon their drooping shoulders; and in the lush grass beetles crawled over their shoes. The brilliant foliage trembled in the breeze, but, glorious as was the evening, the mourners did not raise their eyes, and their hearts were full of sorrow. Again and again they deplored the sad fate of their people in its dispersal. They neither ate nor drank; they did not look at the glories which surrounded them; they only continued to intone lamentations about the destruction of the Temple and the fall of Jerusalem. Though every word they uttered was familiar, they continued their litany to intensify their pain and lacerate their hearts the more. Their only wish, on this day of affliction, the day of the Black Fast, was to intensify their sense of suffering, to become ever more keenly aware of the woes of the Chosen People in which their dead forefathers had participated. They recounted one to another all the tribulations which had befallen the Jews throughout the ages. Even as now in Rome, so everywhere that a Jewish community existed, there crouched on this day and at this hour Hebrews in torn raiment and with ashes on their heads. Among the tombs they lamented, from end to end of the civilized world, uttering the same plaints. Everywhere they reminded one another that the daughters of Zion were fallen and had become a mockery among the nations. They knew that these universal lamentations of the faithful remained their firmest tie.

As they sat and lamented, they did not notice how the sunlight grew more and more golden, while the dark stems of the pines and the cypresses were glowing red, as if illumined from within. They failed to realize that the ninth of Ab, the day of the great mourning, was drawing to its close, and that the hour of evening prayer had come. It was at this moment that the rusty iron hinges of the cemetery gates creaked loudly. The mourners heard it. They knew that someone had entered, but did not rise. The stranger, without a word, stood silent, aware that the hour of prayer had come. Then the leader of the community perceived the newcomer, and greeted him, saying:

"Receive our blessing. Peace be with you, O Jew."

"A blessing upon all here," answered the stranger.

The leader spoke again, asking: "Whence come you, and to what community do you belong?"

"The community to which I belonged no longer exists. I fled hither from Carthage by ship. Great things have happened there. Justinian, Emperor of the East, sent from Byzantium an army to attack the Vandals. Belisarius, his general, took the city by storm. That nest of pirates has fallen. The King of the Vandals is a prisoner, and his realm has been destroyed. Belisarius has seized all that the robbers have got together during the last hundred years, and is taking it to Byzantium. The war is over."

The Jews received this tidings mutely and indifferently, without rising. What was Byzantium to them, and what was Carthage? Edom and Amalek, ever at odds. The heathen were always making war against one another, war without purpose. Sometimes one side conquered, sometimes the other; but never did righteousness prevail. What did such things matter to the Chosen People? What did they care for Carthage, for Rome, or for

Byzantium? Only one town was of any concern to them —Jerusalem.

One member alone of the Roman community, Benjamin Marnefesh, the sorely tried, raised his head with interest, to inquire:

"What has happened to the Lampstand?"

"No harm has come to it, but Belisarius has carried it away with the other trophies. With the rest of his plunder, he is taking it to Byzantium."

Now, in turn, the others were alarmed. They grasped the meaning of Benjamin's question. Once again the Menorah was on its wanderings, from foreign land to foreign land. The stranger's news was like an incendiary torch flung into the dark edifice of their mourning. They sprang to their feet, strode across the tombs, surrounded the man from Carthage, sobbing and weeping:

"Woe! To Byzantium! . . . Again across the seas! . . . To another foreign country! . . . Once more they have carried it off in triumph as did Titus, the accursed. . . . Always to some other land of the Gentiles and never back to Jerusalem. . . . Woe, woe hath befallen us!"

It was as if a branding-iron had been thrust into an old wound. The same unrest, the same fear seized them all. When the furnishings of the Holy of Holies wandered, they too would have to wander; to go anew among strangers; to seek a fresh home which would be no home. Thus had it happened ever since the Temple had been destroyed. Again and again there had been a new phase of the Diaspora. The old pain and the new seized them in a wild medley. They wept, they sobbed, they lamented;

and the little birds which had been sitting peacefully upon the tombstones flew away in alarm.

One only among the assembled Jews, Benjamin, the old, old man, had remained seated upon a moss-grown tombstone, silent while the others shouted and wept. Unconsciously, he had clasped his hands. As if in a dream he sat there, smiling as he looked at the tombstone on which was graven the likeness of the Menorah. There appeared upon his furrowed countenance, encircled with white locks, something of the expression he had had as a child of seven long, long ago. The wrinkles seemed to vanish; the lips grew supple again, while the smile, one could have fancied, spread all over his body as if, bowed forward though he was, he was smiling from within.

At length one of the others grew aware of his expression, and was ashamed of himself for having lost control. Pulling himself together, he looked reverently at Benjamin, and nudged his nearest neighbour, with a nod of direction. One after the other, they silenced their lamentations, and looked breathlessly at the old man, whose smile hung like a white cloud over the darkness of their pain. Soon they were all as quiet as the dead among whose graves they were standing.

The silence made Benjamin aware that they were staring at him. Laboriously, being very frail, he arose from the tombstone on which he was sitting. Suddenly he appeared to radiate power such as he had never before possessed, as he stood there with his silvern locks flowing down across his forehead from beneath his small silk cap. Never had his fellow-believers felt so strongly as at this hour that Marnefesh, the sorely tried man, was a man with a mission. Benjamin began to speak, and his words sounded like a prayer:

"At length I know why God has spared me till this hour. Again and again I have asked myself why I, having grown useless from age, continue to break bread; why death should pass me by, since I am a weary do-nothing of an old man to whom eternal silence would be welcome. I had lost courage and trust, as I watched the excess of affliction with which our people has been visited. Now I understand that there is still a task for me to perform. I saw the beginning, and I am summoned to see the end."

The others listened attentively to these obscure words. After a pause, one of them, the leader of the community, asked in low tones: "What do you propose to do?"

"I believe that God has vouchsafed me life and vision for so long that I may once again set eyes on the Menorah. I must betake myself to Byzantium. Perhaps that which as a child I was unable to achieve will be possible to me in extreme old age."

His hearers trembled with excitement and impatience. Incredible was the thought that a decrepit man of eighty-seven would be able to win back the Lampstand from the mightiest emperor on earth; and yet there was fascination in the dream of this miracle. One of them ventured to ask:

"How could you endure so long a journey? A three weeks' voyage across tempestuous seas. I fear it would be too much for you."

"A man is always granted strength when he has a holy

task to perform. When the eleven elders took me with them eighty years ago from Rome to Portus they did so doubtingly, being afraid that the walk would be beyond my strength; yet I kept pace with them to the end. It is needful, however, since I have a withered arm, that someone shall go with me as helper, a vigorous man and young, that he may bear witness to later generations even as I have borne witness to yours."

He glanced around the circle, letting his eyes rest on one of the young men after another, as if appraising them. Each trembled at this probationary glance, which seemed to pierce him to the soul. Every one of them longed to be chosen, but none would thrust himself forward. They waited eagerly for the decision. But Benjamin hung his head and murmured:

"No, I will not choose. You must cast lots. God will disclose to me the right companion."

The men drew together, cut grasses from the burial mounds, breaking off one much shorter than the others. He who drew the short blade was to go. The lot fell upon Jehoiakim ben Gamaliel, a man of twenty, tall and powerful, a blacksmith by trade, but unpopular. He was not learned in the Law and was of passionate disposition. His hands were stained with blood. At Smyrna, in a brawl, he had slain a Syrian, and had fled to Rome lest the constables should lay hands on him. Ill-pleased, the others silently wondered why the choice had thus fallen upon a man who was savage and mutinous instead of upon one who was reverent and pious. But when Jehoiakim drew the short blade of grass, Benjamin barely glanced at him and said:

Jewish Legends

"Make ready. We sail tomorrow evening."

The whole of the day which followed this ninth of Ab, the Jews of the Roman community were busily at work. Not a man among them plied his ordinary trade. All contributed the money they could spare; those who were poor borrowed upon whatever valuables they owned; the women gave their gold and silver buckles and such jewels as they possessed. Without exception they were sure that Benjamin Marnefesh was destined to liberate the Menorah from its new captivity, and persuade Emperor Justinian, like King Cyrus of old, to send the people of Israel and the furnishings of the Temple back to Jerusalem. They wrote letters to the communities of the East, in Smyrna, Crete, Salonika, Tarsus, Nicæa, and Trebizond, asking them to send emissaries to Byzantium and to collect funds on behalf of the holy deed of liberation. They exhorted the brethren in Byzantium and Galata to accept Benjamin Marnefesh, the sorely tried, as a man chosen by the Lord for a sublime mission and to smooth his path for him. The women got ready wraps and cloaks and cushions for the journey; and also food prepared as the Law directs, that the lips of the pious need not be contaminated by unclean victuals on the voyage. Although the Jews in Rome were forbidden to drive in a cart or to ride on horseback, they secretly provided a vehicle outside the gates, that the old man might reach the harbour without the fatigue of a long walk.

To their surprise, however, Benjamin refused to enter this vehicle. Eighty years before, he had gone on foot from Rome to Portus, completing the march betwixt midnight and morning. He would do the same now, said the determined octogenarian. A foolhardy undertaking, thought his co-religionists to begin with, for a man almost decrepit to attempt so long a march. But they were amazed to see the way in which he stepped out, being as it were transfigured by his vocation. The tidings from Carthage had instilled new energy into his ageing limbs, and invigorated his senile blood. His voice, which for years had been the thin pipe of a very old man, was now deep-toned and masterful as, almost wrathfully, he refused to be coddled. They contemplated him with respectful admiration.

All through the night the Jewish men of Rome accompanied Benjamin Marnefesh upon the road which their ancestors had trod to accompany the Lampstand of the Lord. Privily, under cover of darkness, they had brought with them a litter to carry the old man should his strength give out. But Benjamin led the way lustily. In silence he marched, his mind filled with memories of long ago. At each milestone, at each turn of the road, he recalled more and more clearly those far-distant hours of his childhood. He remembered everything plainly, the voices of those who had generations ago been buried; and he recapitulated the words that had been spoken on that momentous journey. There on the left had risen the pillar of fire from the burning house; this was the milestone opposite which his companions' hearts had failed them when the Numidian lancers were charging down upon them. He recalled each one of his questions, and each one of Rabbi Eliezer's answers. When he reached the place where, at dawning, the elders had prayed at the roadside, he donned, as before, his praying-shawl and his phylacteries, and, turning to the east, intoned the very prayer which fathers and forefathers were accustomed to say morning after morning—the prayer which, handed down from generation to generation, children and grandchildren and great-grandchildren would continue to utter.

His companions wondered. Why should he speak the morning prayer at this hour? As yet there was no hint of dawn in the sky. Why, then, should so pious a man utter the morning prayer at this untimely instant? Contrary to all custom and tradition it was, a defiance of the prescriptions of the Law. Still, however strange a freak it seemed, they watched him reverently. What he, the chosen of the Almighty, did could not be wrong. If, when day had not yet dawned, he chose to thank God for the gift of light, he must have good reason for what he was doing.

Having said his prayer, old Benjamin refolded his praying-shawl, put away his phylacteries, and marched on lustily, as if his act of piety had refreshed him. When they reached Portus, day had begun. He gazed long out to sea, thinking of himself as a child when he had glimpsed the sea for the first time, watching the play of the waves on the shore and gazing out towards the horizon. "The same sea as of old, deep and unfathomable as God's thoughts," he piously reflected. Rejoicing, as before, in the brightness of the sky, he gave his blessing to each of his companions, convinced that he was taking leave of them for ever; then, accompanied by Jehoiakim, he went on board the ship. Like their fathers and grandfathers eighty years before, the Jews now watched with interest and excitement as the ship hoisted her sails and made for the offing. They knew they had set eyes upon the sorely tried Benjamin for the last time, and when the sails vanished in the distance they became aware of a keen sense of loss.

Steadily the merchant vessel proceeded on her course. The waves rose high, and dark clouds gathered in the west. The seamen were exceedingly anxious about the weather. But though once or twice they had baffling winds and rough water which was most uneasy for landsmen, they reached Byzantium safely three days after the arrival of Belisarius's fleet with the spoils of Carthage.

After the fall of the Western Empire and the consequent decline of Rome, Byzantium had become the sole mistress of the occidental civilized world. The streets of the capital were thronged with lively crowds, for it was years since there had been promise of so glorious a spectacle in a town which loved festivals and games far more than it loved God or righteousness. In the circus, Belisarius, conqueror of the Vandals, was to parade his victorious army and display his booty before the Basileus, the Master of the World. Enormous crowds packed the streets, which were gaily decorated with flags; the vast hippodrome was filled to bursting; and the fretful populace, tired of waiting, murmured in its impatience. The gorgeous imperial tribune, the cathisma, remained untenanted. When the Basileus arrived, he would come through the underground passage which connected the dais with his palace; but he was long in coming, and the expectant sightseers grew querulous.

At length a blast of trumpets heralded the great man's approach. The first to appear were the members of the imperial guard, tall soldiers resplendent in red uniforms and with flashing swords; next there rustled in, clad in silken garments, the chief dignitaries of the court, with the priests and the eunuchs; last of all, borne in brightly coloured litters, each with a canopy, came Justinian, the Basileus, the autocrat, wearing a golden crown that looked like a saint's halo, and Empress Theodora, glittering with jewels. As the ruling pair entered the imperial box, a roar of acclamation rose from all the tiers of the huge assembly. Forgotten now was the terrible fight which had broken out in the hippodrome only three years before between the Green and the Blue factions of the circus, when the Greens had proclaimed a rival emperor and thirty thousand had been slain by the imperial forces under Belisarius. Popular memories are short, and the victorious cause is readily acclaimed as the just one. Intoxicated by the display, overwhelmed by the frenzy of their own enthusiasm, the countless spectators shouted and howled and applauded in a hundred tongues, while the stone circles of the hippodrome echoed to their voices. It was a whole city, a whole world, which now adulated its rulers: Justinian, the grandson of a Macedonian peasant; and Theodora, the lovely actress who, before her marriage, had danced totally nude in this same arena, and had sold her favours to any casual lover who could pay a sufficient fee. These escapades, these disgraces, were forgotten, as every shame is wiped away by victory and every deed of violence is excused by a subsequent triumph.

But on the highest tiers, mute above the vociferating crowds, stood spectators of marble, hundreds upon hundreds of the statues of Hellas. From their peaceful temples they had been torn away, the images of the Gods; from Palmyra and Cos, from Corinth and Athens; from triumphal arches and from pedestals they had been snatched, white and shining in their glorious nudity. Unaffected by transient passions, immersed in the perpetual dream of their own beauty, they were dumb and unparticipating, motionless, utterly aloof from human turmoil. With eyes that were sculptured but unseeing, they stared steadfastly across the agitated hippodrome toward the blue waters of the Bosporus.

Now there came another flourish of trumpets, to announce that Belisarius's triumphal procession had reached the outer gates of the hippodrome. The portals were thrown open, and once more the spectators shouted thunderous acclamations. Here they were, the iron cohorts of Belisarius, the men who, under their famous commander, had re-established imperial rule in Northern Africa, conquering all Justinian's enemies, freeing Byzantium from its anxieties, and ensuring for the pleasure-loving crowds an unchecked supply of bread and circuses. Even louder were the shouts of applause at the appearance of the booty, the spoils of Carthage, to which there seemed to be no end. Behold the triumphal cars which the Vandals had seized long, long ago; next, sustained by a framework of poles borne on men's shoulders, came a bejewelled throne; this was followed by the altars of unknown gods, and by lovely statues, the work of artists who had doubtless been famous in other times and other lands; then chests filled to the brim with gold and chalices and vases and silken garments. The vast abundance of plunder which the Vandal pirates had got together from the ends of the earth had now been won by Belisarius for its rightful owner, Emperor Justinian. What could his loyal subjects do but shout themselves hoarse at the sight of so much wealth assembled from all lands for the enrichment of their own mighty ruler?

Amid such splendours, the jubilant onlookers scarcely noticed the coming of a few articles which seemed insignificant when compared with what had gone before; a small table of which the wood had been covered by plates of hammered gold, two silver trumpets, and a seven-branched lampstand. No cheers greeted these seemingly trifling utensils. But on one of the topmost tiers was an old, old man who groaned as, with his left hand, he grasped Jehoiakim's arm. After fourscore years, Benjamin Marnefesh again set eyes upon what he had seen only once before, as a child of seven—the sacred Candelabrum from Solomon's House, the Menorah which his little hand had grasped for a moment, with the result that ever since he had had a withered arm. Happy and glorious sight; the holy emblem was unchanged, uninjured. Invincible did the eternal Lampstand march through the eternity of days, and had now taken a long stride nearer home. The sense of God's grace in granting him another sight of the Menorah was overwhelming. Unable to contain himself, he shouted: "Ours, ours, ours for all eternity!"

But none marked his cry, not even those nearest to him. For at this moment the whole assembly was roaring with excitement. Belisarius, the victorious general, had entered the arena. Far behind the triumphal cars, far behind the vast wealth of spoil, he marched in the simple uniform he had worn on active service. But the populace knew him in an instant, shouting his name so loudly, so exultantly, that Justinian was jealous, and had a wry face when the commander-in-chief made obeisance before the Emperor.

A silence ensued, tense with expectation, and no less striking than the previous uproar. Gelimer, the last King of the Vandals in Africa, mockingly clad in a purple robe, led in behind Belisarius the conqueror, now stood before the Emperor. Slaves tore off the purple garment, and the vanquished monarch prostrated himself. For a moment the myriads of onlookers held their breath, staring at the Basileus's hand. Would he grant grace or give the sign for immediate execution? Would he raise his finger or lower it? Look, Justinian lifted a forefinger, Gelimer's life was to be spared, and the crowd cheered approval. One only among the spectators disregarded this incident. Benjamin could think of nothing but the Menorah, which was slowly being carried round the arena. When, at length, the sacred emblem vanished through the exit, the old man's senses reeled.

"Lead me forth."

Jehoiakim grumbled. A young man, pleasure-loving, he wanted to see the rest of the show. But old Benjamin's bony hand gripped his arm impatiently.

"Lead me forth! Lead me forth!"

As if struck blind, the aged and sorely tried Benjamin Marnefesh groped his way across the town, leaning on Jehoiakim's arm, with the Menorah in imagination ever before his eyes, as he impatiently urged his guide not to tarry, but to bring him quickly to the Jewish quarter of the town. Benjamin had grown anxious lest the feeble flame of his life should flicker out prematurely, before he had had time to fulfil his mission and rescue the Lampstand.

Meanwhile in the synagogue at Pera the community had for hours and hours been awaiting their exalted guest. Just as in Rome the Jews were allowed to dwell only on the farther side of the Tiber, so in Byzantium were they restricted to the farther side of the Golden Horn. Here, as everywhere, to be held aloof was their destiny; but in this aloofness there also lay the secret of their survival as a distinct people.

The synagogue was small and was therefore overcrowded and stuffy. Packed into it were not only the Jews of Byzantium, but others of the congregation assembled from far and from near. From Nicæa and Trebizond, from Odessa and Smyrna, from various towns in Thrace, from every Jewish community within reach, envoys had arrived to take part in the proceedings. Long since had news come that Belisarius had stormed the Vandals' stronghold, and was bringing back to Byzantium, with numerous other treasures, the Seven-Branched Lampstand. To all the coasts of the Mediterranean had the tidings spread, so that there was not a Jew in the Byzantine Empire who had not been made aware of it. Though scattered like chaff over the threshing-floors of the world, and many of them more at home in Gentile tongues than in their own Hebrew, the members of this dispersed people retained a common interest in the holy emblem, suffering on this account common sorrows and hoping for common joys; and though they were sometimes at enmity with one another or mutually forgetful, their hearts beat in unison when danger threatened. Again and again persecution and injustice reforged the chain out of which their unity had been fashioned, so that the strength of these bonds was perpetually renewed; and the more savage the bludgeonings of Fate, the more firmly were the Jews of the Diaspora recemented into the one Chosen People. Thus the rumour that the Menorah, the Lampstand of the Temple, the Light of the Jewish nation, had once more been liberated from duress, and was wandering as of old from Babylon and from Rome across lands and seas, had aroused every Jew as if the thing had happened to his own self. In the streets and in the houses they conversed eagerly about the matter, asking their rabbis and their sages to interpret Scripture and explain the significance of these wanderings. Why had the sacred emblem started on its travels once more? Were they to hope or were they to despair? Was there to be a fresh persecution, or were the old ones to come to an end? Would they be driven from their homes to roam no man knew whither, unresting as of old now that the Menorah was again on the move? Or did the deliverance of the Lampstand betoken their own deliverance likewise? Was the Diaspora at length to come to an end? Were they to regather in their ancient home, in the Land of Promise? Terrible was their impatience. Messengers hastened from place to place to learn what was happening to the Menorah, and intense was the disappointment of the Jews when finally they were informed that, as had happened half a thousand years before in Rome, so now was the Seven-Branched Candlestick to be borne in a triumph at Byzantium beneath the contemptuous eyes of a Gentile emperor.

By this intelligence they had been profoundly moved; but excitement rose to fever-heat when the letter from the Roman community arrived informing them that Benjamin Marnefesh, the man sorely tried, the man who in early childhood had been the last to set eyes upon the Menorah when the Vandals sacked Rome, was on his way to Byzantium. To begin with, amazement was their predominant feeling. For years and for decades every Jew, however far from Rome, had known about the wonderful deed of the seven-year-old boy who, when the Vandals were carrying off the Lampstand, had tried

The Buried Candelabrum

to snatch it from the robbers, and had been struck down with a broken arm. Mothers told their children about Benjamin Marnefesh, whom God's own hand had touched; and Jews learned in the Law told their pupils. This brave exploit of a little boy had become a pious legend like those in Holy Writ, like the tale of David's slaying of Goliath and many others. At eventide, in Jewish houses, the heroic deed was related over and over again by the mothers and the elders of the people, among the stories of Ruth and Samson and Haman and Esther.

Now had come the astounding, the almost incredible news that this legendary child still lived. Old though he was, Benjamin Marnefesh, the last witness, was on his way to Byzantium. This must be a sign from the Almighty. Not without reason could Jehovah have spared him far beyond the allotted span. Was it not likely that he had been preserved for a special mission, that he was to take the sacred emblem back to Jerusalem, and to lead his co-religionists thither as well? The more they talked the matter over among themselves, the less were they inclined to doubt. Faith in the coming of a saviour, a redeemer, was eternal in the blood of this outcast people, ready to blossom at the first warm breath of hope. Now it sprouted mightily and fructified in their hearts. In the towns and the villages the Gentiles among whom the Jews dwelt were mightily puzzled at the aspect of their Hebrew neighbours, who had changed betwixt night and morning. Those who, as a rule, were timid and cringing, ever in expectation of a curse or a blow, were now cheerful and ready to dance for joy. Misers who counted every crumb were buying rich apparel; men who were usually slow to speak stood up in the marketplace to preach and to prophesy; women heavy with child slipped off joyfully to gossip about the news with their neighbours; while the children waved flags and sported garlands. Those who were most powerfully impressed by the report began to make ready for the journey, selling their possessions to buy mules and carts that there should not be a moment's delay when the summons came to set out for Jerusalem. Surely they must travel when the Menorah was travelling; and was it not true that the herald who had once before accompanied the Lampstand for a space when it left Rome, was again on the way? What signs and wonders such as this had there been among the Jews during the latter generations of the Dispersion?

Thus every congregation which received the news in time had appointed an envoy to be on hand when the Menorah should reach Byzantium, and to take part in the deliberations of the Byzantine brethren. All who were thus chosen thrilled with happiness and blessed God's name. How wonderful it seemed to them in their petty and obscure lives of daily need and hourly peril that they, inconspicuous traders or common craftsmen, should be privileged to participate in such marvellous events and to set eyes upon the man whom the Almighty had spared to so great an age for the deed of deliverance. They bought or borrowed sumptuous raiment, as if they had been invited to a great banquet; during the days before departure they fasted and bathed and prayed diligently, that they might be clean of body and pure at heart when they started on their mission; and when they left their homes, the community turned out in force to accompany them for the first stage of the journey. Wherever there were Jewish confraternities on the road to Byzantium, they were proud to entertain the envoys and pressed money upon them for the redemption of the Candelabrum. With all the pomp of a mighty monarch's ambassador did these men of little account, the representatives of a poor and powerless people, proceed on their way; and when they encountered one another, joining forces for the rest of the journey, they eagerly discussed what would happen, excitement growing as they spoke. Naturally, as this fervour grew, each of them reacted on the other, and thus they became increasingly confident that they were about to witness a miracle and that the long-prophesied turn in the fortunes of their nation was to occur.

Behold them assembled, a motley crowd of ardent talkers holding lively converse in the synagogue at Pera. Now the boy whom they had sent to keep watch ran up panting, and waving a white cloth as he came, in token that Benjamin Marnefesh, the expected guest, had come across from Byzantium in a boat. Those who were seated sprang to their feet; those who had been talking most volubly were struck dumb with excitement; and one of them, an exceedingly old man, fell in a faint, being struck down by his emotions. None of the company, not even the leader of the community, ventured to go and meet the new arrival. Holding their breath they stood to await his coming; and when Benjamin, led by Jehoiakim, an imposing figure with his white beard and flashing eyes, drew near to the house, he seemed to them a patriarchal figure, the true lord and master of miracles. Their repressed enthusiasm broke forth.

"Blessed be thy coming! Blessed by thy name!" they shouted to him. In a trice they surrounded him, kissing the hem of his garment while the tears ran down their withered cheeks. They jostled one another to get near him, each of them piously wishing to touch the arm which had been broken in the attempt to rescue the Lord's Lampstand. The leader of the community had to intervene for the visitor's protection lest, in the frenzy of their greeting, they should overturn him and trample him beneath their feet.

Benjamin was alarmed at the exuberance of their welcome. What did they want? What did they expect of him? Anxiety overcame him when he realized the intensity of their anticipations. Gently yet urgently he protested.

"Do not look for so much from me or entertain such exalted ideas which I myself do not harbour. I can work no miracles. Be content with patient hope. It is sinful to ask for a miracle as if its performance were a certainty."

They hung their heads, disconcerted that Benjamin had read their secret thoughts; and they were ashamed of their impetuosity. Discreetly they drew aside, so that their leader could conduct Benjamin to the seat prepared for him, well stuffed with cushions, and raised above the seats of the others. But once more Benjamin protested, saying:

"No, far be it from me to sit above any of you. Not for me to be exalted, who am, perhaps, the lowliest of your company. I am nothing more than a very old man to whom God has left little strength. I came merely to see what would happen to the Menorah, and to take counsel with you. Do not expect me to work a miracle."

They complied with his wishes, and he sat among them, the only patient member of an impatient assembly. The leader of the community rose to give him formal greeting:

"Peace be unto you. Blessed be your coming and blessed your going. Our hearts are glad to see you."

The others maintained a solemn silence. In low tones, the leader resumed:

"From our brethren in Rome we received letters heralding your arrival, and we have done everything in our power. We have collected money from house to house and from place to place to help in the redemption of the Menorah. We have prepared a gift in the hope of softening the Emperor's heart. We are ready to bestow on him the most precious of our possessions, a stone from Solomon's Temple which our forefathers saved when the Temple was destroyed, and this we propose to offer Justinian. At this moment his most cherished purpose is to build a House of God more splendid than there has ever been in the world before, and from all lands and all cities he is collecting the most splendid and most sacred materials to this end. These things we have done willingly and joyfully. But we were terrified when we heard that our Roman brethren wanted us to gain access for you to the Emperor, that you might beg him to restore the sacred Lampstand. We were mightily alarmed, for Justinian, who rules over this land, regards us with disfavour. He is intolerant of all those who differ from him in the smallest particle, whether they be Christians of another sect than his own or heathens or Jews; and perhaps it will not be long before he expels us from his empire. Never has he admitted any member of our community to audience; and it was, therefore, bowed with shame that I came to tell you how impossible it would be for us to fulfil the request of our brethren in Rome—that no Jew would be admitted to the presence of Emperor Justinian."

The leader of the community, who had spoken timidly and deprecatingly, was silent. All present hung their heads. How was the miracle to take place? What change in the situation could be effected if the Emperor were to close his ears to the words of God's messenger, were to harden his heart? But now, when the leader spoke once more, his voice was firmer and clearer:

"Yet magical and comforting is it to learn again and ever again that to God nothing is impossible. When, heavy of heart, I entered this house, there came up to me a member of our community, Zechariah the goldsmith, a pious and just man, who informed me that the wish of our Roman brethren would be fulfilled. While we were aimlessly talking and striving, he set quietly to work, and what had seemed impossible to the wisest among us he was able to achieve by secret means. Speak, Zechariah, and make known what you have done."

From one of the back rows there stood up hesitatingly a small, slender, hunchbacked man, shy because so many eyes were turned on him. He lowered his head to hide his blushes for, a lonely craftsman, used only to his own company, he was little accustomed to conversation. He

The Buried Candelabrum

cleared his throat several times, and, when he began to speak, his voice was as small as a child's.

"No occasion to praise me, Rabbi," he murmured; "not mine the merit. God made things easy for me. For thirty years the treasurer has been well disposed towards me; for thirty years I have been one of his journeymen; and when, three years ago, the mob rose against the Emperor and plundered the mansions of the nobles, I hid him and his wife and child in my house for several days until the danger was past. I felt sure, therefore, that he would do anything I asked him, all the more since I had never asked him anything before. But when I knew that Benjamin was on the way, I ventured to put a request, and he went to tell Justinian that a great and private message was on the way across the sea. By God's grace this moved the Emperor, who wants to see our messenger from Rome. Tomorrow he will give audience to Benjamin and our leader, in the imperial reception room."

Shyly and quietly Zechariah resumed his seat. There was an amazed and reverent silence. Assuredly this was the miracle for which they had been waiting. Never before had it been known that a Jew should be received in audience by the unapproachable Emperor. They trembled, open-eyed, while the conviction that God's grace had been vouchsafed to them presided over their solemn silence. But Benjamin groaned like a sorely wounded man, saying:

"O God, O God! What burdens art thou laying on me? My heart is feeble and I cannot speak a word of the Greek tongue. How can I present myself before the Emperor, and why should I do so more than another? I was

Jewish Legends

sent here only to bear testimony, to look upon the Menorah, not to seize it or get possession of it. Do not choose me. Let another speak. I am too old, I am too weak."

They were all horrified. A miracle had been vouchsafed, and now he who had been chosen to perform it was unwilling. But while they were still wondering what they could do to overcome their visitor's timidity, Zechariah again rose slowly to his feet. When he now spoke it was in a firmer voice than before. The man had grown resolute.

"No, Benjamin, you must go to the audience, and you only. A little thing it was that I did, but I would not have ventured to do it for any other than you. This much do I know, that if any one of us can do so it is you that will bring the Menorah to its resting-place."

Benjamin stared at the speaker.

"How can you tell?"

Zechariah repeated firmly: "I know, and I have long known. Only you, if anyone, can bring the Menorah to its resting-place."

Benjamin's heart was shaken by this definite assurance. He looked full at Zechariah, who was himself looking encouragingly at Benjamin, and smiling as he did so. Suddenly it seemed to Benjamin as if Zechariah's features were familiar, and in Zechariah's eyes there was also a light of recognition, for his smile broadened, and he spoke with reinforced confidence:

"Recall that night eighty years ago. Do you remember one of the old men of your company, Hyrcanus ben Hillel by name?"

Now it was Benjamin's turn to smile.

The Buried Candelabrum

"How could I fail to remember him? I remember every word and every happening of that blessed night as if it had been yesterday."

Zechariah went on: "I am his great-grandson. Goldsmiths have we been for generations. When an emperor or a king has gold and gems, and has need of a cunning craftsman or an appraiser, he chooses one of our race. Hyrcanus ben Hillel, at Rome, kept watch over the Menorah in its imprisonment; and all of his family ever since, no matter in what place, have been awaiting the hour when the Lampstand might come into their charge in some other treasury, for where there are treasures, there are we as valuers and jewellers. My father's father said to my father and my father reported it to me that, after the night on which your arm was broken, Rabbi Eliezer, the pure and clear, proclaimed of you what you yourself could not yet know, being but a little child, that there must be some great meaning in your deed and in your suffering. 'If anyone,' said the Rabbi, 'then this little boy will redeem the Menorah.'"

All trembled. Benjamin looked down. Greatly moved, he said:

"No one has ever been kinder to me than was Rabbi Eliezer that night, and his words are sacred to me. Forgive me my cowardice. Once, long ago, when I was a child, I was courageous; but time and old age have dashed my spirits. I must implore you not to expect a miracle from me. If you ask me to go to the man who now holds the Lampstand in his grip, I will do my best, for woe unto him who should refrain from a pious endeavour. Truth to tell, I am not one of those who have the gift of eloquence, but perhaps God will put words into my mouth."

Benjamin's voice was low and diffident, so that it was plain he felt the burden of the task which had been imposed on him. Still more softly, he said:

"Forgive me if I leave you now. I am an old man, wearied by the journey and by the excitement of this day. With your permission, I will seek repose."

Respectfully they made way for him. One only of the company, the impetuous Jehoiakim, his companion, could not refrain from questioning old Benjamin, on the way to the appointed quarters:

"What will you say to the Emperor tomorrow?"

The old man did not look up, but murmured as if to himself:

"I do not know, nor do I want to know or to think about the matter. In myself there is no power. What I have to say must be given to me, by the Almighty."

Long that night the Jews sat together in Pera. Not one of them could sleep, or had any inclination to seek his couch, so they talked unceasingly, holding counsel. Never had they felt so near the realm of miracles. What if the Diaspora were really drawing to a close; if an end were about to come to the cruel distresses of life among the Gentiles, the everlasting persecutions, in which the Chosen People was trodden underfoot, afraid day after day and night after night of what the next hour would bring forth? What if this old man who had sat among them in the flesh were in very truth the Messiah, one of those mighty of speech such as had lived aforetime among their people, able to touch the hearts of kings and move them to righteousness? What unthinkable happiness, what incredible grace, to be able to bring home the sacred emblem, to rebuild the Temple and to live within its shadow. Like men drunken with wine they talked the matter over throughout the long night, their confidence growing all the while. They had forgotten the old man's warning that they were not to expect a miracle from him. Had they not, as pious Jews, learned from Holy Writ to look always for God's miracles? How could they go on living at all, the outcast and the oppressed, unless in perpetual expectation of this redemption? Interminable seemed the night, and they could no longer restrain their expectations. Again and again they glanced at the hourglass, thinking that its orifice must have become clogged. Again and again one of them went to the window to look for the first glimmer of dawn upon the darkened sea, and for the flames of coming day which would be appropriate to the flames that were burning in their hearts.

It was difficult for the leader to control his usually docile brethren. One and all they wanted, on the coming day, to accompany Benjamin to Byzantium, where they would stand outside the palace, while he, within, conversed with the ruler of the world. They wished to be close to him while this miracle was being worked. The leader had sternly to remind them how dangerous it would be for them to assemble in striking numbers in front of the imperial palace, for the populace was ever hostile to the Jews, upon whom suspicion would easily fall. Only by using threats could he induce them to stay

Jewish Legends

in the synagogue at Pera, where, unseen by their enemies, they could pray to the invisible God, while Benjamin was received in audience by the great ruler. They prayed, therefore, and fasted throughout the day. So earnestly did they pray that it seemed as if all the homesickness of all the Jews of the world must be concentrated within the heart of each one of them. Of nothing

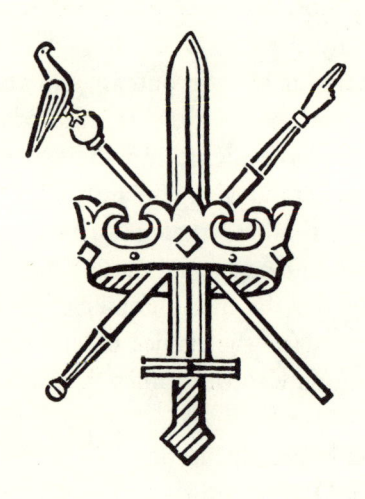

else could they think than of their hopes that this miracle would be performed, and that, by God's grace, the curse of having to live among the Gentiles would be removed for ever from the Chosen People.

Noon was the appointed hour, and a few minutes before noon Benjamin accompanied by the leader of the community entered the colonnades of the square in front

The Buried Candelabrum

of Justinian's palace. Behind them came Jehoiakim, young and vigorous, bearing on his shoulders a heavy burden, which was carefully wrapped. Slowly, quietly, grave of mien, the two old men, plainly dressed in dark robes, made their way through the bronze portals of the reception room, behind which was the ornate throne-room of the Byzantine Emperor. They were, however, kept waiting a long time in the ante-room, for such was the custom at Byzantium, where envoys and suitors were to be taught by this expedient how exceptional was the privilege of being vouchsafed a glimpse of the countenance of the mightiest man on earth. An hour and a second and a third passed, but no one offered either of the old men a stool or a chair. Unfeelingly they were left to stand upon the cold marble. There streamed by in busy idleness an endless train of courtiers, fat eunuchs, guardsmen, and fantastically dressed menials; but no one troubled about the Jews, no one looked at them or spoke to them; while from the walls the impassive mosaics stared down upon them, while from the pillared cupola the lavish gold decorations mingled their splendours with those of the sunlight. Benjamin and the leader of the community stood patiently in silence. Being old men of an oppressed race, they had learned to wait. Too long an experience had they had of the weary hours to trouble about the passing of one or two more. Only Jehoiakim, young and impatient, looked inquisitively at everyone who passed through, irritably counting the fragments of the mosaic, hoping thus to while away the time.

At length, when the sun was manifestly declining, the præpositus sacri cubiculi approached them and initiated them into the practices enjoined by the ritual of the Court upon anyone who was granted the privilege of looking upon the Emperor's countenance.

"As soon as the door opens," he said, "you must, with lowered heads, advance twenty paces to the place where a white vein is inserted into the coloured marble slabs on the floor; but no farther, lest your breath should mingle with that of His Majesty the Emperor. Before you venture to raise your eyes to look upon the autocrat, you must prostrate yourself three times, arms and legs outspread upon the floor. Then only may you draw near to the porphyry steps of the throne, to kiss the hem of the Basileus's purple robe."

"No," interposed Jehoiakim, hotly though in low tones. "Only before God Almighty may we prostrate ourselves in that fashion, not before any mortal. I will not do it."

"Silence," answered Benjamin severely. "Why should I not kiss the earth? Did not God create it? Even if it were wrong to prostrate oneself before a mortal, still we may do wrong in a sacred cause."

At this moment the ivory-inlaid door leading into the throne-room opened. There emerged a Caucasian embassy which had come to pay homage to the Emperor. The door closed noiselessly behind them, and the aliens stood dumbfounded in their fur caps and their silken robes. Their faces were distorted with anxiety. Obviously Justinian had given them a rough reception, because they had offered him an alliance in the name of their people instead of making complete submission. Jehoiakim was staring at the strangers curiously, and taking note of their unusual attire, when the præpositus ordered him to take his burden on his shoulders and instructed the old men to do exactly what he had told them. Then he smote on the door gently with his golden staff, which produced a faint, ringing note. It was opened silently from within, and thereupon the three visitors, joined by an interpreter at a sign from the præpositus, entered the spacious throne-room of the Emperor of Byzantium, the room known as the consistorium.

To right and left from the door to the middle of the huge apartment was ranged on each side a line of soldiers, and it was between these two lines that they had to advance. Each man stood to attention, dressed in a red uniform, sword strapped to his hips, wearing a gilded helmet decorated with a huge red horsetail, holding a long lance in his right hand, and having slung behind his shoulders a formidable battle-axe. As stiff and straight they stood as a wall of stone, all of the same height, and behind them, likewise as if turned to stone, stood the leaders of the cohorts, holding banners. Slowly the three visitors and the interpreter advanced between these walls of impassive figures, whose eyes were as motionless as their bodies, none seeming to notice the newcomers. In silence they reached the farther side of the room where doubtless (though they did not dare to raise their eyes) the Emperor was awaiting them. But when the præpositus, who preceded them with his golden staff uplifted, came to a halt, and, as was now permitted, they could raise their eyes towards the Emperor's throne, lo, there was no throne to be seen and no Emperor, but only a silken curtain stretched across the hall and cut-

Jewish Legends

ting the outlook. Motionless they stood there, staring at this coloured, arresting partition.

Once more the master of the ceremonies raised his staff. Thereupon the curtain parted in the middle and was drawn back to either side by unseen cords. Now, at the top of three porphyry steps, there was seen in the background the bejewelled throne on which sat the Basileus beneath a golden canopy. Stiffly he sat, looking more like a graven image than a human being, a corpulent and powerfully built man whose forehead vanished beneath the glittering crown which haloed his head. No less statue-like were the guardsmen, wearing white tunics, golden helmets, and golden chains round their necks, who formed a double circle round the monarch, while in front of these stood, equally statuesque, the Court dignitaries, the senators, wearing mantles of purple silk. They seemed neither to breathe nor to see; and it was plain that they were thus drilled into motionlessness and sightlessness that any stranger who thus for the first time glimpsed the ruler of the world should himself be petrified with veneration.

In fact both the leader of the Jewish confraternity and Jehoiakim felt as if blinded, like one unexpectedly thrust from darkness into strong sunlight. Only Benjamin, by far the oldest man in the room, looked steadily and imperturbably at Justinian. During his one lifetime, ten emperors and rulers of Rome had mounted the throne and then passed away. He knew well, therefore, that, for all their costly insignia and invaluable crowns, emperors did not really differ from ordinary mortals who eat and drink, attend to the calls of nature, possess women, and die at last like anyone else. His soul was unshaken. Firmly he raised his eyes to look into the eyes of the mighty Emperor, from whom he had come to beg a favour.

At this moment, from behind, he was warningly touched on the shoulder by the golden staff, and was thus reminded of what custom prescribed. Difficult as it was for one whose limbs were stiffened by extreme old age, he flung himself upon the cold marble of the flooring, hands and feet outstretched. Thrice he pressed his forehead against the flooring, while his huge white beard rustled against the unfeeling stone. Then he arose, assisted by Jehoiakim, with lowered head advanced to the steps, and kissed the hem of the Emperor's purple robe.

The Basileus did not move, did not so much as flicker an eyelid. Sternly he looked, as it were, through the old man. It seemed to be indifferent to him, the Emperor, what might happen at his feet, and what worm might dare to touch the hem of his garment.

But the three, at a sign from the master of the ceremonies, had drawn back a little, and stood in a row, with the interpreter at a pace to the front to serve as their mouthpiece. Once more the præpositus raised his staff, and the interpreter began to speak. This man, he said, was a Jew, commissioned by the other members of his fraternity in Rome to bring the Emperor of the world thanks and congratulations for having avenged Rome upon the robbers and having freed seas and lands from these wicked pirates. Inasmuch as all the Jews in the world, who were His Majesty's faithful subjects, had learned that the Basileus, in his wisdom, had determined to build a new House of God in honour of sacred wisdom, Hagia Sophia, which was to be more splendid and more costly than any other temple yet built by the hands of man, they had, poor though they were, done their utmost to contribute a fragment to the sanctification of this edifice. Insignificant was their gift, in contrast with His Majesty's splendours, but still it was the greatest and most sacred object which had been preserved by them from ancient days. Their forefathers, when driven out of Jerusalem, had carried with them a stone from the Temple of Solomon. This they had brought with them today, hoping that it might be inserted among the foundations of the new House of God, that the latter might contain a fragment from King Solomon's Holy House, and be a blessing to the Holy House about to be built by Justinian.

Upon a sign from the præpositus, Jehoiakim carried the heavy stone to place it among the gifts which the Caucasian envoys had heaped up to the left of the throne; furs, Indian ivory, and embroidered cashmeres. But Justinian looked neither at the interpreter nor at the gift brought by the Jewish visitors. Bored and weary he stared into vacancy, and said, with a drowsy irritability mingled with contempt:

"Ask them what they want."

In flowery metaphors the interpreter explained that among the magnificent spoils brought back from Carthage by Belisarius there was a trifle which happened to be peculiarly dear to the Jewish people. The Seven-Branched Lampstand which the Vandals had stolen from Rome and taken to Carthage had originally come from Solomon's Temple, built by the Jews in ancient days as the House of God. Therefore the Jews implored the Emperor to spare them this Lampstand, being ready to redeem it by paying twice its weight in gold, or, if need be, ten times its weight. There would not be a Jewish house or a Jewish hut anywhere in the world where the inmates would not daily pray for the health and welfare of the most gracious of all the Emperors and for his long reign.

The eyes of the Basileus did not soften. Spitefully he answered:

"I do not wish those who are not Christians to pray for me. But ask them to explain more fully what concern they have with this Lampstand, and what they propose to do with it."

The interpreter looked at Benjamin, translating these remarks, and a shudder seized the old man, who was chilled to the soul by Justinian's cold glances. He sensed resistance and hostility, so that he grew afraid that he would not prevail. Imploringly he raised his hand:

"Great Lord, bethink yourself, this is the only one of the holy treasures our people once possessed which still remains on earth. Our city did they batter down, our walls did they raze, our Temple did they destroy. Everything which we loved and owned and honoured has fallen into decay. One object only, this Lampstand, has lasted through the ages. It is thousands of years old, older than anything else on earth; and for centuries has it wandered homeless. While it continues to wander, our people will know no rest. Lord, have pity on us. The Lampstand is the last of our sacred possessions. Restore it to us. Think how God raised you from among the lowly to place you upon the seats of the mighty, to make you wealthier than any other man on earth. It is the will of God that he shall give to whom it has been given. Lord, what is it to you, this wandering Lampstand? Lord, let there be an end of its wanderings and let it go home to rest."

Whatever the interpreter translated, he translated with courtly embellishments, and hitherto the Emperor had listened indifferently. But when, through the mouth of the interpreter, Benjamin reminded him that he had been lifted from a lowly place to become the mightiest of the mighty, his face darkened. Justinian was not fond of being told that he, now accounted semi-divine, had been born the offspring of a poor peasant family in a Thracian village. He frowned, and was about to utter a curt refusal.

But with the watchfulness of anxiety, Benjamin was quick to perceive the signs of imperial disfavour, and already fancied himself hearing the dreadful, the irrevocable No. His fears made him eloquent. As if propelled by an irresistible force from within, and forgetting the etiquette which forbade him to advance beyond the white vein in the marble floor, to the alarm of all present he stepped briskly towards the throne and raised his hands imploringly towards the Emperor, saying:

"Lord, your rule, your city are at stake. Be not presumptuous, nor try to keep what no one yet has been able to keep. Babylon was great, and Rome, and Carthage; but the temples have fallen which hid the Lampstand; and the walls have crashed which enclosed it. It alone, the Lampstand, remained unhurt, while all around it fell in ruins. Should anyone try to seize it, his arm is broken and withered; and anyone who deprives it of rest will himself suffer perpetual unrest. Woe to him who keeps what does not belong to him. God will give him no peace until he has returned this sacred emblem to the Holy City. Lord, I warn you. Give back the Lampstand."

The onlookers were struck dumb. Not one of them had understood the wild words. But the courtiers had witnessed with terror how a suitor had ventured what none had ever ventured before; in the heat of anger he had drawn close to the Emperor, and, with impetuous words, had interrupted the mightiest in the world when about to speak. Shudderingly they contemplated this old, old man, who stood there shaken by the intensity of his pain, with tears glistening in his beard while his eyes flashed with wrath. The leader of the Jewish confraternity, greatly alarmed, had retreated far into the background; the interpreter, too, had withdrawn to a distance. Thus Benjamin stood quite alone, face to face with the Basileus.

Justinian had been startled out of his rigidity. He looked unsteadily at this wrathful old man, and impatiently bade the interpreter translate what had been said. The interpreter did so, toning the words down as much as he dared. Would His Majesty be gracious enough to pardon the aged stranger for a breach of etiquette, seeing that the Jew had in truth been driven beyond all bounds by anxiety for the safety of the Empire? He had wished to warn His Majesty that God had laid a terrible curse upon this Lampstand. It would bring disaster upon any who should keep it, and whatever town should harbour it would be ravaged by enemies. The old man, therefore, had felt it his duty to warn His Majesty that the only way of escaping this curse would be to restore the Lampstand to the land of its origin, to send it back to Jerusalem.

Justinian listened with bent brows. He was angered by the impudence of this irreverent old Jew, who had raised voice and fist in the imperial presence. All the same, he was uneasy. Being of peasant origin, he was superstitious, and like every child of fortune he believed in sorcery and signs. After thinking matters over for a few moments, he said dryly:

"So be it. Let the thing be taken from among the spoils of Carthage and sent to Jerusalem."

The old man quivered as the interpreter translated the Emperor's words. The joyful tidings illuminated his soul like a flash of lightning. His mission was fulfilled. For this moment had he lived. For this moment it was that God had spared his life so long. Almost unwittingly, he raised his left hand, the sound one, stretching it upward as if, in his gratitude, he hoped to touch the Almighty's footstool.

Justinian was quick to see how Benjamin's face was irradiated with joy, and a spiteful desire took possession of him. On no account would he permit the insolent Jew to go back to his own people with the boast: "I have persuaded the Emperor and have won a victory." He smiled maliciously, saying:

"Don't rejoice before you have heard me out. It is not my purpose that the Lampstand shall belong to you

Jews, shall be restored to you as one of the implements of your false religion."

Turning to Bishop Euphemius, who stood at his right hand, he went on:

"When you set forth at the new moon in order to consecrate the church which Theodora has founded in Jerusalem, you will take the Lampstand with you. Not that it may have its lamps lighted and stand upon the altar. You will place it unlighted beneath the altar, that everyone may see how our faith is high above theirs and how truth transcends error. It shall be safeguarded in the True Church, and not by those to whom the Messiah came and who failed to acknowledge him."

The old man was terrified. Of course he had not understood the words spoken in a foreign tongue; but he had seen that Justinian's smile was ill-natured, and knew that the man of might must have said something intended to disappoint him. He wished to prostrate himself once more at the Emperor's feet and implore him to revoke whatever this last order could have been. But Justinian had already glanced at the præpositus. The latter raised his staff of office, and the curtains rustled together. Emperor and throne had vanished. The reception was over.

Benjamin stood dismayed, facing the partition. Then the master of the ceremonies, who was standing behind him, touched him on the shoulder with the golden wand, as a sign that he was dismissed. Aided by Jehoiakim, Benjamin tottered out, his vision clouded. Once more God had rejected him, at the moment when the sacred emblem was almost in his grasp. Again he had failed. The

Jewish Legends

Menorah still belonged to those who regarded might as right.

When he had walked no more than a few paces across the square outside the palace, Benjamin, again sorely tried, staggered and was about to fall. The leader of the community and Jehoiakim had all they could do to get him safe into an adjoining house where they put him to bed. His face was deathly pale as he lay there scarcely breathing. They thought, indeed, that he was about to pass away, for even the uninjured arm hung flaccid, and the leader found it difficult to detect the beating of his heart, which fluttered irregularly. He remained unconscious for several hours, as if his last vain appeal to the Emperor had sapped the remainder of his vital forces; but, when night was falling, to the amazement of the two watchers, the man who had been so near to death came to himself and stared at them with a strange expression which suggested that he must be a visitant from the other world. Gradually recognizing them, he commanded (to their still greater astonishment) that they should remove him as speedily as possible to the synagogue in Pera, for he wished to bid farewell to the community. Vainly did they urge him to rest awhile longer until he had more fully recuperated; he stubbornly told them to do his bidding, and they had no choice but to obey. Hiring a litter, they had him carried to the Golden Horn and ferried across to Pera by boat. During the transit, he lay half asleep, without opening his eyes or uttering a word.

Long ere this had the Jews in Pera heard about the Emperor's decision. They had been so certain that the

Lord would work a miracle that such a grudging return of the Menorah to Jerusalem could by no means satisfy them. This was an utterly inadequate fulfilment of their extravagant hopes. The trouble was not only that the Menorah was to be kept beneath the altar in a Christian church, but that they themselves were to remain in exile. Their own fate concerned them even more than that of the Lampstand. They looked like men stricken with apoplexy as they sat there gloomily, huddled up, and full of secret vexation. Hope told a flattering tale to him who was fool enough to believe it. Miracles were fine things to read about in Holy Writ and were as beautiful as the bow in the cloud which was a token of God's covenant made in the days when the Almighty was near to his creatures; but the time of miracles was over. God had forgotten his people, once the chosen, but now left unheeded in their sorrows and distresses. No longer did Jehovah send prophets to speak in his name. How foolish, then, to believe in uncertain signs or to expect wonders. The Jews in the synagogue at Pera had ceased to pray and ceased to fast. Morose they sat in the corners, munching bread and onions.

Now that the expectation of a miracle no longer made their eyes glisten and their foreheads shine, they had become once more the petty, plaintive beings they had been so long, poor and oppressed Jews; and their thoughts, which so recently had soared Godward, had again become commonplace and earthbound. They were traders and shopkeepers again, with minds according. The envoys openly asked one another of what avail it had been to make a long and arduous journey, which had cost a lot of money. Why had they spent so much upon fine clothes that were now travel-worn? Why had they wasted their time and missed excellent opportunities of doing business? When they got home again, the incredulous would make mock of them, and their wives would nag. And since the human heart is so constituted that it is ever prone, when hopes have been dashed, to show the strongest animus against all who awakened them, vexation was now concentrated upon the Roman brethren and upon Benjamin the false prophet. Sorely tried, was he? Well, he had been a sore trial. God did not love him, so why should they? When, after nightfall, Marnefesh turned up at the synagogue, they showed him plainly enough how their feeling towards him had changed. Not, as before, did they reverently draw near to him with cordial greetings. Deliberately they averted their countenances. Why should they bother themselves about him, the old, old Jew from Rome? He was no stronger than the rest of them; and God was as little interested in him as in their own sad fate.

Benjamin was quick to perceive the anger which underlay their aloofness; to perceive the discontent which alone could explain their cheerless silence. He was distressed to find that they looked at him askance, or would not even meet his eyes; and he could not but feel as if he must be to blame for their disappointment. He therefore begged the leader of the community to call them together, since he still had a word to say to them. Unwillingly, morosely, they came out of their corners. What more could he wish to say to them, the man from Rome, the false prophet? Yet they could not but feel compassion when they saw him rise with difficulty from his seat, and support himself on his stick, leaning forward, by far the oldest man in the company. He barely had the strength to speak.

"I have come once more, brethren, this time to take leave of you. Also to humble myself before you. Not of set purpose have I brought you sorrow. As you all know, I did not wish to present myself before the Emperor, yet I could not but comply with your request. When I was only a little child, the elders of our Roman community took me with them, having snatched me from sleep, I not knowing wherefore or whither. Always, after that night, they continued to tell me and others that the whole meaning of my life was to redeem the Menorah. Believe me, brethren, it is terrible to be one whom God perpetually summons but to whom he never listens, one whom he lures onward with signs which he does not fulfil. Better that such a man should remain in obscurity where none can see him or hearken to him. I beg you, therefore, to forgive me, to forget me, and to make no further inquiries about me. Do not name the name of the failure who did you grievous wrong. Patiently await the coming of him who will, one day, deliver the Chosen People and the Menorah."

Thrice did Benjamin bow before the confraternity like a penitent who acknowledges his wrongdoing. Thrice did he strike his breast with his enfeebled left hand, while the other, the hand of the withered arm, hung motionless by his side; then he drew himself up and strode to the door. No one stirred, no one answered his words. But Jehoiakim, remembering that it was his duty to sustain the old man, hastened after him to the threshold. Benjamin, however, waved the youth away, saying:

"Return to Rome, and when the brethren there ask after me, say: 'Benjamin Marnefesh is no more, and was not appointed by God as a redeemer.' Tell them to forget my name and to say no prayers in memory of me. When I die, I wish to be forgotten. Go in peace, and trouble yourself about me no longer."

Obediently Jehoiakim refrained from crossing the threshold. Uneasily he looked after the old man, wondering why Benjamin, walking with difficulty and supported by the staff, took the uphill direction. But he did not dare to follow, standing his ground at the door to watch the bowed figure out of sight.

That night, in his eighty-eighth year, Benjamin, who never before had lost patience, for the first time arraigned God. Confusedly, regarding himself as a hunted man, he had groped his way through the narrow, winding alleys of Pera, not knowing his destination. His one wish was to flee from the shame of having led his people to entertain immoderate hopes. He would creep into some out-of-the-way corner where no one knew him and where he could die like a sick beast.

"After all, it was not my fault," he murmured again and again. "Why did they lay this burden upon me, expecting me to work a miracle? Why did they pick me out, me of all men?"

But these self-communings did not assuage him, as he was driven farther and farther by the fear that someone might follow him. At length he grew footsore, and his knees trembled with fatigue. Sweat-drops beaded his wrinkled brow, tasted salt as they rolled between his lips while others fell into his beard. His tormented heart beat fitfully, and his breath came in gasps. But like a hunted animal, the old man, still aided by his staff, mounted higher and higher along the steep path which led into the open, away from the houses. Never again did he wish to see or be seen by anyone. Away, away from dwellings and firesides, to lose himself, to be for ever forgotten, enduringly delivered from the persistent illusion of deliverance.

Stumbling along, as unsteady on his feet as a drunkard, Benjamin at length reached the open hill-country behind the town, and there, as he leaned against a pine which, though he knew it not, kept watch over a tomb, he rested and recovered his breath. It was early autumn; the southern night was clear; the sea shone brightly in the moonlight, showing silver scales like a giant fish; while, like a serpent, close at hand was the channel of the Golden Horn. On the other side of this channel, Byzantium slumbered in the moonlight, its white turrets and cupolas shining brightly. Very few lights were moving in the harbour, since it was after midnight; nor did there rise from the city any sound of human toil; but the breeze rustled gently through the vineyards, now and then detaching a yellowed leaf from the withering vines, a leaf that fluttered silently to the ground. Somewhere close at hand must be wine-presses and wine-vaults, for down wind came the sour-sweet smell of must. This smell reminded him of the past, and with quivering nostrils the weary old man snuffed the odour of fermentation. The vine leaves were sinking to earth, and would become earth again. Ah, could but he himself thus perish, be joined to earth as they were. Never did he wish to go back to live among his fellows, address himself to a fruitless task, torment himself anew. Let him be delivered, at length, from the burden of the flesh.

When, now, a sense of the prevailing stillness took possession of him, and he grew aware of being alone, he was more and more overmastered by the longing for eternal rest. Amid the silence, therefore, he raised his voice to God, half in complaint and half in prayer:

"Lord, let me die. Why should I go on living, being useless to myself, and a scorn and a trouble to all with whom I come in contact? Why should you spare my life when you know that I do not wish to live? I have begotten sons, seven of them, each one a strong man in his time and eager for life; yet I, their father, shovelled the first earth into the graves of them all. A grandson didst thou give me, young and fair, too young to know the desire for women and the sweetness of life; but the heathen wounded him unto death. He did not wish to die; he did not wish to die. For four days, though wounded unto death, he struggled against death. Then, at last, didst thou take him, who wished to live, while me, who long to die, thou wilt not take. Lord, what dost thou want of me which I am not willing to do? When I was a little child they snatched me from my bed, and obediently I went whither I was told. Yet now, in my old age, I have had to deceive those who believed in me, and the signs which led them to believe in me were false. Lord, let me be. I have failed, so fling me away. Eighty and eight years have I lived; eighty and eight years have

I vainly waited to find a meaning in the length of my life and to do a deed which should prove me faithful to thy word. But I have grown weary. Lord, I am at the end of my strength. Lord, be content, and let me die."

Thus raising his voice, the old man prayed, with a yearning gaze directed heavenward, as he looked earnestly at the twinkling stars. He stood there, expecting God's answer. Surely an answer would come at last? Patiently he awaited this answer, but by degrees his uplifted hand sank slowly, and fatigue, intense fatigue, overcame him. His temples throbbed; his feet and knees gave way. Involuntarily he sank to the ground, in a pleasant lassitude. Not wholly pleasant, indeed, for he felt as if he were bleeding to death, yet there was pleasure in his overpowering weakness.

"This is death," he thought gratefully. "God has heard my prayer." Piously, tranquilly, he stretched his head upon the earth, which had the decaying odour of autumn.

"I ought to have put on my shroud," he thought, but felt too tired to seek for it in his scrip. Unconsciously he drew his cloak more closely around him. Then, closing his eyes, he confidently awaited the death for which he had prayed.

But not that night was death to visit Benjamin, the sorely tried. Gently he fell asleep, while his mind went on working in the imagery of a dream.

Here is the dream which Benjamin dreamed on that night of his last trial. Once more he was groping his way in flight after darkness had fallen through the narrow al-

Jewish Legends

leys of Pera; but that darkness was now darker than it had been before, while in the skies thick black clouds hung low above the hilltops and the peaks. He had carried fear with him into dreamland, so that his heart throbbed violently when he heard footsteps on his trail; again he was seized with terror at the thought of anyone following him; and as he had fled when awake so did he now flee in his dream. But the footsteps continued, in front of him, behind him, to right and left, all round him in the gloomy, vacant, black landscape. He could not see who those were that marched to right and to left, in front and behind, but there must be very many of them, a huge wandering company; he could distinguish the heavy tread of men, the lighter footsteps of women with clicking buckles on their shoes, and the pitter-patter of childish feet. It must be an entire people that marched along with him through the moonless, metallic night; a mourning and oppressed people. For continually he heard dull groans and murmurs and calls from their invisible ranks; and he felt convinced that they had been marching thus from time immemorial, being long since weary of their enforced wanderings, which led them they knew not whither.

"What is this lost people?" he heard himself asking. "Why do the skies lower over them, especially over them, in this way? Why should they never find rest?"

In his dream, however, he had no inkling who these wanderers might be; but he felt brotherly sympathy for them, and their yearning and groaning in the unseen impressed him more lamentably than would have loud complaint. Unwittingly he murmured:

The Buried Candelabrum

"No one should be kept a-wander like this, always through the darkness, and never knowing whither. No people can continue to live thus without home and without goal, always afoot and always in peril. A light must be kindled for them, a way must be shown them, or else this hunted, lost people will despair and will wither into nothingness. Someone must lead them, must lead them home, throwing light on the path for them all. A light must be found; they need light."

His eyes tingled with pain, so full of compassion was he for this lost people which, gently complaining and already reduced to despair, marched onward through the silent and lowering night. But as he, likewise despairing, plumbed the distance with his gaze, it seemed to him as if, at the farthest limits of his vision, a faint light began to glow, the merest trace of a light, a spark or two, recalling the look of a will-o'-the-wisp.

"We must follow that light," he murmured. "Even if it be no more than a jack-o'-lantern. Perhaps, though it is a small light, we can kindle at it a great one. We must follow it and catch up with it, that light."

In his dream, Benjamin forgot that his limbs were old and feeble. Like an active boy, like the heathen god who was fabled to wear winged sandals, he speeded on his pursuit of the light. He pushed forward fiercely through the murmuring, shadowy crowd, which made way for him mistrustfully and angrily.

"Keep your eyes fixed on the light, that light over there," he called to them encouragingly. Nevertheless this depressed people moved on sluggishly, hanging their heads and groaning as they went. They could not see that distant light; perhaps their eyes were blinded with tears and their hearts enfeebled by their daily distresses. He himself, however, perceived the light ever more plainly. It consisted of seven little sparks which flickered side by side, looking like seven sisters. As he ran on and drew nearer while his heart throbbed violently with exertion and excitement, he saw that in front of him there must be a Lampstand, Seven-Branched, which sustained and fed these little flames. That was but a guess, for the

Lampstand itself was not yet visible. Nor could it be standing still, for it, too, was a-wander, even as the people who surrounded him were a-wander in the darkness, mysteriously hunted and driven by an evil wind. That was why the flames that flew before him did not show a steady light, nor a strong one, but were feeble and flickered uncertainly.

"We must grasp it, must bring it to rest, the Lampstand," thought the dreamer, while the dream-image fled before him, "for it will burn brightly and steadily and clearly as soon as it is at rest."

Blindly he ran onward to reach it, and nearer and nearer did he come to the Lampstand. Already he could see the golden stem and the upstanding branches, and in the seven knops of gold the seven flames, each of them blown flat by the wind, which continued to drive the Lampstand farther and farther across lowland and mountain and sea.

"Stay! Halt awhile!" he shouted. "The people is perishing. It needs the consolation of the light, and cannot for ever and ever wander like this through the darkness."

But the Lampstand continued to advance, while its fleeing flames shone craftily and angrily. Then the hunter, too, grew wrathful. Summoning the last of his forces, for his heart was now beating furiously, he made a huge leap forward to grasp the fugitive Lampstand. Already his grip had closed upon the cool metal; already he had clenched his hand upon the heavy stem—when a thunderbolt struck him to earth, splintering his arm. He yelled with the pain, and as he did so there came an answering cry from the pursuing masses: "Lost! For ever lost!"

Jewish Legends

But see, the storm abated, the Lampstand ceased its wandering flight, to stand still and magnificent. Not to stand on the ground, but in the air, firm and upright as if on an iron pedestal. Its seven flames, which had hitherto been pressed flat by the power of the wind, now streamed steadily upward in their golden splendour, giving off a more and more brilliant light. By degrees, so strong grew this light, that the whole expanse of heaven into which it shone was golden. As the man who had been struck down by the thunderbolt looked up confusedly to see those who had been wandering behind him through the darkness, he became aware that there was no longer night upon a trackless earth, and that those who had been following him were no more a wandering people. Fruitful and peaceful, cradled in the sea and shaded by mountains, was a southern land where palms and cedars swayed in a gentle breeze. There were vineyards, too, teeming with grapes; fields of golden grain; pastures swarming with sheep; gentle-footed gazelles at play. Men were quietly at work upon their own land, drawing water from the wells, driving ploughs, milking cows, sowing and harrowing and harvesting; surrounding their houses with beds of brightly coloured flowers. Children were singing songs and playing games. Herdsmen made music with their pipes; when night fell, the stars of peace shone down upon the slumbering houses.

"What sort of country is this?" the astonished dreamer asked himself in his dream. "Is this the same people that groaned and lamented as it fled through the darkness? Has it at length found peace? Has it, at long last, reached home?"

The Buried Candelabrum

Now the Lampstand rose higher in the sky and shone more gloriously. Its lights were like the light of the sun, illuminating sky and land to the very horizon. The mountain tops were revealed in its sheen; upon one of the lower hills gleamed white with mighty turrets a magnificent city, and amid the turrets projected a gigantic House built of hewn stone. The sleeper's heart throbbed again.

"This must be Jerusalem and the Temple," he panted. Thereupon the Lampstand moved on toward the city and the Temple. The walls gave way as if they had been water to let it pass, and now, as it flamed within the Holy Place, the Temple shone white like alabaster.

"The Lampstand has returned home," muttered the sleeper. "Someone has been able to do what I have ever yearned to do. Someone has redeemed the wandering Lampstand. I must see it with my own eyes, I, the witness. Once more, once more, I shall behold the Menorah at rest in God's Holy Place."

As the winds carry a cloud, so did his wish carry him whither he wanted to go. The gates sprang open to admit him, and he entered the Holy of Holies to behold the Lampstand. Incredibly strong was the light. Like white fire, the seven flames of the Lampstand blazed up together in one huge flame, so bright that it dazzled and hurt, and he cried aloud in his dream. He awoke.

Benjamin had awakened from his dream. But still the intense light of that flame glowed into his eyes, so that he had to close the lids to protect them from the glare, and even then the light shone through them sparkling and purple. Only as he raised his hand to shade them did

Jewish Legends

he become aware that it was the sun which was scorching his forehead; that, in the spot where he had sought to die, he had slept until well on in the morning, when the sun was high; and that it was the sunlight which had wakened him. The tree beneath which he had fallen asleep had not been enough to protect him from the dazzling rays. Having risen to his feet with some difficulty, he leaned against the tree-trunk, looking out into the distance. There lay the sea, blue and boundless, as he had seen it when a child at Portus, even as he was now contemplating the Euxine. Landward shone the marble and other stone buildings of Byzantium. The world displayed the colour and sheen of a southern morning. After all, it had not been God's will that he should die. In a fright the old man leaned forward and lowered his head in prayer.

When Benjamin had finished his prayer to the Almighty, who gives life at his will and does not end it until he chooses, he felt a gentle touch on his shoulder from behind. It was Zechariah who stood there, as Benjamin instantly recognized, being now fully awake. Before the old man could give vent to his astonishment—for he wondered how the goldsmith could have discovered him—Zechariah whispered:

"Since early morn I have been seeking you. When they told me in Pera that, on quitting the synagogue, you had wandered uphill through the darkness, I could not rest until I found you. The others were extremely anxious about you. Not I, however, for I knew that God still has a use for you. Come back with me to my home. I have a message for you."

"What message?" Benjamin had it in mind to say. "I want no more messages"—so ran his stubborn thoughts—"for God has tried me too often."

But he did not utter these refractory words, being still consoled by the wonder of his dream, and by the remembrance of the blessed light which had shone upon that land of peace—the light which seemed to have left a reflection upon the smiling countenance of his friend. Without refusing the invitation, therefore, he walked down the hill with Zechariah. They crossed the Golden Horn in a boat, and soon reached the walled quadrant of the palace. There was a strong guard at the gates, but, to Benjamin's amazement, they allowed Zechariah and his companion to pass freely.

"My workshop," the goldsmith explained, "adjoins the treasury, for there, in secret and fully safeguarded from danger, I can do my work for the Emperor. Enter, and blessed be your coming. There will be no one else to trouble you. We are and shall remain alone."

The two men stepped lightly through the workshop, which was full of artistically fashioned trinkets. In the back wall the goldsmith opened a concealed door, which led down two or three steps into an apartment behind, where he lived and did his more special work. The shutters were closed and heavily barred, the rooms being lighted only by a shaded lamp which cast a golden circle of light upon the table, at the back of which was an object hidden by a purple cloth.

"Sit down, dear Benjamin," said Zechariah to his guest. "You must be hungry and tired."

He thrust aside the work on which he had last been engaged, brought bread and wine and some beautifully worked silver saucers containing fresh fruit, dates, almonds, and other nuts. Then he tilted back the lampshade, so that the greater part of the table was lighted, as were the clasped hands of Benjamin—the gnarled and parchmenty hands of a very old man.

"Please break your fast," said Zechariah encouragingly. To Benjamin, the man sorely tried, the voice of him who had till so recently been a stranger came to his ears as softly as a gentle breeze from the west. He ate some of the fruit, slowly crumbled bread and took a few mouthfuls, washing it down with small gulps of the wine which shone purple in the lamplight. He was glad to hold his peace while collecting his forces, and was content that above the lighted table the room was in darkness. His feelings towards Zechariah were those which a man has to an old and trusted friend. Now and again, though Zechariah's head was in shadow, Benjamin studied what he could see of the face with thoughtful tenderness.

As if recognizing that his guest desired closer scrutiny, Zechariah took the shade right off. Thereupon the whole room was illuminated, and for the first time Benjamin got a clear view of his new friend. Zechariah's face was delicately moulded, and weary, as that of a man whose health left a good deal to be desired; it was deeply furrowed with the marks of suffering silently and patiently borne. When Benjamin looked at him, the goldsmith smiled responsively, and this smile gave the old man courage.

"How differently you feel towards me from the others. They are angry with me because I have not worked a miracle, although I implored them not to expect one from me. You alone are not incensed against me, you, who made it possible for me to have audience of the Emperor. All the same, they are right to make mock of me. Why did I awaken their hopes, why did I come hither? Why should I go on living, merely to see how the Lampstand wanders afresh and eludes us?"

Zechariah continued to smile, a gentle smile which brought balm and healing. He said:

"Do not kick against the pricks. Perhaps it was too soon, and the way we tried was not the right one. After all, what can we do with the Lampstand so long as the Temple lies in ruins and our people is still dispersed among the Gentiles? It may be God's will that the Menorah's destiny shall remain mysterious, and not be plainly disclosed to the people."

The words were consoling, and warmed Benjamin's heart. He bowed his head and spoke as if to himself:

"Forgive me my lack of courage. My life has grown narrow, and I must be very near to death. Eight and eighty years have I lived, so perhaps it is natural that I should lose patience. Since, as a child, I tried to rescue the Lampstand, I have lived only for one thing, its redemption and its return to Jerusalem; and from year to year I have been faithful and patient. But now that I am so old, what can I hope from waiting?"

"You will not have to wait. Soon all will be fulfilled."

Benjamin stared, but his heart beat hopefully.

Zechariah smiled yet more cheerfully, saying: "Do you not feel that I came to bring you a message?"

"What message?"

"The message you expected."

Benjamin quivered to his finger-tips.

"You mean, you mean, that the Emperor might receive me again in audience?"

"No, not that. What he has spoken, he has spoken. He will never eat his words, and will not give us back the Menorah."

"What, then, is the use of my remaining alive? Why should I wait here, plaintive, a burden to everyone, while the holy symbol leaves us, and this time for ever?"

Zechariah continued to smile, yet more confidently—a smile which made his face glow.

"The Lampstand has not yet departed from us."

"How can you tell? How can you say such a thing?"

"I know. Trust me."

"You have seen it?"

"I have seen it. Two hours ago it was still locked in the treasury."

"But now? They must have taken it away."

"Not yet. Not yet."

"Then where is it, now?"

Zechariah did not answer immediately. Twice his lips were tremulous with the beginnings of speech, but the words did not come. At length he leaned forward over the table and whispered:

"Here. In my dwelling. Close to us."

Benjamin's face twitched.

"You have it here?" he asked.

"It is here in my dwelling."

"Here in your dwelling?"

"In this dwelling, in this very room. That is why I sought you out."

Benjamin quivered. In Zechariah's tranquillity there was something which stupefied him. Without knowing it, he folded his hands, and whispered almost inaudibly: "Here in this room? How could that be?"

"Strange as it may seem to you, there is nothing miraculous about it. For thirty years, more than twenty of them before Justinian began to reign, I have worked as goldsmith in the palace, and in all that time nothing has been placed in the treasury, nothing of value, without being sent first to me, for me to weigh it and test it. I knew that all the spoils brought back by Belisarius after he had overthrown the Vandals would take the usual path, and the first of them for which I asked was the Menorah. Yesterday the treasurer's slaves brought it here; it is beneath that purple cloth, and it is entrusted to me for a week."

"And then?"

"Then it will be shipped to Jerusalem."

Benjamin turned pale. Why had Zechariah summoned him? Only that he should once more have the Menorah, the sacred emblem, within his grasp for a moment—to pass anew into the hands of the Gentiles? But Zechariah smiled meaningly, saying:

"I should tell you that I am permitted to make duplicates of all the precious objects in the imperial treasury. Often they specially ask me to make such a replica, for they esteem my craftsmanship. The crown which Justinian wears is a copy of Constantine's, and of my making; in like manner Theodora's diadem is the duplicate

Jewish Legends

of one which Cleopatra used to wear. I therefore begged permission to make a duplicate of the Menorah before it was sent to that church of theirs across the sea, and I actually began the work this morning. The crucibles are already heated, and the gold is made ready. In a week from now the new lampstand will be finished, so like our own that no one will be able to distinguish it, since it will be of precisely the same weight, will show no unlikeness in shape or ornamentation, or even in the graining of the gold. The only difference will be that one will be sacred and the other wholly the work of an ordinary mortal like myself. But as to which is the sacred Lampstand and which the profane, which one we piously cherish and which one we hand over to the keeping of the Gentiles—that will be a secret known only to two persons in the world. It will be your secret and mine."

Benjamin's lips no longer trembled. His whole frame tingled with the rush of blood, his chest expanded, his eyes sparkled, and a cheerful smile which was the reflection of Zechariah's lit up his aged face. He understood. What he had once attempted, this fellow-countryman of his would now achieve. Zechariah would redeem the Lampstand from the Gentiles, handing over to them one exactly alike in gold and in weight, but keeping back the sacred Menorah. Not for a moment did he envy Zechariah the wonderful deed to which he had consecrated his own long life. Humbly he said:

"God be praised. Now I shall gladly die. You have found the path which I vainly sought. God merely called me, but you hath he blessed."

Zechariah protested:

"No, you, and you alone must take the Menorah home."

"Not I, for I am so very, very old. I should be likely to die upon the journey. And then, once more, the Lampstand would fall into the hands of the Gentiles."

Zechariah answered, with a confident smile:

"You will not die. It has already been revealed to you that your life will not pass away until its meaning has been fulfilled."

Benjamin bethought himself. Yesterday he had wished to die, and God had refused to grant him his prayer. Perhaps his mission had, after all, to be fulfilled. He raised no further objection, merely saying:

"I will be guided by your promptings. Why, indeed, should I resist, if God has chosen me? Go on with your work."

For a week Zechariah's workshop was closed to all access. For a week the goldsmith did not set foot in the street nor open his door to any knock. Before him, on a lofty stand, was the eternal Menorah, tranquil and splendid, as of yore it had stood before the Altar of the Lord. In the furnace, the fire licked silently at the crucibles with tongues of flame, melting down rings and clasps and coins to provide gold for the beaten work. Benjamin spoke hardly a word during this week. He looked on while the precious metal fused in the meltingpot, whence it was poured into the mould, and hardened as it cooled. When, with great care, skilfully plying the tools of his trade, Zechariah broke away the mould, the shape of the new lampstand was already recognizable.

Jewish Legends

Strong and proudly rose the stem from the broad base, and, thinning, this stem ran straight upward to the central chalice. On either side curved away three stalks from the main shaft, each ending in its own chalice to hold oil for a burning wick. As the goldsmith hammered and chiselled, the appropriate ornamentations began to show everywhere, the bowls, and the knops, and the

flowers. From day to day the counterfeit came to resemble more and more closely the true Menorah. On the last, the seventh day, the two Seven-Branched Candlesticks stood side by side like twin brethren, indistinguishable from one another, being exactly of the same size and tint, measure and weight. Unrestingly, with practised gaze, Zechariah continued to work at the counterfeit until, down to the minutest traces, it was a truthful representation of the true. At length his hands rested from their task. Indeed, so closely alike were the two lampstands that Zechariah, fearing that even he might be deceived, took up his graving-tool once more, and within the pistil of one of the flowers made a tiny mark to show that this was the new lampstand, his own work, and not the Lampstand of the Jewish people and of the Temple.

This done, he stepped backward, took off his leather apron, and washed his hands. After six days' labour, on the seventh, the Sabbath, he addressed Benjamin once more:

"My work is finished. Yours now begins. Take our Lampstand and do what you think best with it."

But, to his surprise, Benjamin refused:

"For six days you have worked, and for six days I have thought and have questioned my heart. I have grown uneasy with wondering whether we are not cheats. You received one Lampstand, and you will give back another to him who trusted you. It is not meet that we should return the false lampstand and keep, by crooked arts, that which was not freely given to us. God does not approve of force, and when I, as a child, tried to take the sacred emblem by force, he shattered my arm. But I am equally sure that God disapproves of fraud, and that when a man cheats, the Almighty will consume his soul as with fire."

Zechariah reflected, and answered:

"But what if the treasurer should himself choose the false lampstand?"

Benjamin looked up, to answer:

"The treasurer knows that one is old and the other new, and if he should ask which of the two is genuine, we must tell him the truth and restore him the genuine emblem. If God should so dispose that the treasurer asks no questions, considering that the two are precisely the same, because there is no difference in the gold or in the weight, then, to my way of thinking, we should do no wrong. If he, deciding for himself, chooses the lampstand which you have made, then God will have given us a sign. Let not the decision be made by us."

Zechariah, therefore, sent one of the slaves of the treasury to summon the treasurer, and the treasurer came, a corpulent and cheerful man with small but protruding eyes which sparkled above his red cheeks. In the anteroom, with the airs and graces of a connoisseur, he examined two saucers of beaten silver which had recently been finished, tapping each of them with his fingers, and examining the delicate chasing. Inquisitively he lifted one gem after another from the work-table, and held them against the light. So lovingly did he inspect piece after piece, both the finished and the unfinished work of the goldsmith, that Zechariah had to remind him he had come to see the lampstands, which were awaiting his judgment, the Menorah which was thousands of years old and the one which had just been made, the original and the copy.

All attention now, the treasurer stepped up to the table. It was obvious that, as an expert, he would have been glad to find some trifling defect or half-hidden inequality which would enable him to distinguish the newly made lampstand from the one which Belisarius had taken from the Vandals in Carthage. Lifting each in turn, he twisted them in all directions, so that the light fell on them from various angles. He weighed them, he scratched at the gold with his finger-nails. Stepping back and drawing near again, he compared them with increasing interest, acknowledging to himself that he could detect no difference. At length, stooping till he was quite close, and using a magnifying-glass of cut crystal, he studied the minutest marks of the graving-tool. The two lampstands seemed to him precisely alike. Outwearied by this lengthy comparison, he clapped Zechariah on the shoulder, saying:

"You are indeed a master goldsmith, being yourself the greatest treasure of our treasury. For all eternity no one will be able to tell which is the old Lampstand and which the new one, so sure is the work of your hand. You have made a superlative copy."

He turned indifferently away, to scrutinize the cut gems, and choose one of them for himself. Zechariah had to remind him.

"Tell me then, Treasurer, which of the lampstands will you have?"

Without glancing at them again, the treasurer replied: "Whichever you like. I don't care."

Then Benjamin emerged from the dark corner to which he had discreetly retired.

"Lord, we beg you to choose for yourself one of the two."

Jewish Legends

The treasurer looked at the speaker in astonishment. Why did this stranger stare at him so eagerly, so imploringly? But, being a good-natured fellow, and too civil not to accede to an old man's whim, he turned back to the show-table. In merry mood, he took a coin from his pocket and tossed it high in the air. It fell and rolled along the floor, this way and that, but at length settled down towards his left hand. With a smile the treasurer pointed to the lampstand which stood to the left, and said: "That one for me." Then he turned, and charged the slave who was in waiting to carry this lampstand to the Emperor's treasure-chamber. Thankfully and courteously the goldsmith ushered his patron to the door.

Benjamin had stayed in the inner room. With tremulous hand he touched the Menorah. It was the genuine one, the sacred one, for the treasurer had chosen the replica.

When Zechariah came back, he found Benjamin standing motionless in front of the Menorah, looking at it so earnestly that it seemed as if he must be absorbing the sacred emblem into himself. When at length he turned to face Zechariah, the reflection of the gold gleamed, as it were, from his pupils. The man sorely tried had gained that tranquillity which comes from a great and satisfactory decision. Gently he uttered a request:

"May God show you his thanks, my brother. I have one thing more to ask of you, a coffin."

"A coffin?"

"Be not astonished. This matter, too, I have thought over during these seven days and nights—how we can best give the Lampstand peace. Like you, my first thought was that, if we should succeed in rescuing the Menorah, it ought to belong to our people, which should preserve it as the most sacred of pledges. But our people, where is it, and where its abiding-place? We are hunted hither and thither, only tolerated at best whithersoever we go. There is no place known to me where the Lampstand could be kept in safety. When we have a house of our own, we are liable from moment to moment to be driven out of it; where we build a Temple, the Gentiles destroy it; as long as the rule of force prevails, the Menorah cannot find peace on earth. Only under the earth is there peace. There the dead rest from their wanderings; if there be gold there, it is not seen, and therefore cannot stimulate greed. In peace, the Menorah, having returned home after a thousand years of wanderings, can rest under the ground."

"For ever?" Zechariah was astounded. "Do you mean to bury the Menorah for ever?"

"How can a mortal talk of 'for ever'? Who can tell, when man proposes, that God will dispose accordingly for ever? I want to put the Lampstand to rest, but God alone knows how long it will rest. I can do a deed, but what will be the upshot thereof I cannot tell, who, like a mortal, must think in terms of time and not of eternity. God will decide, he alone shall determine the fate of the Menorah. I intend to bury it, for that seems to me the only way to keep it safe—but for how long, I cannot tell. Perhaps God will leave it for ever in darkness, and in that case our people must wander for ever unconsoled, dispersed like dust, scattered over the face of the earth.

Jewish Legends

Maybe, however, and my heart is full of hope, maybe he will one day decide that our people shall return home. Then—you can believe, as I believe—he will choose one who by chance will thrust his spade where the Menorah lies, and will find the buried treasure, as God found me to bring the weary Lampstand to its rest. Do not trouble yourself about the decision, which we shall leave to God and to time. Even though the Lampstand should be accounted lost, we, the Chosen People, fulfilling one of God's mysterious purposes, shall not be lost. Just as the Chosen People will not fade out of existence in the obscurity of time, so gold that is buried underground does not crumble or perish as will our mortal bodies. Both will endure, the Chosen People and the Menorah. Let us have faith, then, that the Menorah which we are about to inter will rise again some day, to shed new light for the Chosen People when it returns home. Faith is the one thing that matters, for only while our faith lasts shall we endure as a people."

For a while the two men were silent, their inward gaze fixed upon the distant prospect. Then Benjamin said once more:

"Now order me the coffin."

The joiner brought the coffin, which was, in appearance, like any other, as Benjamin had requested. It must not be of peculiar aspect so as to attract attention when he took it with him to the land of his fathers. Often the pious Jews bore coffins with them on pilgrimage to Jerusalem, in order to inter the corpse of some near relative in the Holy Land. He need have no anxiety about the Lampstand when it was hidden away in a deal coffin, for no one is inquisitive about the bodies of the dead.

Reverently the two men put the Menorah away in its resting-place, as reverently as if it had been a corpse. The branches were wrapped in silken cloths and heavy brocade, as the Torah is wrapped whenever it is put away, the vacant spaces being stuffed with tow and cotton-wool, that there might be no rattling to betray the secret. Thus softly did they bed the Menorah in the coffin, which is the cradle of the dead, knowing, as they did so, that unless God willed to change the fortune of the Jewish people, they were probably the last who would ever look upon and handle the Lampstand of Moses, the sacred Lampstand of the Temple. Before closing the coffin, they took a sheet of parchment and wrote thereon a statement to the effect that they two, Benjamin Marnefesh, known as the sorely tried, descendant of Abtalion, and Zechariah, of the blood of Hillel, had, at Byzantium, in the eighth year of the reign of Justinian, here deposited the holy Menorah, bearing witness to any who might, peradventure, one day disinter it in the Holy Land that this was the true Menorah. Having rolled up the parchment, they enveloped it in lead which was hermetically sealed by Zechariah, the cunning worker in metal, that the container should be impermeable to damp. With a golden chain he secured it to the shaft of the Lampstand. This done, they closed the coffin with nails and clasps. Not a word more did either say to the other about the matter until the bondmen had brought the coffin to Benjamin on board the ship which was about

Jewish Legends

to set sail for Joppa. The sails were being hoisted when Zechariah took leave of his friend and kissed him, saying: "God bless you and guard you. May he guide you on your path and help you to fulfil your undertaking. To this hour we two and none others have known the fate of the Lampstand. Henceforward that fate will be known to you alone."

Benjamin inclined his head reverently.

"My knowledge cannot last much longer. When I am dead, God alone will know where his Menorah rests."

As usual when a ship enters port, a crowd assembled on the quay in Joppa when the boat from Byzantium came to land. There were some Jews among these onlookers. Recognizing by his appearance and raiment the white-bearded old Benjamin as one of their own people, and perceiving that the shipmen followed him ashore bearing a coffin, they formed up to follow in a silent procession. It was traditional among them, when such an event chanced, to accompany the corpse even of an unknown compatriot a few steps upon the last journey—to be helpful and reverent. When the news spread abroad through the town that an aged member of their people had brought the remains of a relative across the sea to be interred in the Holy Land, all the members of the community left work to join in the procession, which grew continually in length until the bearers reached the inn where Benjamin was to pass the night. Not until the old man had (strangely enough, as it seemed to them) arranged for the coffin to be placed on trestles beside the spot where he was to sleep, did these followers break silence. They invoked a blessing on the traveller, and then asked him whence he had come and whither he was going.

Benjamin was chary of words, being afraid lest tidings might have come from Byzantium and that one of those who had flocked together might identify him. The last thing he desired was to raise fresh hopes among the brethren. Nevertheless he could not bring himself to utter anything that was not absolutely true when he stood so near the Menorah. He begged them, therefore, to excuse his reticence. He had been charged to bring this coffin to Palestine, and was not permitted to say any more. To ward off further inquiries, he asked questions of his own.

"Where," he said, "shall I find a holy place in which I can lay this coffin to rest?"

The Jews of Joppa smiled proudly, and replied:

"This, brother, is the Holy Land, and every spot of ground in it is therefore consecrated."

However, they went on to tell him of all the places where, in caverns, or in the open fields (marked in the latter case only by cairns), were the tombs of their fathers and forefathers, of the mothers of the tribe, of the heroes and kings of the Jewish people; and they vaunted the holiness of these same places. Every pious member of their fraternity visited them from time to time, seeking strength and consolation. Since the old man's appearance inspired respect, they said:

"Gladly, brother, will we show you a suitable place, and go with you to join in prayer when the unknown dead is interred."

Benjamin, however, eager to preserve his secret, declined their aid courteously, saying that privacy for the burial was enjoined on him by the nature of his mission. Only when the visitors had retired, did he ask the innkeeper to find him someone who, on the morrow, for a good wage, would take him to a suitable place and dig a grave. A mule would also be needed to carry the coffin. The host promised that his own servant and his own beast should be ready at dawn to do whatever the visitor required.

This night in the inn at Joppa was marked by the last hours of painful questioning and of holy torment in the life of Benjamin the sorely tried. Once again he doubted; once again did his resolution fail. Once more he asked himself whether it could really be right for him to withhold from his brethren the news of the rescue of the Menorah and of its return to the Holy Land; right to say nothing to the members of the Jewish congregation in Joppa about the sacred emblem which was about to be interred here. For if the members of his afflicted race could draw so much consolation from visiting the tombs of their forefathers, what would it not mean to them, to those who were hunted and persecuted and blown hither and thither by all the winds of heaven, if they could but receive the slightest intimation that the eternal Menorah, the most visible token of their unity, was not really lost, but had been redeemed, and was to rest secure underground in the Holy Land until, in the fullness of time, the whole Jewish Congregation likewise would return home?

"How dare I withhold from them this hope and consolation?" he murmured to himself, as he tossed sleeplessly on his pallet. "How can I dare to keep the secret, taking with me into the tomb information which might give joy to thousands? I know how they thirst for comfort. What a terrible fate is it for a people to be kept in unceasing expectation, feeding upon thoughts of 'some day' and 'perhaps'; relying dumbly upon the written word, and never receiving a sign. Yet only if I keep silent will the Menorah be preserved for the people. Lord, help me in my distress. How can I do right by the brethren? May I tell the servant whom my host has placed at my disposal that we have buried a sacred pledge? Or should I hold my peace, that no one may know where the Lampstand has been laid to rest? Lord, decide for me. Once before thou gavest me a sign. Give me another. Relieve me of the burden of decision."

No voice of answer came through the silence of the night, nor would sleep visit the eyes of the man sorely tried. He lay awake hour after hour, his temples throbbing, as he asked himself the same perpetual round of unanswerable questions, and became more and more entangled in the net of his fears and sorrows. Already light was showing in the eastern sky, and the old man had not yet decided upon his course, when, with troubled countenance, the innkeeper entered the room, to say:

"Forgive me, brother, but I cannot provide you with the servant I spoke of yesterday, the man well acquainted with the neighbourhood. He has fallen sick during the night. Foam issued from his mouth, and now he has been smitten with a burning fever. The only man available is my other servant, a stranger from a far country, and dumb to boot. It has been God's will that since birth he has been able neither to hear nor to speak. Still, if he will serve your turn, he is at your disposal."

Benjamin did not look at the innkeeper, but raised his eyes gratefully heavenward. God had answered his prayer.

A dumb man had been sent to him in sign of silence. A stranger, too, from a far country, that the place of burial might remain for ever hidden. He hesitated no longer, and answered the host, saying thankfully:

"Send me the dumb man. He will suit me excellently, and I shall be able to find my own way."

From morn till eve, Benjamin, with his dumb companion, crossed the open country. Behind them came the patient mule, with the coffin tied across his back. From time to time they passed wayside huts, the dwellings of impoverished peasants, but Benjamin did not pause. When he encountered other travellers, he shunned conversation, merely exchanging the usual greeting of "Peace be unto you." He was eager to finish his task, that he might know the Menorah to be safe underground. The place was still uncertain, and some mysterious intimation withheld him from making his own choice. His thoughts ran as follows:

"Twice I have been given a sign, and I will await a third."

Thus the little procession moved on across the darkling land. The sky was obscured by clouds; though fitfully, through breaks in these, the moon glimmered, nearing the zenith. It was perhaps a league from the next village, where rest and shelter might be found. Benjamin strode on sturdily, followed by the silent servitor who shouldered a spade, and behind the pair walked the mule with its burden.

Suddenly the beast stopped short. The man seized the bridle and tugged, but the mule, planting his forefeet, refused to budge. "I have had enough of it," he seemed to say, "and will go no farther." Angrily the attendant lifted the spade, intending to belabour the animal's flanks, but Benjamin laid a hand upon the raised arm. Perhaps this balking of the packmule was the sign for which he had been waiting.

Benjamin looked around him. The dark, rolling landscape was abandoned. There was no sign either of house or of hut. They must have strayed aside from the road to Jerusalem. Yes, this was a suitable place, where the interment could be effected unobserved. He thrust at the earth with his staff. It was soft, not stony, and would be easy for the digger. But he must find the exact spot.

He glanced uncertainly to right and to left. There, to the right, a hundred paces or so away, stood a tree, recalling the one beneath which he had slept on the hill above Pera, and where he had had the reassuring dream. As he recalled that dream, his heart was uplifted. The third sign had come. He waved to the dumb man, who unbound the coffin from the beast's back, and, on the instant, the mule, relieved of the burden, trotted up to him and nuzzled his fingers. Yes, God had given him a sign. This was the place. He pointed to the ground, and the servitor began to dig busily. Soon the grave was deep enough. Now there remained only the last thing to do, to commit the Lampstand to its tomb. The unsuspecting deaf-mute lifted the burden in his strong arms and carefully lowered it into the grave. There lay the coffin, a wooden vestment for the last sleep of its precious golden contents, soon to be covered by the breathing, life-giving, ever-living earth.

Benjamin stooped reverently.

"I am still the witness, the last," he mused, trembling beneath the burden of his thoughts. "No one on earth save me knows the secret resting-place of the Menorah. Except for me, no one guesses its hidden tomb."

At this moment, the moon shone once more through the clouds. It was as if a huge eye had suddenly appeared in the heavens, lidded by dark vapours. Not like a mortal eye, perishable, and fringed by lashes, but an eye that was hard and round, as if chiselled out of ice, eternal and indestructible. It stared down, throwing its light into the depths of the open grave, disclosing the four corners of the tomb, while the white pinewood of the coffin shone like metal. No more than a momentary glance, and the moon was again obscured; but a glance that seemed to come from an enormous distance before the eye was hidden as the clouds regathered. Benjamin knew that another eye than his had espied the burial of the Menorah. At a fresh sign, the servitor shovelled in the earth, and made all smooth above the tomb. Then Benjamin waved to him to depart, to return home, taking with him the mule. The man wrung his hands, and showed reluctance. He did not wish to leave this aged and fragile stranger by night in so solitary a place, where there was danger of robbers and wild beasts. Let him at least accompany Benjamin to some human habitation, where there would be rest and shelter. Impatiently, however, Marnefesh commanded the underling to depart. It irked him till he should be alone here beside the tomb, when man and beast should have vanished into the darkness, leaving him by himself beneath the expanse of heaven, to the emptiness, the incomprehensibility, of the night.

When his wishes had been obeyed, he bent his head beside the grave to utter the prayer for the dead:

"Great is the name and holy is the name of the Eternal in this world and in other worlds and also in the days of the rising from the dead."

Strongly did he desire, in accordance with the pious custom, to lay a stone or some other recognizable indication upon the freshly shovelled earth; but, reminding himself of the need for secrecy, he refrained, and walked away from the tomb into the darkness, he knew not whither. He no longer had a purpose or a goal, now that he had laid the Menorah to rest. Anxiety had departed from him, and his soul was at peace. He had fulfilled the task laid upon him. Now it was for God to decide whether the Lampstand should remain hidden until the end of days and the Chosen People should remain scattered over the face of the earth, or whether, in the end, he would lead the Jews home and allow the Menorah to arise from its unknown grave.

The old man walked onward through the night, beneath a sky in which the clouds were dispersing, allowing moon and stars to shine. At each step he rejoiced more and more heartily. As by a charm, the burden of his years was falling from him, and he felt a sense of lightness and renewed energy such as he had not known since childhood. As if loosened by friction with warm oil, his aged limbs moved easily once more. He felt as a bird may feel flying free and happy over the waters. Head erect, shoulders squared, he marched joyfully like a young man. His right arm too (or was he dreaming) was again hale, so that he could use it as he willed—the arm that had been useless for eighty years since that morning at Portus. His blood was coursing with renewed energy, as the sap rises in a tree during the springtime; there was a joyous throbbing in his temples; and he could hear the noise of a mighty singing. Was it the dead under the earth who sang a brotherly chorus to him in greeting, to him the wanderer who had returned home; or was it the music of the spheres, was it the stars that sang to him as they shone ever more brightly? He did not know. He walked on and on, through the rustling night, upborne by invisible pinions.

Next morning some traders on their way to market at Ramleh caught sight of a human form lying in an open

The Buried Candelabrum

field close to the road which led from Joppa to Jerusalem. An old man, dead. The unknown lay on his back, with bared head. His arms widespread, seeming ready to grasp the infinite, he had his fingers likewise opened, as if the palms were prepared to receive a bounteous gift. His eyes, too, were wide open and undismayed, his whole expression being peaceful. When one of the traders stooped, with the pious intention of closing the dead man's eyes, he saw that they were full of light, and that in their round pupils the glory of the heavens was reflected.

The lips, however, were firmly closed, as if guarding a secret that was to endure after death.

Jewish Legends

A few weeks later, the spurious lampstand was likewise brought to Palestine, and, in accordance with Justinian's command, was placed beneath the altar in the church at Jerusalem. Not long, however, did it there abide. The Persians invaded the Holy City, seized the seven-branched candlestick, and broke it up in order to make golden clasps for their wives and a golden chain for their king. Time continually destroys the work of human hands and frustrates human design; and so, now, was the emblem destroyed which Zechariah the goldsmith had made in imitation of the Holy Candelabrum, and its trace for ever lost.

Hidden, however, in its secret tomb, there still watches and waits the everlasting Menorah, unrecognized and unimpaired. Over it have raged the storms of time. Century after century the nations have disputed one with another for possession of the Land of Promise. Generation after generation has awakened and then has slept; but no robber could seize the sacred emblem, nor could greed destroy it. Often enough a hasty foot passes over the ground beneath which it lies; often enough a weary traveller sleeps for an hour or two by the wayside close to which the Lampstand slumbers; but no one has the slightest inkling of its presence, nor have the curious ever dug down into the depths where it lies entombed. Like all God's mysteries, it rests in the darkness through the ages. Nor can anyone tell whether it will remain thus for ever and for ever, hidden away and lost to its people, who still know no peace in their wanderings through the lands of the Gentiles; or whether, at length, someone will dig up the Menorah on that day when the Jews come once more into their own, and that then the Seven-Branched Lampstand will diffuse its gentle light in the Temple of Peace.

Rachel Arraigns with God

A LEGEND

Once again had the froward and fickle folk of Jerusalem forgotten the Covenant, once again had they offered up sacrifices to brazen idols. Nor were they satisfied with this impiety; for even in God's Temple, which Solomon His servant had built, they set up an image of Baal, and the gutters ran red with the blood of the victims.

When God saw how they mocked him in the heart of the sanctuary, his wrath found vent. He stretched forth His hand, and His voice made the skies tremble. His patience was exhausted; He would shower destruction upon the sinful city and scatter its inhabitants like chaff. His thunders resounded, announcing this resolve from one end of the world to the other.

Now that the Almighty had given utterance to His anger, the earth quaked with terror. The windows of heaven were opened, as they had been in the days of Father Noah, the fountains of the great deep were broken up, and the high hills tottered. The birds of the air

Jewish Legends

dropped to earth, and even the angels were affrighted by the fury of the Lord.

Far beneath, in the doomed town, men, though they heard the thunder of God's voice, were deaf to the meaning of His words. They knew not that they had been sentenced to destruction. Yet full well they were aware that the foundations of the world were crumbling; that at high noon it had grown dark as midnight; that a hurricane was raging which broke the stems of the mighty cedars like straws. Fearful lest the roofs should fall in upon their heads, they fled from their houses into the open, to be even more panic-stricken by the force of the blast, the driving of the rain, the sulphurous reek of the murky air. Vainly did they rend their garments and put ashes on their heads, vainly did they abase themselves and implore God's forgiveness. The fury of the elements was unabated, the darkness unrelieved.

So fierce had been the thunder of God's wrath that it aroused even the dead from the slumbers in which, as is decreed, they lie awaiting the Last Trump. Believing that this dread summons had sounded, they rose and winged their way heavenward, to find, after they had traversed the fearful storm, that the Last Judgment was not yet. Nevertheless, the souls of the fathers and forefathers gathered in a circle round the Throne, to beseech that the doom might be averted from their children and from the pinnacles of the Holy City. Abraham, Isaac, and Jacob led the prayer. But their voices were drowned by the Voice of the Lord, repeating that too long had He endured the stubbornness of His creatures. Ungrateful though these were, the shattering of the Temple would teach the wicked who could not be taught by love.

Since the ancestors of the Chosen People were thus struck dumb, there now petitioned those who in life had been the mouthpieces of God's Holy Word, the prophets Moses, Samuel, Elijah, and Elisha—men with tongues of fire and burning hearts. But the Lord would not hearken, and the tempest of His anger blew their words back into their faces. Brighter than before flashed the lightnings that were to consume the Temple and raze it to the ground.

The prophets and sages, too, lost courage. Their souls quivered like grass in the tempest; they were as dead leaves trodden under foot. No man among them dared to breathe another syllable. But the soul of a woman spake, that of Rachel, the arch-mother of Israel, who in her tomb at Ramah had likewise heard God's proclamation, and had come weeping for her children, refusing to be comforted. Drawing strength from love, she ventured to take up her parable before Him whose face she could not see—for none but the angels can look upon God's countenance until the Judgment Day. Kneeling, she raised her hands and said her word:

"My heart is like water within me, Almighty, thus to address Thee, but Thou madest this heart so timid; and Thou gavest me lips wherewith, though fearfully, to utter my prayer. The bitter need of my children enables me. Thou didst not gift me with either wisdom or cunning, nor know I how to allay Thine anger. But as for Thee, Thou knowest what I would say, for every word forms itself in Thy mind before it is spoken by human lips, and every human action is foreseen by Thee. Nevertheless, I pray Thee to hear me for those poor sinners' sake."

Having thus spoken, Rachel bowed her head. God saw her humility, and noted the tears that coursed down her cheeks. He restrained His wrath, and was silent, to hear her pleading.

Now when God listens in heaven, space is emptied and time stands still. The wind ceased howling, the thunder roared no longer, creeping and crawling things stayed from creeping and crawling, the birds of the air folded their pinions, no one ventured even to draw breath. The movement of the hours was arrested, and the cherubim were motionless as statues. Even the sun and the moon and the stars rested from their circling, and the rivers from their flow.

Far beneath, the inhabitants of the doomed city knew naught of Rachel's pleading in their behalf, or that the Almighty was hearkening to her prayer. For mortals cannot perceive what passes in heaven. All they were aware of was that the storm had abated. But when, taking heart of grace, they looked skyward, it was to see the black clouds hanging over them like the pall that covers a coffin. In the unrelieved darkness they were still terrified, all the more because the quietude continued to envelop them as a shroud enwraps a corpse.

But Rachel, glad that God was paying heed to her supplication, plucked up courage, raised her head, and continued:

"Lord, as Thou knowest, I dwelt in Haran, the land of the people of the east, where I kept my father Laban's sheep. Came a morning when we maidens drove the sheep to the water, but lacked strength to roll the stone from the well's mouth. Then a youth appeared, a stranger, well-made, who sprang forward to help us, and rolled away the stone so easily that we were astonished at his strength. Jacob was his name, and he was the son of my father's sister Rebekah. When he told us who he was, I led him to my father Laban's house. Within an hour of the meeting by the well, our hearts yearned for one another. At night, I could not sleep for longing—nor am I ashamed to say this, seeing that, if passion flames up in us like the ardours of the Burning Bush, it is through Thy will, Lord, that such things happen. Through Thy will doth it come to pass that a woman craves for a man's embraces, that youth and maiden are magically drawn together. Because these things are so, we did not try to quench the flames, but on that first day of our meeting Jacob and I exchanged vows of betrothal.

"As Thou knowest, Lord, my father Laban was a hard man; hard as the stony ground he ploughed, hard as the horns of the oxen whose necks he bent beneath the yoke. When Jacob asked me of him in marriage, he had it in mind first of all to discover whether this suitor, his nephew, was a man of his own kind, a strenuous worker and endowed with iron patience. Laban demanded of Jacob seven years' service as the price of my hand. My soul trembled, and Jacob's cheeks paled, for to both of us, young and impatient, seven years seemed an infinity of waiting. For Thee, Lord, seven years are but a moment, the flicker of an eyelash, since time is nothing to the Eternal. But for us mortals (deign to remember it, Lord

God) seven years is a tenth of our life. Short is the allotted span, and scarcely have our eyes opened to see Thy holy light, when they are closed in the darkness of death. Like a freshet in springtime races the current of human existence, and a wave that has passed can never return. Seven long years were we to be sundered, though living in close companionship; kept apart, while our lips thirsted for one another's kisses. Nevertheless, Jacob complied with his uncle's wishes, and I obeyed my father's behest. We resolved upon seven years of waiting, of obedience and patience—because we loved one another.

"Yet Thou has made patience difficult to Thy creatures, having given them hot passions, and instilled into them a brooding anxiety because of the shortness of their lives. We know that our autumn follows close upon our springtime, that the season of our summer is brief. That is why we snatch at fleeting hours of joy, and are eager to make the most of evanescent pleasures. How can we be expected to wait without repining, we who grow older day by day? Of course we burn, since, by Thy decree, time perpetually consumes us. Can we fail to be in a hurry, since we know that Death unceasingly dogs our footsteps? Yet we mastered our impulses, while each day of waiting was as long as a thousand. In the end, when the seven years were accomplished, they seemed, as we looked back on them, to have been no more than a single day. Thus, Lord, did I wait for Jacob, and thus did Jacob love me.

"When the seventh year of waiting had drawn to a close, I went joyfully to Laban, my father, and asked him to prepare the wedding tent. But Laban, my father,

Rachel Arraigns with God

looked coldly on my joy. His brows were clouded, and for a space his mouth was sealed. At length he broke silence, and commanded me to summon Leah, my sister.

"Leah, as Thou knowest, Lord, was two years mine elder, and hard-favoured. Hence no man coveted her, whereat she was sorely grieved. Yet I loved her fondly, because of her affliction and her gentleness. When, however, my father bade me summon Leah, it entered my mind in a flash that he had planned to beguile me and Jacob. I therefore hid close to the tent, that I might overhear their conversation. My father spake as follows:

"'Leah, my nephew Jacob has served me faithfully seven years, in order to win Rachel as his wife. Yet for thy sake I will not do this thing, since it must not be so done in our country, to give the younger before the firstborn. In the beginning, the Almighty commanded us to be fruitful and multiply, that we might people His world and raise up many to praise His holy name. He did not desire the soil to lie fallow, or that a woman should bear no children. No ewe and no heifer feeds on my pastures without bringing forth after their kind. Can it be expected of me that I should allow the womb of my elder daughter to remain closed? Make ready, then, Leah. Don the bridal veil, and Jacob (unknowing) shall wed thee in Rachel's stead.' Thus spake my father to Leah, who listened in a timid silence.

"But I, eavesdropping, was filled with anger against Laban, my father, and against Leah, my sister. Forgive me, Lord, for being so undaughterly, so unsisterly; but bethink Thee how Jacob and I had been waiting for one another seven years, and now, after all his service, my

Jewish Legends

sister was to be imposed upon him whose life was dearer to me than my own. I mutinied against my father, even as Thy children in Jerusalem have mutinied against Thee—for thus hast Thou made us, O Lord, that we grow stiff-necked when we deem that we are unjustly treated. Secretly I talked with Jacob, and disclosed my father's plan. That this scheme might be frustrated, I told him of a sign by which he might know me. 'When thou art wedded,' I declared, 'thy bride shall kiss thee thrice on the forehead before she enters the tent.' Jacob understood, and approved the sign.

"That evening, Laban had Leah veiled for the bridal. Also he had her face skilfully made up, lest Jacob should recognize her before he had gone in unto her. He had me barred in the granary, fearing lest one of the servants might warn me of what was afoot. Like an owl, I sat there in the gloom, and as the hours wore on towards nightfall, I ate my heart out with rage and pain. Not, Lord, as Thou knowest, that I bore a grudge against my sister because she was to be possessed by Jacob—but I was wroth that my beloved was to be tricked out of what he had slaved seven years to secure. I bit my wrists, when the cymbals clashed merrily, and my passions gnawed at my vitals as lions tear at their kill.

"Thus prisoned and forgotten I spent the weary hours, consumed with bitterness, until, when the darkness without was as impenetrable as the darkness of my soul, the bolts were drawn back, the door was gently opened, and Leah entered. Yes, Leah, my sister, had stolen away to visit me, before the bridal. I knew her footsteps, but I turned from her in enmity, for my heart was hardened against her. Leah stroked my hair, and, when I looked up, I could see, by the light of the lamp she carried, that her face was overcast. Thereupon, Lord, as I frankly acknowledge, a malicious pleasure stirred within me. It did me good to know that she was uneasy, that Leah (too) was suffering on her wedding day. But she, poor innocent, did not suspect my feelings. Had we not drawn suck from the same breasts, and had we not always loved one another? Confidently, she put her arms around me, saying, with pallid lips:

"'What will be the upshot, Rachel, my sister? I am sore at heart because of this scheme of our father's. He is taking your lover from you and giving Jacob to me; grievous is the thought of tricking him thus. How can I dare to substitute myself for you? My legs will refuse to carry me; and my heart is full of fear, for assuredly, Rachel, he will detect the fraud. How shamefaced I shall be, if thereupon he drives me forth from his tent! Down to the second and third generation, children will make mock of me, saying: "That is Leah, ugly Leah! Don't you know her story? She was thrust upon a husband, who wouldn't have her when he found out the trick, and drove her away like a mangy cur." What am I to do, Rachel, dear? Shall I take the venture, or shall I defy our father (whose hand is heavy)? How can I prevent Jacob discovering the fraud too soon, so that shame will be brought upon my innocent head? Help me, Sister, help me, I implore you, in the name of the All-Merciful!'

"Lord, I was still exceeding wroth; and, much though I loved my sister, the evil within me still made her anxiety sweet to me. Since, however, she had called upon

Thy holy name, the holiest of Thy names, since she had implored me in the name of the All-Merciful, the might of Thy compassion, the power of Thy goodness, flowed through my veins like wine, and entered like a blaze of light into my darkened soul. For this is one of Thy everlasting miracles, O Lord, that the barriers which separate each of us from others are broken down the instant we become sympathetically aware of the suffering of our neighbor and share the pain within our neighbour's tortured breast. My sister's anxiety permeated me, so that, instead of thinking of my private sorrow, I felt her bitter need. Sharing her distress, I, Thy foolish handmaid (mark this, Lord, I pray Thee), had compassion upon her in the hour when she stood before me in tears, even as now, in this hour, I stand before Thee in tears. I had compassion upon her, because she had appealed to me for pity, even as now I appeal to Thee. In my own despite, I taught her how to deceive Jacob, betraying to her the sign I had pledged myself to give him. 'Kiss him thrice on the brow,' said I, 'before thou enterest his tent.' Thus, for love of Thee, the All-Merciful, did I gain the victory over my jealousy, and play the traitor to the man I loved.

"When I had told this secret to Leah, she could no longer contain herself, but prostrated herself before me, fondling my hands and kissing the hem of my raiment; for thus hast Thou fashioned Thy creatures, that always they are filled with humility and gratitude when they discern in another a trace of Thine own goodness. We embraced, making one another's cheeks salt with our mingled tears. Leah was comforted, and prepared to

Rachel Arraigns with God

depart. But as she arose, once more her face became shadowed with sorrow, and again her lips blanched.

"'I thank thee, Sister, for thy loving-kindness,' she said, 'and shall do as thou biddest. But what if the sign fail to convince him? Yet more counsel do I need, Rachel. What shall I do if he address me by thy name? Can I remain stubbornly silent, a bride to whom the bridegroom speaketh? Yet the instant I open my mouth, he will know that it is Leah whom he is taking to wife, and not Rachel. I cannot answer him in thy voice! Help me yet further, Sister, shrewd as thou art; help me in the name of the All-Merciful!'

"Again, Lord, when she thus appealed to me in the holiest of Thy names; again that intoxicating fire flowed through me, so that once more my heart melted, and ruthlessly I trod my own wishes under foot. I was ready for the supreme sacrifice, and answered:

"'Be comforted, Leah. Here, too, I can find a way. For the sake of the All-Merciful I will see to it that Jacob shall not recognize thee as Leah until after he has known thee, believing thee to be Rachel. This is my plan. I shall slip into Jacob's tent, and shall there crouch in the darkness beside the nuptial couch. Should he speak to thee, I shall answer him. Then he will have no suspicion, but will embrace thee, and will fertilize thy body with his seed. This will I do for thee, Leah, because of the love we have borne one another since we were little children together, and for love of the All-Merciful, that He may have compassion on my children and my children's children, whenever they may call upon Him by the holiest of His names.'

"Lord, thereupon Leah embraced me and kissed me on the lips. Another woman, a woman renewed, was she who rose from her knees. Freed from care, she went forth, to offer herself to Jacob, her face hidden behind the deceitful veil. As for me, I drank my cup to the dregs, hiding myself beside the couch on which my lover was to enter into my sister. Soon the cymbals clashed once more, as the musicians attended the wedded pair, who in a minute stood at the entry to the tent. But before Jacob raised the veil to give his bride a blessing, he paused in expectation of the sign I had promised. Then Leah kissed him thrice on the forehead. Jacob, satisfied with the token, clasped his bride lovingly, lifted her in his arms, and carried her to the bed behind which I cowered. Even now, however, as Leah had foreseen, before the final embrace, he asked: 'Is it truly Rachel whom I hold in my arms?' Then, Lord (Thou, the All-Knower, knowest how hard it was for me to utter the words!), I whispered: 'Yes, it is I, Jacob, my husband.' He, recognizing my voice, he, who had waited seven years to possess me, thereupon made Leah my sister his own, with all the vigour of a young man in his prime. Lord, Thou whose vision pierces the darkness as a scythe cuts grass, Thou sawest my plight when I crouched there within touch of them, while passionately he possessed Leah believing himself to be entering into me, who so ardently longed for his embraces. Omnipresent Lord, recall, I pray Thee, that memorable night when I spent seven hours of agony, hearing the transports that should have been mine and were denied me. Seven hours, seven æons, did I lie beside that couch, holding my breath, wrestling against

Rachel Arraigns with God

my longing to cry out, even as Jacob, later, wrestled with Thy angel until the breaking of the day. Longer, far longer, seemed to me these seven night hours than Jacob's seven years of waiting. Never could I have endured it, this night of forbearance, had I not (in the silence of my soul) called repeatedly upon Thy holy name, and strengthened my resolve with the thought of Thine infinite patience.

"This, Lord, was my deed, the only one upon which I plume myself among all that I did during my earthly pilgrimage, for then I rivalled my Creator in forbearance and compassion. I doubt if ever Thou has laid so heavy a burden upon a woman as upon me in the anguish of that night. Yet I endured to the uttermost; and at length, when the cocks crew, I rose up wearily while the pair on the bed were in a profound slumber. Hastily I fled to my father's house, for soon the fraud would be disclosed, and my teeth chattered as I thought of Jacob's fury. Alas, my forebodings were justified. Scarcely was I safely ensconced at my father's, when the shouts of the husband whom we had beguiled rent the air of morning like the bellowing of an enraged bull. Armed with an axe, he rushed hither and thither in search of Laban, my father, who was paralysed with terror at sight of his infuriated son-in-law, and sank upon the ground, calling upon Thy holy name. Once again, Lord, this appeal to Thee revived my flagging courage, inspired me with determination, so that I flung myself between Jacob and Laban, to turn my lover's wrath towards myself, and save my unhappy father. Jacob saw red, and directly his eyes lighted upon me who had helped to deceive him, he struck me in the face with his fist, and I fell. Thou knowest, Lord, that I bore this chastisement without repining, being aware that the greatness of his love accounted for the greatness of his wrath. Had he slain me—and, indeed, he raised the axe to smite me—I should have appeared uncomplainingly before Thy Throne.

"But as soon as he saw me stretched at his feet, bruised and bleeding, pity overcame him. The axe dropped from his nerveless hands. Leaning over me, he tenderly kissed the blood from my lips. For my sake, he forgave my father Laban, and did not drive Leah from his tent. A week later, my father gave me to him as second wife. Jacob opened my womb, and I bare him children, which I nourished upon the milk of my breasts and upon the words of Thy Covenant, children which I bade call upon Thee in their need, with the mystery of Thy ineffable name. Today, Lord, Almighty and All-Merciful, in my own uttermost need, I call upon Thee to do what Jacob did, to drop the axe of Thine anger and to dispel the clouds of Thy wrath. Because Rachel was pitiful to Leah, her sister, wilt not Thou be pitiful to Rachel's children and children's children; wilt not Thou be patient, even as I was patient, and spare the Holy City? Have mercy on them, Lord; have mercy on Jerusalem."

Rachel's voice echoed through the vaults of heaven. Her strength was spent, and she sank back upon her knees, exhausted, while her hair fell in a black flood over her trembling body. Thus did Rachel await God's answer.

But God did not answer. He was silent. And in heaven, upon earth, in the circling spheres between, there is nothing more dreadful than God's silence. When

Rachel Arraigns with God

God is silent, the movement of time ceases; light is merged into darkness, day into night; and throughout all the worlds of the habitable universe there prevails only the chaos of the days before creation. The movable moves no longer, the flow of the rivers is stayed, the flowers do not bloom, even the tides cannot ebb and flow without the power of God's word. No mortal ear can bear God's silence, no mortal heart can continue beating in this awesome void, wherein nothing is but God, and even He, the life of lives, is alive no longer when He is silent.

Rachel, for all her patience, could not endure the endless silence with which God answered her proclamation of infinite need. Once more she lifted her eyes towards the Invisible, once more she lifted her motherly hands, and anger struck words of fire from her lips.

"Hast Thou not heard me, Omnipresent? Hast Thou not understood me, Omniscient? Must Thy handmaid speak yet more plainly to thrust her meaning home? Learn, then (hard of hearing though Thou art), that I was jealous because Jacob had bestowed on my sister what was meant for me, just as Thou art jealous because my children have sacrificed to other gods than Thee. But I, a weak woman, mastered my jealousy, grew pitiful for sake of Thee, whom I have called the All-Merciful. I had pity on Leah, and Jacob had pity on me. Take note of this, Almighty! All of us, poor mortals though we be, control the evil passion of envy. But Thou, Almighty, Creator of the universe, alpha and omega, the beginning and the end, Thou who hast an ocean where we have only droplets—Thou canst not show compassion. Well do I know that my children are a stiff-necked brood, that again and

Jewish Legends

ever again they revolt against the yoke. But since Thou art God, and Lord of Plenty, shall not Thy forbearance match their stubbornness, and shall not Thy forgiveness march with their transgressions? For this must not be, God; this must not be, that before Thine own angels Thou shouldest be put to shame, so that the angels will say: 'Once upon earth there was a woman, a frail mortal, Rachel by name, who held her anger in check. But He, God almighty, Lord and Master of the universe, was the slave of His own wrath.' No, God, that must not be, for unless Thy mercy is infinite, Thou Thyself art not infinite—which means that Thou art not God! Thou art not the God whom I made for myself out of my tears, and whose voice called to me through my sister's tears. Thou Thyself art a 'strange god,' a god of wrath, punishment, and vengeance; and I, Rachel, I, who loved only the Loving God and served only the All-Merciful—I reject Thee before Thine own angels. They and Thy prophets may abase themselves. But I, Rachel, the mother, will not abase me. I stand erect and defy Thee. God, I arraign Thee, before Thou executest Thy will upon my children. Thy word, God, conflicts with Thine own nature, and Thy wrathful mouth gives the lie to the promptings of Thine own heart. Judge, God, betwixt Thyself and Thy word. If Thou art, in very truth, the wrathful and jealous God Thou proclaimest Thyself to be, then will I fling myself down into the darkness to join my children and share their doom. I do not wish to contemplate the visage of an angry God, and I loathe the thought of a jealous one. But if Thou art a merciful God, the God I have loved, and by the guidance of whose teachings I tried to walk, then show Thyself to me in that light; be clement, spare my children, have mercy upon Jerusalem."

When Rachel had uttered this message of defiance, again her strength was spent. She awaited the answer of the Most High, her eyelids closed like those of the dead.

The forefathers and the prophets drew away, in terror of the lightnings which must, they felt assured, blast the impious spirit of her who had arraigned God. Timidly they gazed upward at the Throne. But there was no sign vouchsafed.

The angels, affrighted by the angry aspect of God's visage, hid their heads under their wings. Then (peeping forth) they looked aghast at the woman who had denied the omnipotence of the Lord—and perceived that a light shone on Rachel's forehead. It was as if this radiance emanated from within, and the tears on her motherly cheeks sparkled red like dew-drops in the glow of dawn. What was happening? The angels understood. God was showing Rachel the glory of His loving countenance. They became aware that the Almighty loved this repudiator of His word for the very reason that she was froward and impatient, loved her more than He loved the sages and the prophets, the pious who so servilely complied with His word. Mastering their terror, the angels confidently raised their eyes, to behold that a splendid and luminous calm once more enveloped God's majesty, and that the consoling azure of His smile filled the infinite spaces of heaven. Thereupon the cherubim winked anew their joyful flight, the rustle of their pinions making music in the skies. The sheen upon God's face grew so bright that the firmament glowed with an intensity no mortal eyes could endure. Now the angels sang together, the dead who had arisen from their tombs joined in the chorus of praise, and mingled therein were the innumerable voices of those whom the Almighty had not yet called to live upon earth.

But they who now dwelt thereon, mortals far beneath, ignoring (as ever) the happenings in heaven, knew naught of what was going on overhead. Clad in their shrouds, they bowed their faces sadly towards the darkened earth. Then to one and another of them came the sound of a stirring, like the rustle of a March wind. Looking upward they were astonished. The dense clouds had been riven in sunder, and across the interspace spread an arch, sevenfold in colour, a rainbow, which was made by the light from God's countenance shining upon Mother Rachel's tears.

The Legend of the Third Dove

In the Book of Genesis there is written the story of the first dove and also of the second, which the patriarch Noah sent forth out of the Ark, when the windows of heaven were stopped and the waters of the deep abated. Yet who has told of the travels and the destiny of the third dove? The ship of salvation, carrying within it all life that was spared from the flood, had grounded upon the peak of Mount Ararat, but the patriarch from his mast-head could see nought save the rise and fall of an infinity of water; he therefore sent out a dove, the first dove, to bring him news of any land that might be seen beneath the lowering skies.

The first dove, so we are told, soared upwards and spread her wings. She flew to the East and to the West, but the waters were everywhere. She found no rest for the sole of her foot and gradually her wings began to weaken. So she returned to the one firm place on earth, to the Ark, and she fluttered about the ship which rested on the mountain peak, until Noah put forth his hand, and took her, and pulled her in unto him into the Ark.

Now he waited for seven days, seven days in which no

rain fell and the waters sank; then he took another dove, the second, and sent her out to search. The dove flew out in the morning and when she returned at the eventide she bore in her bill an olive leaf, the first sign that the earth was uncovered once again. Thus Noah learned that the treetops were already clear of the water and that the trial was surmounted.

After another seven days he once again sent forth a dove, the third, and she flew out into the world. In the morning she set forth, yet by evening she had not returned, and though Noah awaited her day after day, she never came back. Thus our ancestor knew that the earth was free and the waters sunken away. But of that dove, the third dove, he never heard again, nor did mankind either, for her legend has not been revealed until to-day.

These were the travels and the destiny of the third dove. In the morning she had flown forth from the ship's musty hold, where the beasts, crowded in darkness, stirred impatiently, hoof to claw, amidst a confusion of roaring and whistling, hissing and lowing; from confinement she flew forth into the infinity of space, from darkness into light. And when she spread her wings in the clear, clean air washed sweet by the rain she felt at once the freedom that was all about her and the grace of boundlessness. The waters of the deep glistened, the forests shone green as dewy moss, the mists of dawn drifted white across the meadows and those meadows were sweetly scented by the opening blossoms. Brightness poured down from the metallic sky to be mirrored below, so that the rising sun was reflected in a pink, eternal dawn upon the rocky mountain tops, while the

The Legend of the Third Dove

sea shone blood-red and the flowering earth, too, steamed warm as blood. It was god-like to watch this awakening, and in an ecstasy of vision the dove floated across the purple world; easily she flew over lands and seas and in her dream slowly became herself a gliding dream. Like God Himself she was now the first to see the earth set free and there was no end to her looking. She had long ago forgotten Noah, the white-bearded captain of the Ark, she had forgotten her mission, she had forgotten that she must return. For the world was now her home, the heavens her very own house.

And so the third dove, the patriarch's faithless messenger, flew across the empty world, on and ever onwards, borne up by the violence of her joy, by the wind of her blissful unrest, ever onwards until her pinions grew heavy and her feathers leaden. The earth drew her down towards itself with a mighty force, her tired wings sank lower and lower so that already they grazed the damp treetops, and at last on the evening of the second day she settled down in the midst of a wood which, like everything else at time's beginning, was without a name. She hid deep in a thicket and rested from her journey through the skies. The twigs sheltered her, the breeze lulled her, the wood was cool by day and a warm dwelling-place by night. She soon forgot the windy heavens and the call of far places; embowered in the green trees, time grew over her, unreckoned.

It was a wood of the world close to us that the last dove had chosen for her home, but there were as yet no human beings within it, and in this solitude she gradually became a dream unto herself. In the darkness, in the green shade she nestled and the years passed her by and death forgot her, for of all those beasts—two of each breed which had seen the first world before the flood—none can ever die nor be harmed by the hunter. Invisible, they shelter in the hidden folds of earth's garment, and even so did this dove live deep in the forest. Sometimes, it is true, forebodings of the presence of man would reach her; a shot would ring out and be re-echoed a hundredfold from the walls of green; axes would be driven into the trunks so that the encircling darkness groaned; the soft laughter of lovers as they stole away together was a murmur in the undergrowth, and the songs of children picking berries came thinly from afar. The lost dove, enmeshed in foliage and in dream, sometimes heard those worldly voices, but they caused her no fear and she remained in her darkness.

But one day the whole wood began to roar and crack as though the very world were falling apart. Black masses of metal screamed through the air and where they fell the earth leapt up in horror and the trees were snapped like grasses. Men in coloured clothes hurled death at one another and fearful machines spewed forth fire and flame. Lightning shot up from earth to clouds and after it thunder; it was as though the land wished to jump into the sky, or the sky to fall upon the land. The dove awakened from her dream. Death was all about her, and destruction; as once the water, so now fire was spread across the world. Quickly she stretched her wings and fluttered upwards, in search of a new home to replace her crashing, crackling wood, in search of a place where there was peace.

She fluttered upwards and flew across our world in search of peace, but go where she would she found everywhere the same man-made lightning, the same man-made thunder, everywhere was war. A sea of fire and blood had once again engulfed the earth, another flood had come, and quickly she flew across the land, searching for a place of rest whence she might return to the patriarch bearing the olive leaf of promise in her bill. But in these days none was to be found, ever higher rose the tide of ruin over mankind, while the flames raced ever on across the face of our world. She has not yet found a restingplace, nor humanity peace, and until then she may not return home, she may not be for ever still.

No man has seen her, the lost and mystical dove in her search for peace, but still she flutters over our heads, frightened and with pinions that are already weary. Sometimes, deep in the night, a man awakening from a startled sleep may hear wings beating high in the air, haste in darkness, anguished, unheeding flight. Upon her is the weight of all our sombre thoughts, in her fear are carried all our wishes, and there, fluttering between heaven and earth, is the lost dove. It is our own destiny that she now must learn, that she now must bear back, that faithless messenger of long ago, to the patriarch of mankind. And once again, as those thousands of years ago, the world is waiting, waiting that a hand be put forth to take her, waiting for the knowledge that the trial has been at last enough.

Virata or the Eyes of the Dying Brother

It is not by shunning action that we can be really freed from action,
Never can we be freed from all activity, even for a moment.
—*Bhagavatgita*, Third Song.

What is action? What is inaction?—These questions have long puzzled the sages.
For we must pay heed to action, must pay heed to forbidden action.
Must pay heed likewise to inaction.—The nature of action is unfathomable.
—*Bhagavatgita*, Fourth Song.

A Legend

This is the Story of Virata who was honoured by his Fellow-Countrymen with the four Names of Virtue. Yet there is no word of him in the Chronicles of the Conquerors or the Books of the Sages, and his Memory has passed from the Minds of Men.

In the days before the sublime Buddha lived on earth to fill his servants with the light of his knowledge, there dwelt in the land of the Birwagher as subject of a king in Rajputana a noble and upright man named Virata. He was known also as the Flashing of the Sword, for he was a great warrior, bold before all others; and he was a great hunter, whose arrow never missed its mark, whose lance never swerved, and whose trusty sword-arm had the strength of a thunderbolt. His countenance was serene, and his eyes did not quail before any man's glance. He never clenched his fist in anger, nor raised his voice in wrath. Himself a loyal servant of the king, his own slaves

Jewish Legends

served him with veneration, for he was deemed preeminent in justice among all who lived in the Land of the Five Rivers. The pious bowed low when they passed before his dwelling, and the children who caught sight of him smiled to see his starry eyes.

But one day misfortune overtook the king his master. The viceroy over half the kingdom, who was brother of the monarch's wife, lusted to make himself ruler of the whole, and by secret gifts had enticed the best warriors of the realm to espouse his cause. He had induced the priests to bring him under cover of darkness the herons of the lake, the sacred herons which for thousands of years had been the insignia of royalty among the Birwagher. He marshalled his elephants in the field, summoned to his army the malcontents from the hills, and marched against the capital.

From morning till evening, by the king's orders, the copper cymbals were beaten and the ivory horns were sounded. At night, fires were lighted upon the towers, and fish-scales were cast into the flames, which flared yellow in the starlight as an alarm signal. Few answered the summons, for the news of the theft of the sacred herons had been bruited abroad, and the leaders' hearts were faint within them. The commander-in-chief and the head of the elephant corps, who had been the most trusted among the king's warriors, had gone over to the enemy. Vainly did the forsaken monarch look around him seeking friends. Alas, he had been a harsh master, ever ready to punish, and strict in the exaction of feudal dues. None of the tried and trusted chiefs were now in

Virata or the Eyes of the Dying Brother

attendance at the palace, where only a helpless rabble of slaves and underlings was to be seen.

In this extremity, the king's thoughts turned to Virata, from whom a pledge of loyal service had come the instant the horns had been sounded. He entered his ebony litter, and was borne to the dwelling of his faithful subject. Virata prostrated himself when the king stepped forth from the litter. But the king's mien was that of a petitioner as he besought Virata to take command of the army and lead it against the enemy. Virata made obeisance, and said:

"I will do it, Lord, and will not return to the shelter of this roof until the flames of revolt shall have been stamped out beneath the feet of thy servants."

Thereupon, he assembled his sons, his kinsmen, and his slaves, and, going forth with them to join the loyal remnant, he marshalled his forces for the campaign. They made their way through the jungle and came at eventide to the river on whose opposite shore the enemy was drawn up in countless numbers. Confident in their strength, the rebels were felling trees to build a bridge, by which they hoped to cross next morning, and drown the land in blood. But Virata, when hunting the tiger, had discovered a ford above the place of the bridge-building. At dead of night he led his men across the stream, and took the enemy by surprise. With flaming torches, the loyalists scared the elephants and buffaloes in the hostile camp, so that the beasts stampeded, and spread disorder among the sleeping horde. Virata was the first to reach the tent of the would-be usurper; and ere the inmates were fully awake, he put two of them to the sword, and then a third who was reaching out for his own weapon. With a fourth and a fifth he strove man to man in the darkness, cutting down one by a blow on the head, and piercing the other through the unarmoured breast. As soon as they all lay motionless, shade beside shade, Virata stationed himself at the entry of the tent, to defend it against any who might seek to carry off the white herons, the sacred emblem of royalty. But none came to attempt the deed, for the foe were in flight, hard pressed by the jubilant and victorious loyalists. Soon the din of the chase grew faint in the distance. Virata seated himself tranquilly in front of the tent, sword in hand, to await the return of his fellow-soldiers.

Ere long, God's day dawned behind the forest. The palm trees were golden red in the early sunlight, and were mirrored like torches in the river. The sun showed all bloody, a fiery wound in the east. Virata arose, laid aside his raiment, and walked to the stream, hands uplifted. Having bowed in prayer before the glowing eye of God, he went down into the waters for the prescribed ablutions, and cleansed the blood from his hands. Now, in the white light of morning, he returned to the bank, wrapped himself in his garment, and, serene of countenance, made his way back to the tent to contemplate the deeds of the night. The dead lay there with eyes staring and faces contorted with terror. The usurper's head was cloven; and the traitor who had been commander-in-chief in the land of the Birwagher who perished from a sword-thrust in the breast. Closing their eyes, Virata moved on to look at those whom he had killed as they slumbered.

Virata or the Eyes of the Dying Brother

These lay half-wrapped in their mats. Two of them were strangers to him, slaves of the traitor, men from the south with woolly hair and black faces. But when he looked upon the last of the dead men, Virata's eyes grew dim, for he saw before him the face of his elder brother Belangur, the Prince of the Mountains, who had come to the aid of the usurper, and whom Virata had struck down all unwitting. Trembling he stooped to feel for the heart-beat of the misguided man. The heart was stilled forever; the dead man's eyes encountered his with a glassy stare—dark eyes which seemed to pierce his very soul. Hardly able to breathe, Virata sat down among the dead, feeling as if he himself were one of them, and turning away his eyes from the accusing gaze of his mother's first-born.

Soon, shouts were heard without. Glad at heart, enriched with plunder, and with wild and gleeful cries like those of birds of prey, the returning soldiers came to the tent. Finding the would-be usurper slain amid his adherents, and learning that the sacred herons were safe, they leapt and danced, kissed the garment of the unheeding Virata, and acclaimed him the Flashing of the Sword. As more came back of them and more, they loaded carts with their booty. So deep sank the wheels beneath the burden that they had to scourge the buffaloes with thorns, and the boats were in danger of sinking. A messenger forded the stream, and hastened to bear tidings to the king; but the others tarried beside the spoil, and rejoiced over the victory.

Virata, meanwhile, sat silent, as if in a dream. Once only did he uplift his voice, when the soldiers were about to strip the dead. Thereupon, rising to his feet, he commanded that funeral pyres should be built, in order that the slain might be burned and their souls go forth cleansed to the transmigration. The underlings were amazed that he should deal thus tenderly with conspirators, who should have been torn limb from limb by the jackals, and whose bones should have been left to bleach in the sun: nevertheless, they did as they were bidden. When the pyres had been built, Virata himself kindled them, and cast spices and sandalwood into the flames. Then, turning away his face, he stood in silence until the blazing platforms fell in and the glowing ashes sank to the ground.

Meanwhile the slaves had finished the bridge whose building had been vauntingly begun the day before by the servitors of the usurper. The first to cross it were the warriors, crowned with flowers of the plantain; then came the slaves; then the nobles on horseback. Virata sent most of the warriors in advance, for their shouts and songs were discordant with his mood. Halting in the middle of the bridge, he gazed for a long time to right and to left over the flowing waters, while the soldiers who had crossed in front of him and those who had still to cross and who, by their commander's orders, were keeping well to the rear, marvelled as they looked at him. They saw him raise his sword, as if to threaten heaven, but when he lowered his arm, his fingers loosed their grip, and the weapon sank into the river. From either bank, naked boys jumped into the water, supposing that the sword had been accidentally dropped, and hoping to recover it by diving; but Virata forbade the attempt, and

Virata or the Eyes of the Dying Brother

strode forward, sad of mien, between the wondering servitors. No word passed his lips during the long homeward march.

The jasper gates and pinnacled towers of Birwagha were still far distant when a white dust-cloud was seen advancing, heralded by runners and riders who had outstripped the dust. They halted at sight of the army and spread carpets athwart the road as a sign of the advent of the king, the sole of whose foot must never press the common clay from the day of his birth to that hour when the flames of the funeral pyre would enwrap his illustrious corpse. Now the monarch came in sight, borne by the lord of the elephants, and surrounded by youths. Obedient to the ankus, the great beast kneeled, and the king stepped down upon the carpet. Virata wished to prostrate himself before his master, but the king hastened to embrace him—an honour that had never yet been paid to an inferior. Virata had the herons brought, and when they flapped their white wings there was such a clamour of rejoicing that the chargers reared and the mahouts were hard put to it to control the elephants. At sight of these emblems of victory, the king embraced Virata once more, and beckoned an attendant, who was carrying the sword of the primal hero of the Rajputs. For seven times seven hundred years, this weapon had been preserved in the treasuries of the kings. The hilt glittered with jewels, and on the blade was inscribed in golden characters a mystic assurance of victory, in the ancient writing which none but sages and priests of the great temple could now decipher. The king offered this sword of swords to Virata

Jewish Legends

as a token of gratitude, and to show that henceforward Virata was to be the chief of his warriors and the leader of his armies.

But Virata made a deep obeisance, saying:

"May I ask a grace from the most gracious and a favour from the most generous of monarchs?"

Looking down on the petitioner's bowed head, the king answered:

"Your request is granted, even before you raise your eyes to meet mine. You have but to ask, and the half of my kingdom is yours."

Thereupon Virata said:

"Grant then, O King, that this sword may be taken back to your treasury, for I have vowed in my heart never again to wield a sword, now that I have slain my brother, the only fruit besides myself which my mother bore in her womb, and whom my mother dandled together with me."

The king looked at him in amazement. Then he replied:

"In that case, be the commander of my armies, though without a sword, that I may know my realm to be safe from its enemies, for never has a hero led an army more wisely against overwhelming odds. Take my sash as a token of power, and my charger likewise, that all may know you as chief among my warriors."

But Virata prostrated himself once more, and rejoined:

"The Invisible One has sent me a sign, and my heart has understood. I have slain my brother, and this has taught me that everyone who slays another human being kills his brother. I cannot lead the armies in war, for the sword is the embodiment of force, and force is the enemy of right. Whosoever participates in the sin of slaying, is himself a slayer. It is not my wish to inspire dread in others, and I would rather eat the bread of a beggar than deny the sign which has been vouchsafed to me. Short is our life amid the unending flux of things, and I would fain live out my days without further wrongdoing."

For a space, the king's brow was dark, and there was the silence of terror where before there had been tumult, for never yet had it happened since the days of fathers and forefathers that a nobleman had renounced war or that a prince had refused to accept his king's gift. But at length the monarch looked upon the sacred herons which Virata had wrested from the insurgents. At sight of these emblems of victory, his face cleared, and he said:

"I have always known you to be brave in conflict with my enemies, and to excel as a just man among the servants of my kingdom. If I must indeed do without your aid in war, I cannot dispense with your services in another field. Since, yourself a just man, you know and can appraise wrongdoing, you shall be the chief among my judges, and shall pass sentence from the threshold of my palace, so that truth may prevail within my walls and right be maintained throughout the land."

Virata prostrated himself before the king, who commanded him to mount the royal elephant. Side by side they entered the sixty-towered town, amid acclamations which thundered like the surges of a stormy sea.

Henceforward, from dawn to sunset, at the summit of the rose-coloured stairway in the shade of the palace,

Jewish Legends

Virata delivered justice in the name of the king. His decisions were like those of a balance whose pointer trembles long before it sways this way or that. His clear eyes searched deeply into the soul of the accused, and his questions burrowed into the profundities of the offence as a badger burrows in the underground darkness. His sentences were rigorous, but were never delivered on the day of the hearing. He always allowed the cool span of night to intervene before passing judgment. During the long hours ere the sun rose, the members of his household could hear his footsteps as he paced the roof of the house while pondering the rights and wrongs of the matter. Before passing sentence, he laved his hands and his brow, that his decision might be free from the heat of passion. Always, too, after passing sentence, he would ask the culprit whether there was any reason to complain of the justice of the decision. Rarely was any objection raised. Silently the offender would kiss the step of the judgment seat, and with bowed head would accept the punishment as if it had been God's decree.

Never did Virata pass sentence of death, even for the most heinous of crimes, resisting all solicitations that he should do so. He dreaded to stain his hands with blood. The basin of the ancient fountain of the Rajputs, over whose margin the headsman would make the criminals lean before he delivered the death-blow, and whose stones had been blackened with blood, were washed white by the rains during the years of Virata's justiceship. Yet there was no increase of evil throughout the land. He confined ill-doers in the prison hewn out of the rock, or sent them to the mountains where they had to quarry

Virata or the Eyes of the Dying Brother

stones for the walls of the gardens, or to the rice mills on the river bank where they turned the wheels side by side with the elephants. But he reverenced life, and men reverenced him, for never was any decision of his shown to be wrong, never was he weary of searching out the truth, and never did his words betray anger. From the remotest parts of the country, the peasants would come in buffalo carts bringing their disputes for his settlement; the priests obeyed his admonitions, and the king hearkened to his counsel. His fame grew as the young bamboo grows, and folk forgot they had once named him the Flashing of the Sword. Now, throughout Rajputana, he was known as the Wellspring of Justice.

In the sixth of the years of Virata's judgeship it came to pass that certain plaintiffs brought a youth of the tribe of the Kazars, the wild men who dwelt beyond the rocky hills and served other gods. His feet were bloodstained, for they had compelled him to make long marches during many days. His mighty arms were strongly bound, lest he should use them to do the harm that his fierce and sullen eyes threatened. Bringing him to the seat of judgment, they forced their prisoner to his knees before Virata, and then, prostrating themselves, they lifted up their hands as a sign that they were petitioners.

The judge looked questioningly at the strangers, saying:

"Who are ye, brothers, that come to me from afar, and who is this man whom ye bring to me thus fettered?"

The eldest of the company made obeisance, and answered:

"We are herdsmen, Lord, living peacefully in the eastern land. He whom we bring you is the most evil of an evil stock, a wretch who has slain more men than he has fingers on his hands. A dweller in our village, whose daughter he had asked in marriage, refused, because the men of his tribe have impious customs, being dog-eaters and cow-killers; instead, the father gave her for wife to a merchant in the lowlands. In his wrath, thereupon, this fellow drove off many of our cattle; one night he killed the father of the girl, and her three brothers; and whenever anyone of that household went to herd cattle in the foothills, this man slew him. Eleven from our village had he thus done to death, when at length we assembled our forces and hunted him like a wild beast until we had made him prisoner. Now, most just among judges, we have brought him to you that you may rid the land of the evildoer."

Virata, raising his head, looked at the bound man.

"Is it true, what they say of you?"

"Who are you? Are you the king?"

"I am Virata, servant of the king and servant of justice, that I may atone for my own wrongdoings and sift the true from the false."

The accused was silent for a space, and then gave Virata a piercing look.

"How, on your distant judgment seat, can you know what is true, and what is false, seeing that all your knowledge comes from what people tell you?"

"Give your rejoinder to their accusation, that from the two I may learn the truth."

The prisoner raised his eyebrows contemptuously.

"I shall not dispute with them. How can you know

Virata or the Eyes of the Dying Brother

what I did, inasmuch as I myself do not know what my hands do when anger seizes me? I did justice on him who sold a woman for money, and I did justice on his children and his servants. Let these men bring a charge against me if they will. I despise them, and I despise your judgment."

A storm of anger burst forth from the accusers when they heard the prisoner express his scorn of the just judge. The apparitor raised his cudgel for a blow. Virata signed to them to restrain their anger, and resumed his questions. Each time the accusers returned to the charge, the judge asked the prisoner to reply. But the latter clenched his teeth in an angry grip, and spoke only once more, saying:

"How can you learn the truth from the words of others?"

The noon-day sun was directly overhead when Virata had finished his examination. Rising to his feet, he said, as was his custom, that he would return home and would deliver sentence on the following day. The accusers raised their hands in protest.

"Lord," said they, "we have journeyed seven days to see the light of your countenance, and it will take us another seven days to return to our homes. How can we wait till the morrow when our cattle are athirst and our land needs the plough? We beseech you to deliver judgment forthwith."

Thereupon Virata seated himself once more and was plunged for a while deep in thought. His brow was furrowed like that of one who bears a heavy burden upon his head, for never before had he been constrained to pass

Jewish Legends

sentence upon any who did not sue for pardon or upon one who remained defiant. His meditation lasted a long time, and the shadows grew as the hours passed. Then he went to the fountain, and, having laved his forehead and his hands in the cool water that his words might be free from the heat of passion, he returned to the judgment seat and said:

"May the decision I shall deliver be a just one. A deadly sin lies upon this offender, who has hunted eleven living souls from their warm human bodies into the world of transmigration. For a year the life of man ripens unseen in the mother's womb, and for this reason, for each one of those whom he has slain the guilty man must remain hidden for a year in the darkness of the earth. And because by his deed the blood has been drained from eleven human bodies, eleven times every year he shall be given one hundred lashes, that he may pay in accordance with the number of his victims. But his life shall not be taken from him, for life is the gift of the gods, and man must not lay his hand on divine things. May this judgment be just, this judgment which I have uttered in pursuance of no man's orders, but only for the sake of the great retribution."

When he had spoken, the plaintiffs kissed the step of his seat in token of respect. But the prisoner met his inquiring glance with a gloomy silence. Virata said:

"I exhorted you to speak, that you might give me reasons for passing a light sentence, and that you might help me against your accusers, but your lips were sealed. Should there be any error in my judgment, you must not charge me with it before the Eternal; you must lay it to the account of your own silence. I would fain have been merciful to you."

The prisoner answered:

"I seek no mercy from you. What mercy can you give to compare with the life that you take from me in the drawing of a breath?"

"I am not taking your life."

"Nay, but you are taking my life, and are taking it more cruelly than do the chiefs of my tribe whom these lowlanders term savages. Why do you not kill me? I killed, man to man; but you bury me like a corpse in the darkness of the earth, to rot as the years pass; and you do it because your craven heart fears to shed blood, and because your bowels are weak as water. Your law is caprice, and your sentence is a martyrdom. Slay me, for I have slain."

"I have given you a just measure of punishment . . ."

"A just measure? But what, O Judge, is the measure by which you measure? Who has scourged you, that you may know what scourging is? How is it that you can tick off the years upon your fingers, as if a year passed in the light of day were the same thing as a year prisoned in the darkness of the earth? Have you dwelt in prison, that you may know how many springs you are taking from my days? You are an ignorant man and no just one, for he only who feels the blow knows what a blow is, not he who delivers it; and none but the sufferer can measure suffering. In your pride you presume to punish the offender, and are yourself the most grievous of all offenders, for when I took life it was in anger, in the thraldom of my passion, whereas you rob me of my life in cold blood and mete me a measure which your hand has not weighed and whose burden you have never borne. Step down from the seat of judgment ere you fall headlong! Woe unto him who measures haphazard, and woe to the ignorant man who fancies he knows what justice is. Step down from the judgment seat, O ignorant Judge, nor continue to pass sentence on living men with the death of your word!"

Pale with wrath was the prisoner as he flung forth these invectives, and once more the angry onlookers were about to fall upon him. Again Virata stayed them, and, turning his face from the prisoner, he said gently:

"It is not in my power to quash the sentence that I have spoken here. My hope is that the doom is just."

Virata moved to depart, while they seized the prisoner, who struggled in his bonds. But, halting after a few steps, the judge turned back towards the condemned man, only to encounter his resolute and angry eyes. With a shudder it was borne in upon Virata that these eyes were exactly like those of his dead brother, the brother he had slain with his own hand, and whom he had found lying dead in the tent of the would-be usurper . . .

That evening, Virata spake no word to anyone. The stranger's look had pierced his soul like an arrow of fire. The folk of his household heard him hour after hour as, the livelong night, he strode sleepless to and fro on the roof of his house, until day dawned red behind the palms.

At sunrise, Virata performed his ablutions in the sacred pool of the temple. Turning eastward, he prayed,

Virata or the Eyes of the Dying Brother

and then, having returned to the house, he donned a ceremonial robe of yellow silk. He greeted the members of his household, who were amazed at his formality but did not venture to question him, and went alone to the king's palace, where he had leave of entry at any time of the day or night. Bowing before the king, Virata touched the hem of the monarch's garment in token of petition.

The king looked at him cordially, saying:

"Your wish has touched my vesture. It is granted before it is spoken."

Virata continued to stand with bowed head.

"You have made me the chief among your judges. For six years I have passed judgment in your name, and know not whether I have judged justly. Grant me a month of rest and quiet that I may find the road to truth; and permit me, in this matter, to keep my own counsel from you and all others. I wish to do a deed free from injustice and to live without sin."

The king was astonished.

"Poor will be my realm in justice from this moon to the next. Nevertheless, I will not ask you what path you wish to follow. May it lead you to the truth."

Kissing the foot of the throne as a sign of his gratitude, and having made a final obeisance, Virata left the presence.

He entered his house and summoned his wife and children.

"For a month you will see me no more. Bid me farewell, and ask no questions. Go to your rooms and

Jewish Legends

shut yourselves in there that none of you may watch whither I go when I leave the house. Make no inquiries for me until the month has passed."

Silently, they did as was commanded.

Virata clad himself in dark attire, prayed before the divine image, and wrote a long letter upon palm leaves which he rolled into a missive. At nightfall he left the silent house and went to the great rock where the mines were and the prisons. He knocked until the sleeping jailer rose from his mat to ask who was without.

"I am Virata, the chief of the judges. I have come to see the prisoner who was brought here yesterday."

"His cell is in the depths, Lord, in the lowest darkness of the prison. Shall I lead you thither?"

"I know the place. Give me the key, and return to your slumbers. Tomorrow you will find the key outside your door. Let no one know that you have seen me tonight."

The jailer fetched the key and also a torch. At a sign from Virata he withdrew, and threw himself on his mat. Virata opened the bronze door which closed the archway of the rocky vault, and descended into the depths of the prison. A century earlier the kings of Rajputana had begun to confine prisoners within this rock. Day by day each of the captives had to quarry deeper into the cold stone, fashioning new cells for the inmates of the morrow.

Virata took a final glance at the quadrant of sky with its sparkling stars visible through the rocky arch. Then he closed the door, and the damp darkness rose to enwrap him, the darkness through which the unsteady light of his torch leaped like a beast of prey. He could still hear the rustling of the trees and the shrill clatter of the monkeys. At the bottom of the first flight of steps, the rustling sound came from a great distance. Lower still, the silence was as profound as if he had been in the depths of the sea, motionless and cold. From the stones there breathed nothing but dampness, without any aroma of the fresh earth, and the farther he descended the more harshly did his footsteps echo amid the silence.

The cell of the prisoned hill-man was five flights from the surface, deeper beneath the earth than the height of the tallest palm tree. Virata entered and held his torch aloft over the dark mass which hardly stirred for a while. Then a chain rattled.

Bending over the prostrate figure, Virata said:
"Do you know me?"
"I know you. You are he whom they made master of my fate, and you have trodden it under your foot."
"I am no master. I am servant of the king and of justice. It is to serve justice that I have come."

The prisoner looked at the judge with a fixed and gloomy stare:
"What do you want of me?"
After a long silence, Virata answered:
"I hurt you with the words of my judgment, and you have likewise hurt me with your words. I do not know if my decision was just; but there was truth in what you said, for no one ought to measure with a measure he does not know. I have been ignorant, and would gladly learn. I have sent hundreds into this abode of darkness; much have I done to many persons, without knowing what I did. Now I wish to find out, now I desire to learn, that I

Jewish Legends

may grow just, and may encounter the day of transmigration free from all taint of sin."

The prisoner remained motionless, so that nothing was heard beyond a faint clanking of his chains. Virata continued:

"I wish to know what it is that I have doomed you to suffer; I wish to feel the bite of the scourge upon my own body, and to experience in my own soul what imprisonment means. For a month I shall take your place, that I may be taught how much I have exacted by way of atonement. Then I shall once again deliver sentence in the place of judgment, aware at length of the weight of my decisions. Meanwhile, you will go free. I shall give you the key by which you can open the door leading into the world of light, and shall accord you a month of liberty, provided only that you promise to return. Then from the darkness of these depths, light will enter my mind."

The prisoner stood as if carven out of stone. The clanking of his chains was no longer audible.

"Swear to me by the pitiless Goddess of Vengeance, who spares no one, that you will keep silence throughout this month, and I will give you the key and my own clothing. The key you must leave outside the porter's lodge, and then you can go free. But you remain bound by your oath that as soon as the month has sped you will take this missive to the king, in order that I may be delivered from prison, and once more judge righteously. Do you swear by the most high gods to fulfil this my bidding?"

"I swear," came the answer in tremulous tones as if from the depths of the earth.

Virata unloosed the chain and stripped off his own garment.

"Wear this," he said, "and give me your clothing. Muffle your face, that the jailer may take you for me. Now clip my hair and beard, that I also may remain unknown."

Tremblingly and reluctantly, under the compelling glance of Virata, the prisoner did as he was told. Then, for a long time, he was silent. At length, throwing himself on the ground, he cried passionately:

Lord, I cannot endure that you should suffer in my stead. I killed. My hand is red with blood. The doom was just."

"Neither you nor I can appraise the justice of that doom, but soon the light will break in upon my mind. Go forth, as you have sworn, and when the moon is again full present my letter to the king that he may set me free. When the time is ripe I shall know what are the deeds I am doing, and my decisions thenceforward will be free from injustice. Go forth."

The prisoner knelt and kissed the ground. The closing door clanged in the darkness. Once again, through a loophole, a ray from the torch flickered across the walls, and then the night engulfed the hours.

Next morning, Virata, whom no one recognized, was publicly scourged. At the first stroke of the scourge upon his bared back, he uttered a cry; but thenceforward was silent, with clenched teeth. At the seventieth stroke, his senses grew dim, and he was carried away like a dead beast.

When he recovered consciousness he was lying in his cell, and it seemed to him as if he were stretched upon a bed of glowing charcoal. But his brow was cool, and he breathed the odour of wild herbs. Half-opening his eyes he saw that the jailer's wife was beside him, gently bathing his forehead. As he looked at her more attentively he perceived that the star of compassion shone down upon him in her glance! Amid his bodily torments he realized that the meaning of sorrow dwelt in the grace of kindliness! He smiled up at her and forgot his pain.

Next day he was able to rise to his feet and to grope his way round the cell. At each step a new world seemed to fashion itself beneath his feet. On the third day his wounds were easier and strength was returning to body and mind. Henceforward he sat without moving, and noted the passage of time only by the falling of the waterdrops from the rocky roof. The great silence was subdivided into many little spaces, which were pieced together, to form day and night as out of thousands of days our life grows to manhood and old age. None came to speak with him, and the darkness entered into his very soul. Yet within, the manifold springs of memory were opened. Flowing gently, they filled a quiet pool of contemplation wherein his whole life was mirrored. What he had experienced bit by bit, coalesced now into a unity. Never had his mind been so limpid as during this motionless insight into a reflected world.

Day by day Virata's vision grew clearer; things shaped

Virata or the Eyes of the Dying Brother

themselves in the darkness, displaying their forms to his gaze. In like manner everything grew clearer to the eye of inward vision. The gentle delight of contemplation, spreading-unsolicited beyond the illusive appearances of memory, played amid the forms of changing thought as the prisoner's hand played with the irregularities in the walls of his rocky cell. Withdrawn from self, and in the darkness and solitude unaware of the intimacies of his own nature, he grew ever more conscious of the might of the multiform divinity, and was able to wander freely amid these constructions of the imagination, in perfect independence, liberated from servitude to the will, dead in life and living in death. All the anxieties of the passing hour were dissipated in the serene joy of deliverance from the body. It seemed to him as if hour by hour he was sinking deeper into the darkness, down towards the stony and black roots of the earth, but as if he were none the less pregnant with a new germinal life. Perhaps it was the life of a worm, blindly burrowing in the clods; or perhaps that of a plant, striving upwards with its stem; or perhaps only that of a rock, cool, quiet, and blissfully unconscious of its own being.

For eighteen nights Virata enjoyed the divine mystery of devout contemplation, detached from his individual will and freed from the goading of life. What he had undertaken as atonement seemed to him blessedness, and he was already beginning to feel that sin and retribution were no more than dream images as contrasted with the eternal wakefulness of knowledge. But during the nineteenth night he was startled out of sleep by the prick of an earthly thought, boring into his brain like a red-hot needle. His body was shaken with terror, and his fingers trembled as leaves tremble in the wind. The terrifying thought was that the prisoner might be faithless and foresworn, might forget him, might leave him to spend a thousand and yet a thousand and yet another thousand days in prison, until the flesh dropped from his bones and his tongue grew stiff from perpetual silence. The will-to-live sprang up like a panther in his body, tearing at the wrappings in which it was enclosed. The current of time resumed its flow in his soul, and therewith came fears and hopes, and all the turmoil of earthly existence. No longer could he concentrate upon the thought of the multiform and everlasting deity. He could think only of himself. His eyes craved for the daylight; his limbs, recoiling from the hard stone, longed for wide expanses, for the power to leap and to run. His mind was filled with thoughts of his wife and his sons, of his house and his possessions, of the ardent allurements of the world, which must be enjoyed with full awareness and must be felt with the waking warmth of the blood.

From now onwards, time, which had hitherto lain silent at his feet like the black waters of a quiet pool passively mirroring events, was magnified in his thoughts, and took on the movement of a stream against which he had unceasingly to struggle. His longing was that it should overpower him, should carry him away like a floating tree to the predestined moment of liberation. But the flow was directed against him; panting for breath he swam desperately up-stream hour after hour. He felt as if the interval between the falling of the water-drops from the roof was being indefinitely prolonged. He could

Virata or the Eyes of the Dying Brother

not lie patiently in his lair. The thought that the hill-man would forget him and that he would be doomed to rot in this crypt of silence, made him prowl round and round his narrow cell like a beast in a cage. The stillness choked him; he volleyed words of abuse and complaint at the walls; he cursed himself and the gods and the king. With bleeding fingers he tore at the obdurate rock, and ran with lowered head against the door until he fell insensible. Only recovering consciousness, he would spring to his feet once more, only to repeat the ceaseless round.

During these days from the eighteenth of his confinement until the moon was full, Virata lived through æons of horror. He loathed food and drink, for his body was racked with anxiety. Thought had become impossible, though with his lips he continued to count the drops of water as they fell, that he might punctuate the interminable time from one day to another. Meanwhile, though he did not know it, the hair on his throbbing temples turned grey.

But on the thirtieth day there was a noise without, followed by silence. Then came the sound of footsteps on the stair; the door was flung open, a light broke in, and the king stood before the man entombed in darkness. With a loving embrace the monarch greeted him and said:

"I have learned of your deed, which is greater than any recorded in the chronicles of our fathers. It will shine like a star above the dead levels of our life. Come forth that the fire of God may light you with its glow, and that the happy people may behold a righteous man."

Virata shaded his eyes with his hand, for the unaccustomed glare was painful. He rose to his feet un-

Jewish Legends

steadily, like a drunkard, and the servants had to support him. Before going to the door he said:

"O King, you have called me a righteous man, but now I know full well that he who passes judgment on another does injustice and grievous wrong. In these depths there still languish human beings who are here by my decision. Now, for the first time, do I know what they suffer. Now at length I know that the law of retaliation is itself unjust. Set the prisoners free, and tell the people to be gone, for their acclamations fill me with shame."

The king gave a sign, and his servitors dispersed the throng. Once again all was quiet. Then the king said:

"Until now your seat of justice has been at the summit of the stairway leading to my palace. But through your knowledge of suffering you have become wiser than any judge has ever been before you, and henceforward you shall sit beside me that I may hearken to your words and may myself drink in wisdom from your justice."

Virata embraced the king's knee in token of petition.

"Discharge me from my office. No longer can I give true decisions, now that I realize that no one can judge another. Punishment is in God's hands, not man's, for whoever interferes with the working of destiny commits a crime. I wish to live out my life free from sin."

"So be it," answered the king. "Instead of the chief of my judges, you shall be my chief counsellor, deciding for me the issues of peace and war, and advising me in matters of taxation, that all my undertakings may be guided by your wisdom."

Again Virata clasped the king's knee.

"Do not give me power, O King, for power urges to

Virata or the Eyes of the Dying Brother

action; and what action can be just, or what action can fail to counteract that which has been decreed by fate? If I counsel war, I am sowing the seeds of death. What I say, grows into actions; and every act of mine has a significance which I cannot foresee. He only can be just and righteous, who refrains from all activities, and who lives alone. Never have I been nearer wisdom, and never have I been freer from sin than here in solitude, exchanging words with no man. Let me live tranquilly in my own dwelling, doing no other service than that of making sacrifice to the gods, that thus I may remain free from sin."

"I am loath to relinquish your services," replied the king, "but who can venture to argue with a sage, or to constrain the will of a righteous man? Live as you think best. It will be an honour to my kingdom that within its bounds there should be one living without sin."

They parted at the gate of the prison. Virata walked homeward alone, drinking in the fragrance of the sunlit air. Never before had he felt so light of heart as now when freed from all service. Behind him sounded the soft tread of naked feet, and when he turned he saw the condemned man whose punishment he had taken upon himself. The hill-man kissed the ground where the sometime judge had trodden, made a timid obeisance, and vanished. Virata smiled for the first time since he had looked upon the staring eyes of his dead brother, and he entered his house glad at heart.

After returning home, Virata lived through a time that was full of happiness. His awakening was a prayer of thanksgiving that he could look upon the light of heaven instead of upon darkness, that he could see the colours and inhale the aroma of the lovely earth, and that he could listen to the sweet music with which the morning is alive. Each day he accepted as a new and splendid gift the wonder of breath and the charm of free movement. With pious affection he would pass his hands over his own body, over the soft frame of his wife, and over the sturdy limbs of his sons, rapturously aware of the imminence of the multiform God in one and all of them. His soul was winged with gentle pride that he never had occasion to pass beyond the boundaries of his own life to interfere with a stranger's destiny, that he never made a hostile onslaught upon any of the numberless embodiments of the invisible God. From morn till eve he read the books of wisdom and practised the different varieties of devotion: the silence of meditation; loving absorption into the spirit; benefaction to the poor; and sacrificial prayer. He had grown cheerful. His speech was gracious even to the humblest of his servants, and all the members of his household were more devoted to him than ever they had been before. He brought help to the needy and consolation to the unfortunate. The prayers of the multitude hovered over his sleep and no longer did men call him as of old the Flashing of the Sword or the Wellspring of Justice, for now he had become the Field of Good Counsel. Not only did his neighbours ask his advice. Though he was no longer a judge in the land, strangers sought him out from afar that he might settle their disputes, and complied unhesitatingly with his words. Virata rejoiced thereat, feeling that counsel was better than command,

and mediation better than judgment. It seemed to him that his life was blameless, now that he no longer held forcible sway over anyone's destiny and could none the less adjust the fates of many. Thus he delighted in this high noon of his life.

Three years passed by, and yet another three, and the speeding of them all was like that of one bright day. Gentler and ever gentler grew the disposition of Virata. When a quarrel was brought to him for adjustment, he found it hard to understand why there was so much bickering upon earth, and why men pressed hard on one another with the petty jealousies of ownership when the expanses of life were open to them and the sweet aroma of existence. He envied none and none envied him. His house stood, an island of peace in the level sea of life, untouched by the torrents of passion or by the stream of sensual appetite.

One evening, in the sixth year of this period of calm, Virata had already retired to bed when he heard harsh cries and the thud of blows. He sprang from his couch and saw that his sons were chastising one of the slaves. They had forced the man to his knees, and were lashing him with a leathern thong until the blood gushed forth. The eyes of the victim stared Virata in the face, and once again he seemed to see the eyes of the brother he had slain. Hastening forth, he arrested the arm of the son wielding the whip and asked what was afoot.

From a medley of answers he gathered that this slave, whose duty it was to draw water from the rocky spring and bring it to the house in wooden buckets, had on several occasions during the noontide heat, pleading ex-

Jewish Legends

haustion, arrived too late with his burden. Each time, he had been punished; and yesterday, after a severer chastisement than usual, he had absconded. Virata's sons had pursued him on horseback, and had not overtaken him until he had crossed the river. They had tied him with a rope to the saddle of one of the horses, so that, half-dragged and half-running, he had reached home with lacerated feet. Now they were giving him an exemplary punishment for his own good and for that of the other slaves, who looked on trembling. This was the explanation of the scene which their father had interrupted. Virata glanced down at the slave. His eyes were widely opened like those of an animal awaiting its death-blow from the slaughterman, and behind their dark stare Virata sensed the horror that he had himself once lived through.

"Loose the man," he said to his sons. "The transgression is atoned."

The slave kissed the dust in front of the master's feet. For the first time the sons parted from their father in dudgeon. Virata returned to his room. Unwittingly he began to lave forehead and hands. At the touch of the cold water he suddenly grew aware of what he was doing, and realized that for the first time since leaving the rocky prison-house he had become a judge and had interfered in another's destiny. For the first time, too, during these six years, sleep forsook his pillow. As he lay awake in the darkness, he saw in fancy the terrified eyes of the slave (or were they the eyes of his own slain brother?); and he saw the angry eyes of his sons; and again and again he asked himself whether his children had not wreaked an injustice upon this servant. On account of a trifling neglect of duty, blood had moistened the sandy precincts of his house. For a petty act of omission, the lash had been laid upon living flesh, and this wrongdoing seared him more deeply than had the strokes of the scourge which aforetime had tortured his own back like scorpions. True, the chastisement he had witnessed that evening had befallen, not a nobleman, but a slave, whose body by the king's law belonged to the master from the very day of birth. But was the king's law right in the eyes of the multiform God? Could it be right in the eyes of God that the body of one human being should pass into the absolute power of another; and could that other be held guiltless before God if he injured or destroyed the life of the slave?

Virata rose from his bed and kindled a light, that he might seek instruction in the books of the sages. He found, indeed, distinctions between man and man established in the ordering of the castes and the estates; but nowhere amid the manifestations of the multiform being was there warrant for any difference in fulfilling the demands of love. More and more eagerly did he drink in wisdom, for never had his soul been more tensely alive to a problem. But now the flame leaped for a moment in the socket of the torch, and then the light went out.

As darkness fell between him and the walls, Virata became strangely aware that the enclosed space his eyes were blindly searching was no longer that of his familiar room, but that of his erstwhile dungeon, where, awestricken, he had acquired the certainty that freedom is the most intimate right of human beings, and that no one is entitled to prison another, be it for a lifelong term or only for a single year. Yet he, Virata, had prisoned this slave within the invisible confines of his own will. He had chained this slave to the chances of his own decisions, so that the underling could no longer take a single footstep in freedom. Clearness came to him as he sat and pondered, feeling how thought was enlarging his comprehension, until from some invisible altitude the light entered into him. Now he became aware that he had still been blameworthy in this, that he had allowed his fellows to be subject to his will, and to be named his slaves in accordance with a law which was but a fragile human construction and not one of the eternal decrees of the multiform God. He bowed himself in prayer:

"I thank thee, O God of a thousand shapes, for that thou sendest me messengers from all thy shapes, to hunt me out of my sins and draw me ever nearer to thee upon the invisible path of thy will. Grant me power to recognize them in the ever-accusing eyes of the undying brother, who encounters me everywhere, who sees with my vision, and whose sufferings I suffer, that I may purify my life and may breathe without sin."

Virata's countenance was again cheerful. Cleareyed he went forth into the night, to enjoy the white greeting of the stars, and to inhale the breath of the breeze that freshens before dawn. Passing through the garden, he went down to the river. When the sun appeared in the east, he plunged into the sacred stream, and then returned homewards to join the members of his household, who were assembled for morning prayer.

He greeted them with a kindly smile, signed to the women to withdraw, and then said to his sons:

"You know that for years I have had but one care, to be a just and righteous man, and to live my life on earth without sin. Yesterday blood flowed upon the ground within the precincts of my dwelling, the blood of a living man, and I wish to be innocent of this blood and to atone for the wrong that has been done under the shadow of my roof. The slave who was punished unduly for a trifling fault shall be free from this hour, free to go whither he lists, so that at the Last Judgment he may not bear testimony against you and me."

His sons remained silent, and Virata felt that their silence was hostile.

"You make no answer. I do not wish to act against your will without hearing what you have to say."

"You propose to bestow freedom upon an offender, to reward him instead of punishing him," said the eldest. "We have many servants in the house, so one will not be missed. But a deed works beyond its own confines, and is no more than a link in a chain. If you set this man free, how can you keep the others in bondage should they also wish to depart?"

"Should they wish to depart from out my life, I must let them go. I will not fashion anyone's destiny, for whosoever fashions another's destiny is a wrongdoer."

"You are loosening the sanctions of the law," the second son broke in. "These slaves are our own, as our land is our own, and the trees that grow thereon, and the fruit of the trees. Inasmuch as they serve you, they are bound

Jewish Legends

to you, and you are bound to them. That which you are touching is part of a traditional ordinance which dates back many thousands of years. The slave is not lord of his own life, but servant of his master."

"We have but one right from God, and it is the right to live, which is breathed into all of us with the divine breath. You did well to exhort me, for I was still in blindness when I thought I was cleansing myself of sin. All these years I have been taking away the lives of others. Now at length I see clearly, and I know that a righteous man may not turn men into beasts. I shall free them all, that I may free myself of sin towards them."

The brows of his sons grew dark with defiance. The eldest returned a stubborn answer:

"Who will irrigate our fields to keep the rice from withering? Who will drive forth the cattle? Are we to become serving men because of your whims? You yourself have never done a hand's turn of work throughout your life, nor have you ever troubled because that life was sustained by the labour of others. Nevertheless, there was others' sweat in the plaited straw on which you were lying, and a slave had to fan you while you slept. Now, of a sudden, you would dismiss them all, that none may labour except your sons, the men of your own blood. Would you have us unyoke the oxen and pull the ploughs ourselves, that the beasts may be free from the goad? Into these dumb beasts, likewise, the multiform God has breathed the breath of life. Touch not that which is ordained, for it also comes from God. Earth yields her fruits unwillingly, yields them only at the spell of force. The law of the world is force, and we cannot evade it."

"But I will evade it, for might is seldom right, and I wish to live out my life in righteousness."

"Might underlies all possession, be it the ownership of man or of beast or of the patient earth. Where you are master, you must be conqueror as well; he who owns is bound to the destiny of men."

"But I will loose myself from everything which binds me to sin. I command you, therefore, to set the slaves free, and yourselves to do the labour that is needful."

The sons' eyes flashed, and they could hardly control their anger. The eldest answered:

"You told us that you wished to constrain no man's will. You would not give orders to your slaves lest thereby you should fall into sin; but you command us to do this and that, and meddle with our lives. In which respect are you doing right before God and man?"

Long time Virata was silent. When he raised his eyes he saw the flame of greed in theirs, and his soul was heavy within him. He said gently:

"You have taught me a lesson. It is not for me to constrain you in any way. Take the house and the other possessions. Divide them among you as you think fit. No longer shall I have part or lot in these things, or in the sin that goes with them. You have said sooth: He who rules, deprives others of their liberty; but, worst of all, he enslaves his own soul. Whoever wishes to live without sin must be free from the ownership of a house and from the management of another's fate. He must not be fed by others' labour, and must not get the wherewithal to drink because others have sweated to supply his need. The joys of carnal intercourse with women and the inertia of satiety must be far from him. He only who lives alone, lives with God; only the active worker feels God; nought but poverty knows God to the full. It is more to me to be near the Invisible One than to be near my own land, for I desire to live without sin. Take the house and share it among you peacefully."

Virata turned and left them. His sons stood amazed. Satisfied greed was sweet to them in the flesh, but in spirit they were ashamed.

At nightfall Virata made ready for the road, taking a staff, a begging bowl, an axe for work, a little fruit for provender, and palm leaves, inscribed with the writings of the sages. Kilting his raiment above the knee, he silently left the house, without taking leave of wife, children, or any others of his household. Afoot all night, he came to the river into which he had once flung his sword in the terrible hour of his awakening, made his way through the ford, and turned up stream along the farther bank, where there were no habitations and where the earth had never yet been broken by the plough.

At dawn he reached a place where the lightning had struck an ancient mango tree, and where the consequent fire had made a clearing in the jungle. The stream flowed softly past the spot in a wide curve, and numerous birds were drinking fearlessly from its waters. Thus the river offered a clear prospect in front, while the trees gave shade behind. Scattered over the ground was wood which had been split off by the lightning blast, together with fragments of the undergrowth. Virata contemplated this lonely clearing in the jungle, and resolved to built a hut there. He would devote the rest of his life to meditation, far from his fellows and free from sin.

It took him five days to build his hut, for his hands were unaccustomed to labour. Even when it was finished, his days were full of toil. He had to seek fruit for food. Hard work was needed to keep back the jungle, which continually tended to encroach. A palisade had to be built as a protection from the hungry tigers, prowling in the jungle at night. But no noise of human beings intruded into his life or disturbed his serenity. The days flowed peacefully like the waters of the river, ever gently renewed from an unfailing spring.

The birds found nothing to alarm them in the quiet doings of the newcomer, and ere long they built their nests on the roof of his hut. He strewed seeds from the great flowers, and set out fruits for their repast. Growing more friendly by degrees, they would fly down from the palm trees at his call. He played with them, and they were not afraid to let him handle them. In the forest, one day, he found a young monkey, lying on the ground with a broken leg and crying like a child. Picking the creature up, he brought it to his hut, and trained it as soon as it was better. The monkey was docile, sportively imitated him, and served him faithfully. Thus he was surrounded by gentle living creatures, but he never forgot that in the animal, no less than in the human kind, force and evil slumber. He saw how the alligators would bite one another and hunt one another in their wrath, how the birds would snatch fish from the river, and how the snakes would encircle and crush the birds. The dreadful enchainment of destruction with which the hostile goddess of destruction had fettered the world became manifest to him as a law whose truth knowledge was forced to admit. Still, it was good to be merely an observer of these struggles, to be blameless amid the enlarging circle of destruction and of liberation.

For a year and many months he had not seen a human face. And then it happened one day that a hunter following the spoor of an elephant, came to the place where the beast had drunk, on the opposite bank. A marvellous sight met his gaze. In the yellow glimmer of evening, a white-bearded man was seated in front of a little hut; birds were perching on his head; a monkey at his feet was breaking nuts for him with a stone. But the man was looking up at the tree tops where the multicoloured parrots were snorting, and when he beckoned to them they fluttered down in a golden cloud and alighted on his hands. The hunter fancied that he was looking at the saint of whom it is written: "The beasts will talk to him with the voice of man, and the flowers grow under his footsteps; he can pluck the stars with his lips, and can blow away the moon with his breath." Forgetting his guest, the elephant-hunter hastened to the city to relate what he had beheld.

The very next day quidnuncs arrived to glimpse the wonder from the other side of the stream. More, and ever more, flocked to contemplate the marvel, until at length there arrived one who recognized Virata. Spreading far and wide, the tidings at length reached the king, who had grievously missed his loyal servant. The monarch ordered a boat to be made ready with four times seven rowers. Lustily they plied the oars up stream until the

Virata or the Eyes of the Dying Brother

vessel reached the site of Virata's hut. A carpet was spread for the king, who landed and approached the sage. For eighteen months, now, Virata had not listened to human speech. He greeted his guest timidly and with diffident mien, forgot the obeisance due from a subject to a ruler, and said simply:

"A blessing on your coming, O King."

The king embraced him.

"For years I have marked your progress towards perfection, and I have come to look upon the rare miracle of righteousness, that I myself may learn how a righteous man lives."

Virata bowed.

"All my knowledge is but this, that I have unlearned how to live with men, in order that I may remain free from all sin. The solitary can teach none but himself. I do not know if what I am doing is wisdom; I do not know if what I am feeling is happiness. I have no counsel to give and nothing to teach. The wisdom of the solitary is different from the wisdom of the world; the law of contemplation is another law than the law of action."

"But merely to see how a righteous man lives is to learn something," answered the king. "Since I have looked upon your face, I am filled with innocent joy. I ask nothing more."

"Can I fulfil any wish of yours in my kingdom, or carry any tidings to your own folk?"

"Nothing is mine any more, Lord King—or everything on this earth is mine. I have forgotten that I ever had a house among other houses, or children among other children. He who is homeless has the world for home; he who has cut loose from the ties of life has all life for his portion; he who is innocent has peace. My only wish is that my life on earth may be free from sin."

"Farewell, then, and think of me in your devotions."

"I think of God, and thus I think of you and of all on this earth, who are part of him and who breathe with his breath."

The king's boat passed away down the stream, and many months were to go by before the recluse was again to hear the voice of man.

Once more Virata's fame took wings unto itself and flew like a white falcon over the land. To the remotest villages and to the huts by the seashore came the news of the sage who had left house and lands that he might live the life of devout contemplation, and it was now that he was given the fourth name of virtue, becoming known as the Star of Solitude. In the temples, the priests extolled his renunciation; the king spoke of it to his servants; and when any judge uttered his decision, he added, "May my words be as just as those of Virata, who now lives wholly for God and knows all wisdom."

It often happened, and more frequently as the years sped by, that a man who came to realize the unrighteousness of his actions and to feel the vanity of his life, would leave house and home, give away his possessions, and wander off into the jungle, to build a hut like Virata and devote himself to God's service. Example is the strongest bond on earth; every deed arouses in others the will to righteousness, the will that now wakens from dreams and turns to vigorous action. Those who were thus wakened grew aware of the futility of their lives. They saw the blood that stained their hands and the sin that flecked their souls. They rose up and went forth to solitude, satisfied with enough for the barest needs of the body, plunged in perpetual meditation. If they chanced to encounter one another on their walks abroad to gather fruit, they uttered no word of greeting lest they should form new bonds thereby, but they smiled cordially at one another, and their souls exchanged greetings of peace. The common folk spoke of this forest as the Abode of the Pious. No hunter ranged its paths, fearing to defile the sanctuary by slaughter.

One morning, when Virata was walking in the jungle, he found an anchorite stretched motionless on the ground. Stooping to lift the fallen man, he perceived that the body was lifeless. Virata closed the eyes of the dead, murmured a prayer, and endeavoured to carry the corpse out of the thicket, intending to build a funeral pyre that the body of this brother might pass duly purified into the transmigration. But his meagre diet of fruits had weakened him, and the burden was beyond his strength. In search of help, he crossed the river by the ford, and made his way to the nearest village.

When the villagers saw the sublime figure of him they had named the Star of Solitude, they came in all humility desiring to know his will, and, on being informed, they hastened to make ready for the task. Whithersoever Virata went, the women prostrated themselves before him. The children remained standing, and regarded his silent progress with astonishment. The men came out of their houses to kiss the raiment of their august visitor and to

Jewish Legends

invoke the blessing of the saint. Virata passed through this gentle wave of humanity with a smile of contentment, feeling how pure and ardent was his love for his fellows now that he was no longer bound to them by any tie.

But when he reached the last of the humble cottages, having everywhere cordially returned the kindly salutations of those who accosted him, he saw that in this hut a woman was seated, and that her eyes as she looked at him were full of hatred. He shrank back in horror, for it seemed to him that he had again encountered the eyes which for so long he had forgotten, the rigid, accusing eyes of his slain brother. During these years of solitude, his spirit had grown unused to enmity, and he tried to persuade himself that he had mistaken the meaning of the stare. But when he looked again, the eyes were still gazing forth upon him with the same fixed malevolence. When, having recovered his self-command, he stepped forward towards the cottage, the woman withdrew into the passage, but from its dark recesses her eyes continued to glare at him with the ferocity of the burning eyes of a tiger in the jungle.

Virata plucked up heart, saying to himself:

"How can I have injured this woman whom I have never seen? Why should her hatred stir against me? There must be some mistake, and I will search out the error."

Moving forward, he knocked at the door. There was no sound in answer to his knock, and yet he could feel the malevolent proximity of the stranger woman. Patiently he knocked once more, waited awhile, and knocked again

Virata or the Eyes of the Dying Brother

like a beggar. At length, with hesitating step, the woman came to the door, and her face as she looked at him was still dark and hostile.

"What more do you want of me?" she fiercely inquired.

He saw that she had to grip the door posts to steady herself, so shaken was she by anger.

Nevertheless, when Virata glanced at her face his heart grew light, for he was sure that he had never seen her before. She was young, and he was far on the road through life; their paths had never crossed, and he could never have done her an injury.

"I wished to give you the greeting of peace, stranger woman," answered Virata; "and I wished to ask you why you look at me so fiercely. Am I your enemy? Have I done you any harm?"

"What harm have you done me?" She smiled maliciously. "What harm have you done me? A trifle only, a mere trifle. My house was full, and you have made it empty; you have robbed me of my beloved; you have changed my life to death. Go, that I may see you no more, or I shall be unable to contain my wrath."

Virata looked at her again. So frenzied were her eyes that it seemed to him she must be beside herself. He turned to depart, saying only:

"I am not the person you suppose. I live far from the haunts of men, and have no part in anyone's destiny. You mistake me for another."

But she screamed after him in her hatred:

"Full well do I know you, as all know you! You are Virata, whom they call the Star of Solitude, whom they extol with the four names of virtue. But I will not extol you. My mouth will cry aloud against you until my plaint reaches the last judge of the living. Come, since you have asked me; come and see what you have done."

Grasping the sleeve of the amazed Virata, she dragged him into the house and opened the door leading into a dark low-ceilinged chamber. She drew him towards the corner where a motionless form was lying upon a mat. Virata stooped over the form, and then drew back shuddering, for a boy lay there dead, a boy whose eyes stared up at him like the accusing eyes of the undying brother. Close beside him stood the woman racked with pain, and she moaned:

"He was the third, the last fruit of my womb; and you have murdered him as well as the others, you whom they call saint, and servant of the gods."

When Virata wished to open his mouth in protest, she broke out once more:

"Look at this loom, look at the empty stool. Here sat Paratika, my husband, day after day, weaving white linen, for there was no more skilful weaver in the land. People came from afar to give him orders, and his work was our life. Our days were joyful for Paratika was a kindly man, and ever industrious. He shunned bad company and kept away from the loafers in the street. By him I bore three children, and we reared them in the hope that they would become men like their father, kindly and upright. Then came a hunter—would to God he had never set foot in the village—from whom Paratika learned of one who had left house and possessions to devote himself, while still leading this earthly life, wholly to the service of God. With his own hands, said the hunter, he had built himself a hut. Paratika grew more and more reserved. He meditated much in the evenings, and rarely spoke. One night I awakened to find that he had left my side and had gone to the forest in which you dwell that you may meditate on God, the forest men call the Abode of the Pious. But while he thus thought of himself, he forgot us, and forgot that we lived by his labour. Poverty visited us; the children lacked bread; one died after another; today the last of the three has died, and through your act. You led Paratika astray. That you might come nearer to the true essence of God, the three children of my body have gone down to dust. How will you atone, O Arrogant One, when I charge you before the judge of the quick and the dead with the pangs their little bodies suffered, while you were feeding the birds and were living far from all suffering? How will you atone for having lured an honest man from the work which fed him and his innocent boys, for having deluded him with the mad thought that in solitude he would be nearer to God than in active life among his fellows?"

Virata blenched, and his lips quivered.

"I did not know that my example would be an incitement to others. The course I took, I meant to take alone."

"Where is your wisdom, O Sage, if you do not know what every boy knows, that all acts are the acts of God, and that no one can by his own will escape from action or evade responsibility? Your mind was swelled with pride when you fancied that you could be lord of your own actions and could teach others. What was sweet to you has become gall to me, and your life has occasioned the death of this child."

Virata reflected for a while, and then bowed his head in assent.

"What you say is true, and I see that there is more knowledge of the truth in a single throb of pain than in all the aloofness of the sages. What I know I have learned from the unfortunate; and what I have seen has been made visible to me by the glance of those who suffer, by the eyes of the undying brother. Indeed, I have not been humble before God, as I fancied, but proud; this is borne in on me by the sorrow I now feel. It is true that he who remains inactive none the less does a deed for which he is responsible on earth; and even the solitary lives in all his brethren. Again, I beseech you to forgive me. I shall return from the forest, in the hope that Paratika will likewise return to implant new life in your womb."

He bent forward once more and touched the hem of her garment with his lips. All sense of anger faded from her mind as, bewildered, she followed with her eyes the retreating figure.

Virata spent one more night in his hut. Once again he looked at the stars, watching at sunset the appearance of their white flames in the depths of heaven, and watching them pale at dawn. Once more he summoned his birds to their feast, and caressed them. Then, taking the staff and the bowl he had brought with him years before, he made his way back to the town.

Hardly had the tidings spread that the holy man had left his lonely hermitage and was once more within the gates of the city, when the people flocked to see the rare and wondrous spectacle, although many were filled with

Virata or the Eyes of the Dying Brother

a secret dread lest the return of this man from the divine presence might bode disaster. As if between living walls of veneration, Virata made his progress, and he endeavoured to greet the onlookers with the serene smile that usually graced his lips. But for the first time he found it impossible to smile; his eyes remained grave and his lips were closed.

At length he reached the palace. The hour of the council was over, and the king was alone. Virata entered, and the monarch stood up to embrace his visitor. But Virata prostrated himself to the earth, and touched the hem of the king's mantle in token of petition.

"Your request is granted," said the king, "before you form it in words on your lips. It is an honour to me that I am empowered to serve a pious man and to help a sage."

"Call me not a sage," answered Virata, "for I have not followed the right path. I have been wandering in a circle, and now stand as a petitioner before your throne. I wished to be free from sin, and I shunned all action; but none the less I was entangled in the net which the gods spread for mortals."

"Far be it from me to believe your words," replied the king. "How could you do wrong to the human beings whose presence you shunned; and how did you fall into sin when your life was devoted to God's service?

"Not wittingly did I do wrong, for I fled from sin; but our feet are chained to earth, and our deeds are in bondage to the eternal laws. Inaction is itself an action. I could not elude the eyes of the undying brother on whom our actions for ever bear, be they good or be they evil, and in defiance of our own will. But I am seven times guilty, for

Jewish Legends

I fled from God and refused to serve life; I was useless, for I nourished my own life merely, and did no service to any other. Now I wish to serve again."

"Your words are strange to me, Virata, and beyond my understanding. But tell me your wish that I may fulfil it."

"No longer do I desire to be free in my will. The free man is not free, and he who is inactive does not escape sin. Only he who serves is free, he who gives his will to another, who devotes his energies to a work, and who acts without questioning. Only the middle of the deed is our work; its beginning and its end, its cause and its effect, are on the knees of the gods. Make me free from my own will, for all willing is confusion, and all service is wisdom."

"I cannot understand you. You ask me to make you free, and at one and at the same time you ask me to give you service. Then he only is free who enters the service of another, whereas that other who takes the first into his service is not free? This passes my comprehension."

"It is just as well, O King, that you cannot understand this in your heart. How could you remain a king and issue commands if you understood?"

The king's face darkened with anger.

"Is it your meaning that the ruler is a lesser thing in the sight of God than the servant?"

"No one is less than another in the sight of God, and no one is greater. He who serves, and unquestioningly surrenders his own will, has relieved himself of responsibility, and has given it back to God. But he who wills, and who fancies that wisdom can enable him to avoid what is hostile, falls into temptation and falls into sin."

Virata or the Eyes of the Dying Brother

The king's countenance was still darkened.

"Then one service is the same as another, and there is neither greater service nor lesser service in the eyes of God and man?"

"It may well happen that one service seems greater than another in the eyes of man, but all service is equal in the eyes of God."

The king gazed at Virata long and sombrely. Pride stirred fiercely in his soul. When he looked once more at the worn face, and the white hair surmounting the wrinkled forehead, it seemed to him that the old man must be in his dotage. To test the matter, he said mockingly:

"Would you like to be keeper of the hounds in my palace?"

Virata bowed, and kissed the step of the throne in sign of gratitude.

From that day forward the old man whom the country had once extolled with the four names of virtue was keeper of the hounds in the kennels adjoining the palace, and he dwelt with the servitors in the menial quarters. His sons were ashamed of him. They made a wide circuit when they had to pass his abode, for they wished to avoid the sight of him and would fain escape having to acknowledge kinship in the presence of others. The priests turned their backs upon him as unworthy. For a few days the common people would stand and stare when the old man who had once been the first of the king's subjects came by habited as a servant and leading the hounds in leash. But he paid no heed to these

Jewish Legends

onlookers, so they soon went their ways and ceased to think of him.

Virata did faithful service from dawn to sunset. He washed the hounds' muzzles and cleansed their coats; he brought their food and made up their litter; he cleared away their droppings. Soon the beasts came to love him more than any other inmate of the palace, and this did his heart good. His old and shrivelled mouth, with which he rarely spoke, smiled as of yore at his charges' pleasure. He took delight in the passing of the years, which were many and uneventful. The king died. A new king came who knew not Virata, and who struck him once with a stick because one of the hounds growled when his majesty went by. A day came when he was forgotten of all his fellow-men.

When the tale of his years was told, when at length he died, and his body was consigned to the common burial ground of the slaves, there was no one among the folk to remember him who had once been famous throughout the land where he had been known by the four names of virtue. His sons kept out of sight, and no priest sang the song of death over his remains. The dogs, indeed, howled for two days and two nights; but then they, too, forgot Virata, whose name is not inscribed in the chronicles of the conquerors and is not to be found in the books of the sages.

Buchmendel

Having just got back to Vienna, after a visit to an out-of-the-way part of the country, I was walking home from the station when a heavy shower came on, such a deluge that the passers-by hastened to take shelter in doorways, and I myself felt it expedient to get out of the downpour. Luckily there is a café at almost every street-corner in the metropolis, and I made for the nearest, though not before my hat was dripping wet and my shoulders were drenched to the skin. An old-fashioned suburban place, lacking the attractions (copied from Germany) of music and a dancing-floor to be found in the centre of the town; full of small shopkeepers and working folk who consumed more newspapers than coffee and rolls. Since it was already late in the evening, the air, which would have been stuffy anyhow, was thick with tobacco-smoke. Still, the place was clean and brightly decorated, had new satin-covered couches, and a shining cash-register, so that it looked thoroughly attractive. In my haste to get out of the rain, I had not troubled to read its name—but what matter? There I rested, warm and comfortable, though looking rather impatiently through the blue-tinted window panes to see when the shower would be over, and I should be able to get on my way.

Thus I sat unoccupied, and began to succumb to that inertia which results from the narcotic atmosphere of the typical Viennese café. Out of this void, I scanned various individuals whose eyes, in the murky room, had a greyish look in the artificial light; I mechanically contemplated the young woman at the counter as, like an automaton, she dealt out sugar and a teaspoon to the waiter for each cup of coffee; with half an eye and a wandering attention I read the uninteresting advertisements on the walls—and there was something agreeable about these dull occupations. But suddenly, and in a peculiar fashion, I was aroused from what had become almost a doze. A vague internal movement had begun; much as a toothache sometimes begins, without one's being able to say whether it is on the right side or the left, in the upper jaw or the lower. All I became aware of was a numb tension, an obscure sentiment of spiritual unrest. Then, without knowing why, I grew fully conscious. I must have been in this café once before, years ago, and random associations had awakened memories of the walls, the tables, the chairs, the seemingly unfamiliar smoke-laden room.

The more I endeavoured to grasp this lost memory, the more obstinately did it elude me; a sort of jellyfish glistening in the abysses of consciousness, slippery and unseizable. Vainly did I scrutinize every object within the range of vision. Certainly when I had been here before the counter had had neither marble top nor cash-register; the walls had not been panelled with imitation rosewood;

these must be recent acquisitions. Yet I had indubitably been here, more than twenty years back. Within these four walls, as firmly fixed as a nail driven up to the head in a tree, there clung a part of my ego, long since overgrown. Vainly I explored, not only the room, but my own inner man, to grapple the lost links. Curse it all, I could not plumb the depths!

It will be seen that I was becoming vexed, as one is always out of humour when one's grip slips in this way, and reveals the inadequacy, the imperfections, of one's spiritual powers. Yet I still hoped to recover the clue. A slender thread would suffice, for my memory is of a peculiar type, both good and bad; on the one hand stubbornly untrustworthy, and on the other incredibly dependable. It swallows the most important details, whether in concrete happenings or in faces, and no voluntary exertion will induce it to regurgitate them from the gulf. Yet the most trifling indication—a picture postcard, the address on an envelope, a newspaper cutting—will suffice to hook up what is wanted as an angler who has made a strike and successfully imbedded his hook reels in a lively, struggling, and reluctant fish. Then I can recall the features of a man seen once only, the shape of his mouth and the gap to the left where he had an upper eye-tooth knocked out, the falsetto tone of his laugh, and the twitching of the moustache when he chooses to be merry, the entire change of expression which hilarity effects in him. Not only do these physical traits rise before my mind's eye, but I remember, years afterwards, every word the man said to me, and the tenor of my replies. But if I am to see and feel the past thus

Jewish Legends

vividly, there must be some material link to start the current of associations. My memory will not work satisfactorily on the abstract plane.

I closed my eyes to think more strenuously, in the attempt to forge the hook which would catch my fish. In vain! In vain! There was no hook, or the fish would not bite. So fierce waxed my irritation with the inefficient and mulish thinking apparatus between my temples that I could have struck myself a violent blow on the forehead, much as an irascible man will shake and kick a penny-in-the-slot machine which, when he has inserted his coin, refuses to render him his due.

So exasperated did I become at my failure, that I could no longer sit quiet, but rose to prowl about the room. The instant I moved, the glow of awakening memory began. To the right of the cash-register, I recalled, there must be a doorway leading into a windowless room, where the only light was artificial. Yes, the place actually existed. The decorative scheme was different, but the proportions were unchanged. A square box of a place, behind the bar—the card-room. My nerves thrilled as I contemplated the furniture, for I was on the track, I had found the clue, and soon I should know all. There were two small billiard-tables, looking like silent ponds covered with green scum. In the corners, card-tables, at one of which two bearded men of professorial type were playing chess. Beside the iron stove, close to a door labelled "Telephone," was another small table. In a flash, I had it! That was Mendel's place, Jacob Mendel's. That was where Mendel used to hang out, Buchmendel. I was in the Café Gluck! How could I have forgotten Jacob

Mendel. Was it possible that I had not thought about him for ages, a man so peculiar as wellnigh to belong to the Land of Fable, the eighth wonder of the world, famous at the university and among a narrow circle of admirers, magician of book-fanciers, who had been wont to sit there from morning till night, an emblem of bookish lore, the glory of the Café Gluck? Why had I had so much difficulty in hooking my fish? How could I have forgotten Buchmendel?

I allowed my imagination to work. The man's face and form pictured themselves vividly before me. I saw him as he had been in the flesh, seated at the table with its grey marble top, on which books and manuscripts were piled. Motionless he sat, his spectacled eyes fixed upon the printed page. Yet not altogether motionless, for he had a habit (acquired at school in the Jewish quarter of the Galician town from which he came) of rocking his shiny bald pate backwards and forwards and humming to himself as he read. There he studied catalogues and tomes, crooning and rocking, as Jewish boys are taught to do when reading the Talmud. The rabbis believe that, just as a child is rocked to sleep in its cradle, so are the pious ideas of the holy text better instilled by this rhythmical and hypnotizing movement of head and body. In fact, as if he had been in a trance, Jacob Mendel saw and heard nothing while thus occupied. He was oblivious to the click of billiard-balls, the coming and going of waiters, the ringing of the telephone bell; he paid no heed when the floor was scrubbed and when the stove was refilled. Once a red-hot coal fell out of the latter, and the flooring began to blaze a few inches from Mendel's feet; the room was full of smoke, and one of the guests ran for a pail of water to extinguish the fire. But neither the smoke, the bustle, nor the stench diverted his attention from the volume before him. He read as others pray, as gamblers follow the spinning of the roulette board, as drunkards stare into vacancy; he read with such profound absorption that ever since I first watched him the reading of ordinary mortals has seemed a pastime. This Galician second-hand book dealer, Jacob Mendel, was the first to reveal to me in my youth the mystery of absolute concentration which characterizes the artist and the scholar, the sage and the imbecile; the first to make me acquainted with the tragical happiness and unhappiness of complete absorption.

A senior student introduced me to him. I was studying the life and doings of a man who is even today too little known, Mesmer the magnetizer. My researches were bearing scant fruit, for the books I could lay my hands on conveyed sparse information, and when I applied to the university librarian for help he told me, uncivilly, that it was not his business to hunt up references for a freshman. Then my college friend suggested taking me to Mendel.

"He knows everything about books, and will tell you where to find the information you want. The ablest man in Vienna, and an original to boot. The man is a saurian of the bookworld, an antediluvian survivor of an extinct species."

We went, therefore, to the Café Gluck, and found Buchmendel in his usual place, bespectacled, bearded, wearing a rusty black suit, and rocking as I have de-

Buchmendel

scribed. He did not notice our intrusion, but went on reading, looking like a nodding mandarin. On a hook behind him hung his ragged black overcoat, the pockets of which bulged with manuscripts, catalogues, and books. My friend coughed loudly, to attract his attention, but Mendel ignored the sign. At length Schmidt rapped on the table-top, as if knocking at a door, and at this Mendel glanced up, mechanically pushed his spectacles on to his forehead, and from beneath his thick and untidy ashen-grey brows there glared at us two dark, alert little eyes. My friend introduced me, and I explained my quandary, being careful (as Schmidt had advised) to express great annoyance at the librarian's unwillingness to assist me. Mendel leaned back, laughed scornfully, and answered with a strong Galician accent:

"Unwillingness, you think? Incompetence, that's what's the matter with him. He's a jackass. I've known him (for my sins) twenty years at least, and he's learned nothing in the whole of that time. Pocket their wages—that's all such fellows can do. They should be mending the road, instead of sitting over books."

This outburst served to break the ice, and with a friendly wave of the hand the bookworm invited me to sit down at his table. I reiterated my object in consulting him; to get a list of all the early works on animal magnetism, and of contemporary and subsequent books and pamphlets for and against Mesmer. When I had said my say, Mendel closed his left eye for an instant, as if excluding a grain of dust. This was, with him, a sign of concentrated attention. Then, as though reading from an invisible catalogue, he reeled out the names of two or three dozen titles, giving in each case place and date of publication and approximate price. I was amazed, though Schmidt had warned me what to expect. His vanity was tickled by my surprise, for he went on to strum the keyboard of his marvellous memory, and to produce the most astounding bibliographical marginal notes. Did I want to know about sleepwalkers, Perkins's metallic tractors, early experiments in hypnotism, Braid, Gassner, attempts to conjure up the devil, Christian Science, theosophy, Madame Blavatsky? In connexion with each item there was a hailstorm of book-names, dates, and appropriate details. I was beginning to understand that Jacob Mendel was a living lexicon, something like the general catalogue of the British Museum Reading Room, but able to walk about on two legs. I stared dumbfounded at this bibliographical phenomenon, which masqueraded in the sordid and rather unclean domino of a Galician second-hand book dealer, who, after rattling off some eighty titles (with assumed indifference, but really with the satisfaction of one who plays an unexpected trump), proceeded to wipe his spectacles with a handkerchief which might long before have been white.

Hoping to conceal my astonishment, I inquired:

"Which among these works do you think you could get for me without too much trouble?"

"Oh, I'll have a look round," he answered. "Come here tomorrow and I shall certainly have some of them. As for the others, it's only a question of time, and of knowing where to look."

"I'm greatly obliged to you," I said; and, then, wishing to be civil, I put my foot in it, proposing to give him a list of the books I wanted. Schmidt nudged me warningly, but too late. Mendel had already flashed a look at me—such a look, at once triumphant and affronted, scornful and overwhelmingly superior—the royal look with which Macbeth answers Macduff when summoned to yield without a blow. He laughed curtly. His Adam's apple moved excitedly. Obviously he had gulped down a choleric, an insulting epithet.

Indeed he had good reason to be angry. Only a stranger, an ignoramus, could have proposed to give him, Jacob Mendel, a memorandum, as if he had been a bookseller's assistant or an underling in a public library. Not until I knew him better did I fully understand how much my would-be politeness must have galled this aberrant genius—for the man had, and knew himself to have, a titanic memory, wherein, behind a dirty and undistinguished-looking forehead, was indelibly recorded a picture of the title-page of every book that had been printed. No matter whether it had issued from the press yesterday or hundreds of years ago, he knew its place of publication, its author's name, and its price. From his mind, as if from the printed page, he could read off the contents, could reproduce the illustrations; could visualize, not only what he had actually held in his hands, but also what he had glanced at in a bookseller's window; could see it with the same vividness as an artist sees the creations of fancy which he has not yet reproduced upon canvas. When a book was offered for six marks by a Regensburg dealer, he could remember that, two years before, a copy of the same work had changed hands for four crowns at a Viennese auction, and he recalled the name of the purchaser. In a word, Jacob Mendel never forgot a title or a figure; he knew every plant, every infusorian, every star, in the continually revolving and incessantly changing cosmos of the book-universe. In each literary specialty, he knew more than the specialists; he knew the contents of the libraries better than the librarians; he knew the book-lists of most publishers better than the heads of the firms concerned—though he had nothing to guide him except the magical powers of his inexplicable but invariably accurate memory.

True, this memory owed its infallibility to the man's limitations, to his extraordinary power of concentration. Apart from books, he knew nothing of the world. The phenomena of existence did not begin to become real for him until they had been set in type, arranged upon a composing stick, collected and, so to say, sterilized in a book. Nor did he read books for their meaning, to extract their spiritual or narrative substance. What aroused his passionate interest, what fixed his attention, was the name, the price, the format, the title-page. Though in the last analysis unproductive and uncreative, this specifically antiquarian memory of Jacob Mendel, since it was not a printed book-catalogue but was stamped upon the grey matter of a mammalian brain, was, in its unique perfection, no less remarkable a phenomenon than Napoleon's gift for physiognomy, Mezzofanti's talent for languages, Lasker's skill at chess-openings, Busoni's musical genius. Given a public position as teacher, this man with so marvellous a brain might have taught thousands and hundreds of thousands of students, have trained others to become men of great learning and of incalculable value to

Buchmendel

those communal treasure-houses we call libraries. But to him, a man of no account, a Galician Jew, a book-pedlar whose only training had been received in a Talmudic school, this upper world of culture was a fenced precinct he could never enter; and his amazing faculties could only find application at the marble-topped table in the inner room of the Café Gluck. When, some day, there arises a great psychologist who shall classify the types of that magical power we term memory as effectively as Buffon classified the genera and species of animals, a man competent to give a detailed description of all the varieties, he will have to find a pigeonhole for Jacob Mendel, forgotten master of the lore of book-prices and book-titles, the ambulatory catalogue alike of incunabula and the modern commonplace.

In the book-trade and among ordinary persons, Jacob Mendel was regarded as nothing more than a second-hand book dealer in a small way of business. Sunday after Sunday, his stereotyped advertisement appeared in the "Neue Freie Presse" and the "Neues Wiener Tagblatt." It ran as follows: "Best prices paid for old books, Mendel, Obere Alserstrasse." A telephone number followed, really that of the Café Gluck. He rummaged every available corner for his wares, and once a week, with the aid of a bearded porter, conveyed fresh booty to his headquarters and got rid of old stock—for he had no proper bookshop. Thus he remained a petty trader, and his business was not lucrative. Students sold him their textbooks, which year by year passed through his hands from one "generation" to another; and for a small percentage of the price he would procure any additional book that was wanted. He charged little or nothing for advice. Money seemed to have no standing in his world. No one had ever seen him better dressed than in the threadbare black coat. For breakfast and supper he had a glass of milk and a couple of rolls, while at midday a modest meal was brought him from a neighbouring restaurant. He did not smoke; he did not play cards; one might almost say he did not live, were it not that his eyes were alive behind his spectacles, and unceasingly fed his enigmatic brain with words, titles, names. The brain, like a fertile pasture, greedily sucked in this abundant irrigation. Human beings did not interest him, and of all human passions perhaps one only moved him, the most universal—vanity.

When someone, wearied by a futile hunt in countless other places, applied to him for information, and was instantly put on the track, his self-gratification was overwhelming; and it was unquestionably a delight to him that in Vienna and elsewhere there existed a few dozen persons who respected him for his knowledge and valued him for the services he could render. In every one of these monstrous aggregates we call towns, there are here and there facets which reflect one and the same universe in miniature—unseen by most, but highly prized by connoisseurs, by brethren of the same craft, by devotees of the same passion. The fans of the book-market knew Jacob Mendel. Just as anyone encountering a difficulty in deciphering a score would apply to Eusebius Mandyczewski of the Musical Society, who would be found wearing a grey skull-cap and seated among multifarious musical MSS., ready, with a friendly smile, to solve the most obstinate crux; and just as, today, anyone in search of information about the Viennese theatrical and cultural life of earlier times will unhesitatingly look up the polyhistor Father Glossy; so, with equal confidence did the bibliophiles of Vienna, when they had a particularly hard nut to crack, make a pilgrimage to the Café Gluck and lay their difficulty before Jacob Mendel.

To me, young and eager for new experiences, it became enthralling to watch such a consultation. Whereas ordinarily, when a would-be seller brought him some ordinary book, he would contemptuously clap the cover to and mutter, "Two crowns"; if shown a rare or unique volume, he would sit up and take notice, lay the treasure upon a clean sheet of paper; and, on one such occasion, he was obviously ashamed of his dirty, ink-stained fingers and mourning finger-nails. Tenderly, cautiously, respectfully, he would turn the pages of the treasure. One would have been as loath to disturb him at such a moment as to break in upon the devotions of a man at prayer; and in very truth there was a flavour of solemn ritual and religious observance about the way in which contemplation, palpation, smelling, and weighing in the hand followed one another in orderly succession. His rounded back waggled while he was thus engaged, he muttered to himself, exclaimed "Ah" now and again to express wonder or admiration, or "Oh, dear" when a page was missing or another had been mutilated by the larva of a book-beetle. His weighing of the tome in his hand was as circumspect as if books were sold by the ounce, and his snuffling at it as sentimental as a girl's smelling of a rose. Of course it would have been the

Jewish Legends

height of bad form for the owner to show impatience during this ritual of examination.

When it was over, he willingly, nay enthusiastically, tendered all the information at his disposal, not forgetting relevant anecdotes, and dramatized accounts of the prices which other specimens of the same work had fetched at auctions or in sales by private treaty. He looked brighter, younger, more lively at such times, and only one thing could put him seriously out of humour. This was when a novice offered him money for his expert opinion. Then he would draw back with an affronted air, looking for all the world like the skilled custodian of a museum gallery to whom an American traveller has offered a tip—for to Jacob Mendel contact with a rare book was something sacred, as is contact with a woman to a young man who has not had the bloom rubbed off. Such moments were his platonic love-nights. Books exerted a spell on him, never money. Vainly, therefore, did great collectors (among them one of the notables of Princeton University) try to recruit Mendel as librarian or book-buyer. The offer was declined with thanks. He could not forsake his familiar headquarters at the Café Gluck. Thirty-three years before, an awkward youngster with black down sprouting on his chin and black ringlets hanging over his temples, he had come from Galicia to Vienna, intending to adopt the calling of rabbi; but ere long he forsook the worship of the harsh and jealous Jehovah to devote himself to the more lively and polytheistic cult of books. Then he happened upon the Café Gluck, by degrees making it his workshop, headquarters, post-office—his world. Just as an astronomer, alone in an observatory, watches night after night through a telescope the myriads of stars, their mysterious movements, their changeful medley, their extinction and their flaming-up anew, so did Jacob Mendel, seated at his table in the Café Gluck, look through his spectacles into the universe of books, a universe that lies above the world of our everyday life, and, like the stellar universe, is full of changing cycles.

It need hardly be said that he was highly esteemed in the Café Gluck, whose fame seemed to us to depend far more upon his unofficial professorship than upon the godfathership of the famous musician, Christoph Willibald Gluck, composer of *Alcestis* and *Iphigenia*. He belonged to the outfit quite as much as did the old cherrywood counter, the two billiard-tables with their cloth stitched in many places, and the copper coffee-urn. His table was guarded as a sanctuary. His numerous clients and customers were expected to take a drink "for the good of the house," so that most of the profit of his farflung knowledge flowed into the big leathern pouch slung round the waist of Deubler, the waiter. In return for being a centre of attraction, Mendel enjoyed many privileges. The telephone was at his service for nothing. He could have his letters directed to the café, and his parcels were taken in there. The excellent old woman who looked after the toilet brushed his coat, sewed on buttons, and carried a small bundle of underlinen every week to the wash. He was the only guest who could have a meal sent in from the restaurant; and every morning Herr Standhartner, the proprietor of the café, made a point of coming to his table and saying "Good morn-

Jewish Legends

ing!"—though Jacob Mendel, immersed in his books, seldom noticed the greeting. Punctually at half-past seven he arrived, and did not leave till the lights were extinguished. He never spoke to the other guests, never read a newspaper, noticed no changes; and once, when Herr Standhartner civilly asked him whether he did not find the electric light more agreeable to read by than the malodorous and uncertain kerosene lamps they had replaced, he stared in astonishment at the new incandescents. Although the installation had necessitated several days' hammering and bustle, the introduction of the glow-lamps had escaped his notice. Only through the two round apertures of the spectacles, only through these two shining and sucking lenses, did the milliards of black infusorians which were the letters filter into his brain. Whatever else happened in his vicinity was disregarded as unmeaning noise. He had spent more than thirty years of his waking life at this table, reading, comparing, calculating, in a continuous waking dream, interrupted only by intervals of sleep.

A sense of horror overcame me when, looking into the inner room behind the bar of the Café Gluck, I saw that the marbletop of the table where Jacob Mendel used to deliver his oracles was now as bare as a tombstone. Grown older since those days, I understood how much disappears when such a man drops out of his place in the world, were it only because, amid the daily increase in hopeless monotony, the unique grows continually more precious. Besides, in my callow youth a profound intuition had made me exceedingly fond of Buchmendel. It was through the observation of him that I had first become aware of the enigmatic fact that supreme achievement and outstanding capacity are only rendered possible by mental concentration, by a sublime monomania that verges on lunacy. Through the living example of this obscure genius of a second-hand book dealer, far more than through the flashes of insight in the works of our poets and other imaginative writers, had been made plain to me the persistent possibility of a pure life of the spirit, of complete absorption in an idea, an ecstasy as absolute as that of an Indian yogi or a medieval monk; and I had learned that this was possible in an electric-lighted café and adjoining a telephone box. Yet I had forgotten him, during the war years, and through a kindred immersion in my own work. The sight of the empty table made me ashamed of myself, and at the same time curious about the man who used to sit there.

What had become of him? I called the waiter and inquired.

"No, Sir," he answered, "I'm sorry, but I never heard of Herr Mendel. There is no one of that name among the frequenters of the Café Gluck. Perhaps the head-waiter will know.""Herr Mendel?" said the head-waiter dubiously, after a moment's reflection. "No, Sir, never heard of him. Unless you mean Herr Mandl, who has a hardware store in the Florianigasse?"

I had a bitter taste in my mouth, the taste of an irrecoverable past. What is the use of living, when the wind obliterates our footsteps in the sand directly we have gone by? Thirty years, perhaps forty, a man had breathed, read, thought, and spoken within this narrow room; three or four years had elapsed, and there had

Jewish Legends

arisen a new king over Egypt, which knew not Joseph. No one in the Café Gluck had ever heard of Jacob Mendel, of Buchmendel. Somewhat pettishly I asked the head-waiter whether I could have a word with Herr Standhartner, or with one of the old staff.

"Herr Standhartner, who used to own the place? He sold it years ago, and has died since. . . . The former head-waiter? He saved up enough to retire, and lives upon a little property at Krems. No, Sir, all of the old lot are scattered. All except one, indeed, Frau Sporschil, who looks after the toilet. She's been here for ages, worked under the late owner, I know. But she's not likely to remember your Herr Mendel. Such as she hardly know one guest from another."

I dissented in thought.

"One does not forget a Jacob Mendel so easily!"

What I said was:

"Still, I should like to have a word with Frau Sporschil, if she has a moment to spare."

The "Toilettenfrau" (known in the Viennese vernacular as the "Schokoladenfrau") soon emerged from the basement, white-haired, run to seed, heavy-footed, wiping her chapped hands upon a towel as she came. She had been called away from her task of cleaning up, and was obviously uneasy at being summoned into the strong light of the guest-rooms—for common folk in Vienna, where an authoritative tradition has lingered on after the revolution, always think it must be a police matter when their "superiors" want to question them. She eyed me suspiciously, though humbly. But as soon as I asked her about Jacob Mendel, she braced up, and at the same time her eyes filled with tears.

"Poor Herr Mendel . . . so there's still someone who bears him in mind?"

Old people are commonly much moved by anything which recalls the days of their youth and revives the memory of past companionships. I asked if he was still alive.

"Good Lord, no. Poor Herr Mendel must have died five or six years ago. Indeed, I think it's fully seven since he passed away. Dear, good man that he was; and how long I knew him, more than twenty-five years; he was already sitting every day at his table when I began to work here. It was a shame, it was, the way they let him die."

Growing more and more excited, she asked if I was a relative. No one had ever inquired about him before. Didn't I know what had happened to him?

"No," I replied, "and I want you to be good enough to tell me all about it."

She looked at me timidly, and continued to wipe her damp hands. It was plain to me that she found it embarassing, with her dirty apron and her tousled white hair, to be standing in the full glare of the café. She kept looking round anxiously, to see if one of the waiters might be listening.

"Let's go into the card-room," I said, "Mendel's old room. You shall tell me your story there."

She nodded appreciatively, thankful that I understood, and led the way to the inner room, a little shambling in

Jewish Legends

her gait. As I followed, I noticed that the waiters and the guests were staring at us as a strangely assorted pair. We sat down opposite one another at the marble-topped table, and there she told me the story of Jacob Mendel's ruin and death. I will give the tale as nearly as may be in her own words, supplemented here and there by what I learned afterwards from other sources.

"Down to the outbreak of war, and after the war had begun, he continued to come here every morning at half-past seven, to sit at this table and study all day just as before. We had the feeling that the fact of a war going on had never entered his mind. Certainly he didn't read the newspapers, and didn't talk to anyone except about books. He paid no attention when (in the early days of the war, before the authorities put a stop to such things) the newspaper-venders ran through the streets shouting 'Great Battle on the Eastern Front' (or wherever it might be), 'Horrible Slaughter,' and so on; when people gathered in knots to talk things over, he kept himself to himself; he did not know that Fritz, the billiard-marker, who fell in one of the first battles, had vanished from this place; he did not know that Herr Standhartner's son had been taken prisoner by the Russians at Przemysl; never said a word when the bread grew more and more uneatable and when he was given bean-coffee to drink at breakfast and supper instead of hot milk. Once only did he express surprise at the changes, wondering why so few students came to the café. There was nothing in the world that mattered to him except his books.

"Then disaster befell him. At eleven one morning, two policemen came, one in uniform, and the other a

Buchmendel

plainclothes man. The latter showed the red rosette under the label of his coat and asked whether there was a man named Jacob Mendel in the house. They went straight to Herr Mendel's table. The poor man, in his innocence, supposed they had books to sell, or wanted information; but they told him he was under arrest, and took him away at once. It was a scandal for the café. All the guests flocked round Herr Mendel, as he stood between the two police officers, his spectacles pushed up under his hair, staring from each to the other bewildered. Some ventured a protest, saying there must be a mistake—that Herr Mendel was a man who wouldn't hurt a fly; but the detective was furious, and told them to mind their own business. They took him away, and none of us at the Café Gluck saw him again for two years. I never found out what they had against him, but I would take my dying oath that they must have made a mistake. Herr Mendel could never have done anything wrong. It was a crime to treat an innocent man so harshly."

The excellent Frau Sporschil was right. Our friend Jacob Mendel had done nothing wrong. He had merely (as I subsequently learned) done something incredibly stupid, only explicable to those who knew the man's peculiarities. The military censorship board, whose function it was to supervise correspondence passing into and out of neutral lands, one day got its clutches upon a postcard written and signed by a certain Jacob Mendel, properly stamped for transmission abroad. This postcard was addressed to Monsieur Jean Labourdaire, Libraire, Quai de Grenelle, Paris—to an enemy country, therefore. The writer complained that the last eight issues of

Jewish Legends

the monthly "Bulletin bibliographique de la France" had failed to reach him although his annual subscription had been duly paid in advance. The jack-in-office who read this missive (a high-school teacher with a bent for the study of the Romance languages, called up for "war-service" and sent to employ his talents at the censorship board instead of wasting them in the trenches) was astonished by its tenor. "Must be a joke," he thought. He had to examine some two thousand letters and postcards every week, always on the alert to detect anything that might savour of espionage, but never yet had he chanced upon anything so absurd as that an Austrian subject should unconcernedly drop into one of the imperial and royal letterboxes a postcard addressed to someone in an enemy land, regardless of the trifling detail that since August 1914 the Central Powers had been cut off from Russia on one side and from France on the other by barbed-wire entanglements and a network of ditches in which men armed with rifles and bayonets, machine-guns and artillery, were doing their utmost to exterminate one another like rats. Our schoolmaster enrolled in the Landsturm did not treat this first postcard seriously, but pigeon-holed it as a curiosity not worth talking about to his chief. But a few weeks later there turned up another card, again from Jacob Mendel, this time to John Aldridge, Bookseller, Gold Square, London, asking whether the addressee could send the last few numbers of the "Antiquarian" to an address in Vienna which was clearly stated on the card.

The censor in the blue uniform began to feel uneasy. Was his "class" trying to trick the schoolmaster? Were the cards written in cipher? Possible, anyhow; so the subordinate went over to the major's desk, clicked his heels together, saluted, and laid the suspicious documents before "properly constituted authority." A strange business, certainly. The police were instructed by telephone to see if there actually was a Jacob Mendel at the specified address, and, if so, to bring the fellow along. Within the hour, Mendel had been arrested, and (still stupefied by the shock,—brought before the major, who showed him the postcards, and asked him with drill-sergeant roughness whether he acknowledged their authorship. Angered at being spoken to so sharply, and still more annoyed because his perusal of an important catalogue had been interrupted, Mendel answered tartly:

"Of course I wrote the cards. That's my handwriting and signature. Surely one has a right to claim the delivery of a periodical to which one has subscribed?"

The major swung half-round in his swivel-chair and exchanged a meaning glance with the lieutenant seated at the adjoining desk.

"The man must be a double-distilled idiot" was what they mutely conveyed to one another.

Then the chief took counsel within himself whether he should discharge the offender with a caution, or whether he should treat the case more seriously. In all offices, when such doubts arise, the usual practice is, not to spin a coin, but to send in a report. Thus Pilate washes his hands of responsibility. Even if the report does no good, it can do no harm, and is merely one useless manuscript or typescript added to a million others.

In this instance, however, the decision to send in a

report did much harm, alas, to an inoffensive man of genius, for it involved asking a series of questions, and the third of them brought suspicious circumstances to light.

"Your full name?"

"Jacob Mendel."

"Occupation?"

"Book-pedlar"(for, as already explained, Mendel had no shop, but only a pedlar's license).

"Place of birth?"

Now came the disaster. Mendel's birthplace was not far from Petrikau. The major raised his eyebrows. Petrikau, or Piotrkov, was across the frontier, in Russian Poland.

"You were born a Russian subject. When did you acquire Austrian nationality? Show me your papers."

Mendel gazed at the officer uncomprehendingly through his spectacles.

"Papers? Identification papers? I have nothing but my hawker's license."

"What's your nationality then? Was your father Austrian or Russian?"

Undismayed, Mendel answered:

"A Russian, of course."

"What about yourself?"

"Wishing to evade Russian military service, I slipped across the frontier thirty-three years ago, and ever since I have lived in Vienna."

The matter seemed to the major to be growing worse and worse.

"But didn't you take steps to become an Austrian subject?"

"Why should I?" countered Mendel. "I never troubled my head about such things."

"Then you are still a Russian subject?"

Mendel, who was bored by this endless questioning, answered simply:

"Yes, I suppose I am."

The startled and indignant major threw himself back in his chair with such violence that the wood cracked protestingly. So this was what it had come to! In Vienna, the Austrian capital, at the end of 1915, after Tarnow, when the war was in full blast, after the great offensive, a Russian could walk about unmolested, could write letters to France and England, while the police ignored his machinations. And then the fools who wrote in the newspapers wondered why Conrad von Hötzendorf had not advanced in seven-leagued boots to Warsaw, and the general staff was puzzled because every movement of the troops was immediately blabbed to the Russians.

The lieutenant had sprung to his feet and crossed the room to his chief's table. What had been an almost friendly conversation took a new turn, and degenerated into a trial.

"Why didn't you report as an enemy alien directly the war began?"

Mendel, still failing to realize the gravity of his position, answered in his singing Jewish jargon:

"Why should I report? I don't understand."

The major regarded this inquiry as a challenge, and asked threateningly:

"Didn't you read the notices that were posted up everywhere?"

"No."

"Didn't you read the newspapers?"

"No."

The two officers stared at Jacob Mendel (now sweating with uneasiness) as if the moon had fallen from the sky into their office. Then the telephone buzzed, the typewriters clacked, orderlies ran hither and thither, and Mendel was sent under guard to the nearest barracks, where he was to await transfer to a concentration camp. When he was ordered to follow the two soldiers, he was frankly puzzled, but not seriously perturbed. What could the man with the gold-lace collar and the rough voice have against him? In the upper world of books, where Mendel lived and breathed and had his being, there was no warfare, there were no misunderstandings, only an ever-increasing knowledge of words and figures, of book-titles and authors' names. He walked good-humouredly enough downstairs between the soldiers, whose first charge was to take him to the police station. Not until, there, the books were taken out of his overcoat pockets, and the police impounded the portfolio containing a hundred important memoranda and customers' addresses, did he lose his temper, and begin to resist and strike blows. They had to tie his hands. In the struggle, his spectacles fell off, and these magical telescopes, without which he could not see into the wonderworld of books, were smashed into a thousand pieces. Two days later, insufficiently clad (for his only wrap was a light summer cloak), he was sent to the internment camp for Russian civilians at Komorn.

I have no information as to what Jacob Mendel suffered

during these two years of internment, cut off from his beloved books, penniless, among roughly nurtured men, few of whom could read or write, in a huge human dunghill. This must be left to the imagination of those who can grasp the torments of a caged eagle. By degrees, however, our world, grown sober after its fit of drunkenness, has become aware that, of all the cruelties and wanton abuses of power during the war, the most needless and therefore the most inexcusable was this herding together behind barbed-wire fences of thousands upon thousands of persons who had outgrown the age of military service, who had made homes for themselves in a foreign land, and who (believing in the good faith of their hosts) had refrained from exercising the sacred right of hospitality granted even by the Tunguses and Araucanians—the right to flee while time permits. This crime against civilization was committed with the same unthinking hardihood in France, Germany, and Britain, in every belligerent country of our crazy Europe.

Probably Jacob Mendel would, like thousands as innocent as he, have perished in this cattle-pen, have gone stark mad, have succumbed to dysentery, asthenia, softening of the brain, had it not been that, before the worst happened, a chance (typically Austrian) recalled him to the world in which a spiritual life became again possible. Several times after his disappearance, letters from distinguished customers were delivered for him at the Café Gluck. Count Schönberg, sometime lord-lieutenant of Styria, an enthusiastic collector of works on heraldry; Siegenfeld, the former dean of the theological faculty, who was writing a commentary on the works of St.

Jewish Legends

Augustine; Edler von Pisek, an octogenarian admiral on the retired list, engaged in writing his memoirs—these and other persons of note, wanting information from Buchmendel, had repeatedly addressed communications to him at his familiar haunt, and some of these were duly forwarded to the concentration camp at Komorn. There they fell into the hands of the commanding officer, who happened to be a man of humane disposition, and was astonished to find what notables were among the correspondents of this dirty little Russian Jew, who, half-blind now that his spectacles were broken and he had no money to buy new ones, crouched in a corner like a mole, grey, eyeless, and dumb. A man who had such patrons must be a person of importance, whatever he looked like. The C.O. therefore read the letters to the short-sighted Mendel, and penned answers for him to sign—answers which were mainly requests that influence should be exercised on his behalf. The spell worked, for these correspondents had the solidarity of collectors. Joining forces and pulling strings they were able (giving guarantees for the "enemy alien's" good behaviour) to secure leave for Buchmendel's return to Vienna in 1917, after more than two years at Komorn—on the condition that he should report daily to the police. The proviso mattered little. He was a free man once more, free to take up his quarters in his old attic, free to handle books again, free (above all) to return to his table in the Café Gluck. I can describe the return from the underworld of the camp in the good Frau Sporschil's own words:

"One day—Jesus, Mary, Joseph; I could hardly believe my eyes—the door opened (you remember the way he had) little wider than a crack, and through this opening he sidled, poor Herr Mendel. He was wearing a tattered and much-darned military cloak, and his head was covered by what had perhaps once been a hat thrown away by the owner as past use. No collar. His face looked like a death's head, so haggard it was, and his hair was pitifully thin. But he came in as if nothing had happened, went straight to his table, and took off his cloak, not briskly as of old, for he panted with the exertion. Nor had he any books with him. He just sat there without a word, staring straight in front of him with hollow, expressionless eyes. Only by degrees, after we had brought him the big bundle of printed matter which had arrived for him from Germany, did he begin to read again. But he was never the same man."

No, he was never the same man, not now the miraculum mundi, the magical walking book-catalogue. All who saw him in those days told me the same pitiful story. Something had gone irrecoverably wrong; he was broken; the blood-red comet of the war had burst into the remote, calm atmosphere of his bookish world. His eyes, accustomed for decades to look at nothing but print, must have seen terrible sights in the wire-fenced human stockyard, for the eyes that had formerly been so alert and full of ironical gleams were now almost completely veiled by the inert lids, and looked sleepy and red-bordered behind the carefully repaired spectacle-frames. Worse still, a cog must have broken somewhere in the marvellous machinery of his memory, so that the working of the whole was impaired; for so delicate is the structure of the brain (a sort of switchboard made of the most fragile substances, and as easily jarred as are all instruments of precision) that a blocked arteriole, a congested bundle of nerve-fibres, a fatigued group of cells, even a displaced molecule, may put the apparatus out of gear and make harmonious working impossible. In Mendel's memory, the keyboard of knowledge, the keys were stiff, or—to use psychological terminology—the associations were impaired. When, now and again, someone came to ask for information, Jacob stared blankly at the inquirer, failing to understand the question, and even forgetting it before he had found the answer. Mendel was no longer Buchmendel, just as the world was no longer the world. He could not now become wholly absorbed in his reading, did not rock as of old when he read, but sat bolt upright, his glasses turned mechanically towards the printed page, but perhaps not reading at all, and only sunk in a reverie. Often, said Frau Sporschil, his head would drop on to his book and he would fall asleep in the daytime, or he would gaze hour after hour at the stinking acetylene lamp which (in the days of the coal famine) had replaced the electric lighting. No, Mendel was no longer Buchmendel, no longer the eighth wonder of the world, but a weary, worn-out, though still breathing, useless bundle of beard and ragged garments, which sat, as futile as a potato-bogle, where of old the Pythian oracle had sat; no longer the glory of the Café Gluck, but a shameful scarecrow, evil-smelling, a parasite.

That was the impression he produced upon the new proprietor, Florian Gurtner from Retz, who (a successful profiteer in flour and butter) had cajoled Standhartner into selling him the Café Gluck for eighty thousand rapidly depreciating paper crowns. He took everything into his hard peasant grip, hastily arranged to have the old place redecorated, bought fine-looking satin-covered seats, installed a marble porch, and was in negotiation with his next-door neighbour to buy a place where he could extend the café into a dancing-hall. Naturally while he was making these embellishments, he was not best pleased by the parasitic encumbrance of Jacob Mendel, a filthy old Galician Jew, who had been in trouble with the authorities during the war, was still to be regarded as an "enemy alien," and, while occupying a table from morning till night, consumed no more than two cups of coffee and four or five rolls. Standhartbner, indeed, had put in a word for this guest of long standing, had explained that Mendel was a person of note, and, in the stock-taking, had handed him over as having a permanent lien upon the establishment, but as an asset rather than a liability. Florian Gurtner, however, had brought into the café, not only new furniture, and an up-to-date cash register, but also the profit-making and hard temper of the post-war era, and awaited the first pretext for ejecting from his smart coffee-house the last troublesome vestige of suburban shabbiness.

A good excuse was not slow to present itself. Jacob Mendel was impoverished to the last degree. Such banknotes as had been left to him had crumbled away to nothing during the inflation period; his regular clientele had been killed, ruined, or dispersed. When he tried to resume his early trade of book-pedlar, calling from door to door to buy and to sell, he found that he lacked strength to carry books up and down stairs. A hundred little signs showed him to be a pauper. Seldom, now, did he have a midday meal sent in from the restaurant, and he began to run up a score at the Café Gluck for his modest breakfast and supper. Once his payments were as much as three weeks overdue. Were it only for this reason, the headwaiter wanted Gurtner to "give Mendel the sack." But Frau Sporschil intervened, and stood surety for the debtor. What was due could be stopped out of her wages!

This staved off disaster for a while, but worse was to come. For some time the head-waiter had noticed that rolls were disappearing faster than the tally would account for. Naturally suspicion fell upon Mendel, who was known to be six months in debt to the tottering old porter whose services he still needed. The head-waiter, hidden behind the stove, was able, two days later, to catch Mendel red-handed. The unwelcome guest had stolen from his seat in the card-room, crept behind the counter in the front room, taken two rolls from the bread-basket, returned to the card-room, and hungrily devoured them. When settling-up at the end of the day, he said he had only had coffee; no rolls. The source of wastage had been traced, and the waiter reported his discovery to the proprietor. Herr Gurtner, delighted to have so good an excuse for getting rid of Mendel, made a scene, openly accused him of theft, and declared that nothing but the goodness of his own heart prevented his sending for the police.

"But after this," said Florian, "you'll kindly take yourself off for good and all. We don't want to see your face again at the Café Gluck."

Jacob Mendel trembled, but made no reply. Abandoning his poor belongings, he departed without a word.

"It was ghastly," said Frau Sporschil. "Never shall I forget the sight. He stood up, his spectacles pushed on to his forehead, and his face white as a sheet. He did not even stop to put on his cloak, although it was January, and very cold. You'll remember that severe winter, just after the war. In his fright, he left the book he was reading open upon the table. I did not notice it at first, and then, when I wanted to pick it up and take it after him, he had already stumbled out through the doorway. I was afraid to follow him into the street, for Herr Gurtner was standing at the door and shouting at him, so that a crowd had gathered. Yet I felt ashamed to the depths of my soul. Such a thing would never have happened under the old master. Herr Standhartner would not have driven Herr Mendel away for pinching one or two rolls when he was hungry, but would have let him have as many as he wanted for nothing, to the end of his days. Since the war, people seem to have grown heartless. Drive away a man who had been a guest daily for so many, many years. Shameful! I should not like to have to answer before God for such cruelty!"

The good woman had grown excited, and, with the passionate garrulousness of old age, she kept on repeating how shameful it was, and that nothing of the sort would have happened if Herr Standhartner had not sold the business. In the end I tried to stop the flow by asking her what had happened to Mendel, and whether she had ever seen him again. These questions excited her yet more.

"Day after day, when I passed his table, it gave me the creeps, as you will easily understand. Each time I thought to myself: 'Where can he have got to, poor Herr Mendel?' Had I known where he lived, I would have called and taken him something nice and hot to eat—for where could he get the money to cook food and warm his room? As far as I knew, he had no kinsfolk in the wide world. When, after a long time, I had heard nothing about him, I began to believe that it must be all up with him, and that I should never see him again. I had made up my mind to have a mass said for the peace of his soul, knowing him to be a good man, after twenty-five years' acquaintance.

"At length one day in February, at half-past seven in the morning, when I was cleaning the windows, the door opened, and in came Herr Mendel. Generally, as you know, he sidled in, looking confused, and not 'quite all there'; but this time, somehow, it was different. I noticed at once the strange look in his eyes; they were sparkling, and he rolled them this way and that, as if to see everything at once; as for his appearance, he seemed nothing but beard and skin and bone. Instantly it crossed my mind: 'He's forgotten all that happened last time he was here; it's his way to go about like a sleepwalker noticing nothing; he doesn't remember about the rolls, and how shamefully Herr Gurtner ordered him out of the place, half in mind to set the police on him.' Thank goodness, Herr Gurtner hadn't come yet, and the head-waiter was drinking coffee. I ran up to Herr Mendel, meaning to tell him he'd better make himself scarce, for otherwise that ruffian" [she looked round timidly to see if we were overheard, and hastily amended her phrase], "Herr Gurtner, I mean, would only have him thrown into the street once more. 'Herr Mendel,' I began. He started, and looked at me. In that very moment (it was dreadful), he must have remembered the whole thing, for he almost collapsed, and began to tremble, not his fingers only, but to shiver and shake from head to foot. Hastily he stepped back into the street, and fell in a heap on the pavement as soon as he was outside the door. We telephoned for the ambulance, and they carried him off to hospital, the nurse who came saying he had high fever directly she touched him. He died that evening. 'Double pneumonia,' the doctor said, and that he never recovered consciousness—could not have been fully conscious when he came to the Café Gluck. As I said, he had entered like a man walking in his sleep. The table where he had sat day after day for thirty-six years drew him back to it like a home."

Frau Sporschil and I went on talking about him for a long time, the two last persons to remember this strange creature, Buchmendel: I to whom in youth the book-pedlar from Galicia had given the first revelation of a life wholly devoted to the things of the spirit; she, the poor old woman who was caretaker of a café-toilet, who had never read a book in her life, and whose only tie with this strangely matched comrade in her subordinate, poverty-stricken world had been that for twenty-five years she had brushed his overcoat and had sewn on buttons for him. We, too, might have been considered strangely assorted, but Frau Sporschil and I got on very well together, linked, as we sat on the forsaken marble-topped

Jewish Legends

table, by our common memories of the shade our talk had conjured up—for joint memories, and above all loving memories, always establish a tie. Suddenly, while in the full stream of talk, she exclaimed:

"Lord Jesus, how forgetful I am. I still have the book he left on the table the evening Herr Gurtner gave him the key of the street. I didn't know where to take it. Afterwards, when no one appeared to claim it, I ventured to keep it as a souvenir. You don't think it wrong of me, Sir?"

She went to a locker where she stored some of the requisites for her job, and produced the volume for my inspection. I found it hard to repress a smile, for I was face to face with one of life's little ironies. It was the second volume of Hayn's *Bibliotheca Germanorum erotica et curiosa*, a compendium of gallant literature known to every book-collector. "Habent sua fata libelli!" This scabrous publication, as legacy of the vanished magician, had fallen into toilworn hands which had perhaps never held any other printed work than a prayer-book. Maybe I was not wholly successful in controlling my mirth, for the expression of my face seemed to perplex the worthy soul, and once more she said:

"You don't think it wrong of me to keep it, Sir?"

I shook her cordially by the hand.

"Keep it, and welcome," I said. "I am absolutely sure that our old friend Mendel would be only too delighted to know that someone among the many thousands he has provided with books, cherishes his memory."

Then I took my departure, feeling a trifle ashamed when I compared myself with this excellent old woman, who, so simply and so humanely, had fostered the memory of the dead scholar. For she, uncultured though she was, had at least preserved a book as a memento; whereas I, a man of education and a writer, had completely forgotten Buchmendel for years—I, who at least should have known that one only makes books in order to keep in touch with one's fellows after one has ceased to breathe, and thus to defend oneself against the inexorable fate of all that lives—transitoriness and oblivion.